Library of
Davidson College

THE SYMBOLIC METHOD OF

COLERIDGE
■
BAUDELAIRE
■
AND YEATS

Anca Vlasopolos

THE SYMBOLIC METHOD OF

COLERIDGE
▪
BAUDELAIRE
▪
AND YEATS

Wayne State University Press · Detroit 1983

COPYRIGHT © 1983 BY WAYNE STATE UNIVERSITY PRESS

DETROIT, MICHIGAN 48202. ALL RIGHTS ARE RESERVED.

NO PART OF THIS BOOK MAY BE REPRODUCED WITHOUT

FORMAL PERMISSION.

LIBRARY OF CONGRESS CATALOGING IN PUBLICATION DATA

Vlasopolos, Anca, 1948–
The symbolic method of Coleridge, Baudelaire, and Yeats.

Bibliography: p.
Includes index.
1. English poetry—19th century—History and criticism. 2. Symbolism in literature. 3. Coleridge, Samuel Taylor, 1772–1834—Criticism and interpretation. 4. Baudelaire, Charles, 1821–1867—Criticism and interpretation. 5. Yeats, W. B. (William Butler), 1865–1939—Criticism and interpretation. 6. Romanticism. I. Title.
PR585.S9V55   1983   821'.009'15   82-20079
ISBN 0-8143-1730-8

TO
JOSEPH PRESCOTT
FOR ALL HE HAS TAUGHT ME

As, without continuous transition, there can be no Method, so without a pre-conception there can be no transition without continuity. The term, Method, cannot therefore, otherwise than by abuse, be applied to a mere dead arrangement, containing in itself no principle of progression.

>Coleridge, *Essays on the Principles of Method*

CONTENTS

ACKNOWLEDGMENTS 11

ONE INTRODUCTION 13

TWO COLERIDGE
THE SYMBOL AS TRANSLUCENCE 29

THREE BAUDELAIRE
HUNGER FOR THE TRUE PARADISE 87

FOUR YEATS
THE QUEST FOR UNITY OF BEING 135

NOTES 192

BIBLIOGRAPHY 203

INDEX 213

ACKNOWLEDGMENTS

I owe a huge debt of gratitude to the multitude of scholars, editors, and compilers of variorum editions and concordances who have lighted my way from Coleridge to Baudelaire to Yeats. I wish to thank Professors George Bornstein and Marcel Muller of the University of Michigan for their invaluable advice and for the attention with which they read the manuscript at various stages of its development. I am indebted to Professor Alfred Schwarz of Wayne State University for encouraging me to investigate the special connotations of Coleridge's terminology. As always, my husband, Anthony Ambrogio, has given me such sustained and considered assistance that it amounts almost to a collaboration. I owe the deepest debt to the person to whom this book is dedicated.

I acknowledge permissions to quote from the following:

Excerpts from Coleridge's clasped-vellum notebook in the Berg Collection of the New York Public Library. Published with the permission of the Henry W. and Albert A. Berg Collection, The New York Public Library, Astor, Lenox and Tilden Foundations.

Excerpts from *The Flowers of Evil*, edited by Marthiel Mathews and Jackson Mathews, copyright 1955, © 1962 by New Directions Publishing Corporation. Reprinted by permission of New Directions, New York.

Excerpts from Yeats's *Autobiography*, copyright 1916, 1935 by Macmillan Publishing Co., Inc., renewed 1944, 1963 by Bertha Georgie Yeats. Reprinted with the permission of the Macmillan Company.

Excerpts from *Essays and Introductions*, copyright Mrs.

Acknowledgments

W. B. Yeats, 1961. Reprinted with the permission of the Macmillan Company.

Excerpts from *Explorations,* copyright Mrs. W. B. Yeats, 1962. Reprinted with the permission of the Macmillan Company.

Excerpts from *The Letters of W. B. Yeats,* edited by Allan Wade, copyright 1953, 1954 Anne Butler Yeats. Reprinted with the permission of Anne Yeats and the Macmillan Company.

Excerpts from *Memoirs,* copyright M. B. Yeats and Anne Yeats. Reprinted with the permission of M. B. Yeats and Anne Yeats.

Excerpts from *Mythologies,* copyright Mrs. W. B. Yeats, 1959. Reprinted with the permission of the Macmillan Company.

Excerpts from the *Variorum Edition of the Poems of W. B. Yeats,* edited by Peter Allt and Russell K. Alspach, copyright 1903, 1906, 1907, 1912, 1916, 1918, 1919, 1924, 1928, 1931, 1933, 1934, 1935, 1940, 1944, 1945, 1946, 1950, 1956, 1957 by the Macmillan Company; 1940 by George Yeats. Reprinted with the permission of the Macmillan Company.

Excerpts from *The Uncollected Prose by W. B. Yeats,* edited by John P. Frayne and Colton Johnson, copyright 1970 John P. Frayne and Michael Yeats, copyright 1975 John P. Frayne, Colton Johnson, and Michael Yeats. Reprinted with the permission of Columbia University Press.

ONE INTRODUCTION

> They and they only can acquire the philosophic imagination, the sacred power of self-intuition, who within themselves can interpret and understand the symbol, that the wings of the air-sylph are forming within the skin of the caterpillar.
>
> Coleridge,
> *Biographia Literaria*

When Coleridge writes this formidable sentence culminating in the image of the emerging psyche,[1] he establishes a new context of associations for the word "symbol." Henceforth, the symbol will gain increasing currency in the vocabulary of nineteenth- and twentieth-century art. For critics, the symbol represents an ideal of art to be opposed to allegory, which itself stands for the abstractions of earlier poetics. For poets and artists, the symbol becomes the unit in a system of recurring imagery which gives coherence to the work. Historically, it becomes the rallying point for a movement whose name it has inspired—Symbolism. Despite the increasing diversity of its meanings by the *fin de siècle*, the symbol stands in clear relation to the imagination as product of the creative process.

An aesthetic of the symbolizing imagination emerges in English Romanticism with the writings of Coleridge, becomes ab-

The Symbolic Method

sorbed and modified by Baudelaire in mid-nineteenth-century France, and redevelops out of the poetics of the Symbolist and Aesthetic movements and away from them in the poetry of Yeats. Arising initially in opposition to eighteenth-century theories of the mind, this new enterprise seeks to unify a psyche divided from itself and divorced from the universe by mechanism and its nineteenth-century offspring, scientific positivism. In studies of movements, influence, or individual poets in the nineteenth and twentieth centuries, the process of symbolization by which the artist translates experience or vision into language becomes the crucial point of vital controversy about man's relationship with the world, with himself, and with others. The opposition of mechanism to organicism and allegory to symbol represents, therefore, much more than a historical change in terminology; it describes a process that supplants external nature in favor of the perceiving mind. To the eighteenth-century ideal gleaned from observation and generalized into composite types, this new aesthetic opposes a sometimes unattainable ideal corresponding to the mind's desire for a revelation of universal coherence exceeding the scientific understanding of natural processes. Instead of imitating nature, the artist creates a world whose structure can be accessible to the mind, hence the frequency of metaphors of artistic object as natural product and of artist as God. As the structuring unit in a system of recurrent patterns which constitute an *oeuvre,* the symbol accumulates layers of meaning and gives unity to art. Its function of fusing the ideal and the concrete challenges traditional uses of poetic diction and traditional forms. Poets strive to express the coincidence of two levels of perception—imaginative and sensory—without loss of referentiality on the one hand and without a lapse into description or abstraction on the other. Psychic integration through art becomes a criterion for composition.

A radical change in poetic diction and the creation of two new genres, the Greater Romantic Lyric and the Romantic Quest, characterize this shift in aesthetics.[2] These new genres and diction mark those poems of Coleridge which exert the most far-reaching influence on literary heirs; they appear with significant modifications in Baudelaire, and his work, which enlarges Coleridge's use of the unconscious and introduces the city, not the pastoral landscape, as the object-world of sensations, represents, as Walter

Introduction

Benjamin noted,[3] the lyric work with European (and, I would add, American) repercussions. The new diction and forms appear transformed again in Yeats, the most canonized of twentieth-century descendants of Romanticism, whose *Collected Poems* contains in hitherto unapprehended ways connections and distortions of Coleridgean Romanticism and its Baudelairian translation. *Collected Poems* is a modern lyric work that exhibits unexpected continuities with Romanticism but also distinctly un-Romantic, antihuman modes of thought. Its influence is such that its relation to the Romantic aesthetic announces the sometimes ambiguous, often directly inimical stance of twentieth-century poets toward the Romantic predecessors who continue to obsess them with the sublimity of both their successes and their failures.[4]

In the larger picture of literary history, the Romantic innovations and transformations effected by Coleridge, Baudelaire, and Yeats extend their influence not only over poetry but over all genres of imaginative writing in the twentieth century. In fact, one could argue, though I shall only hint at such possibilities here, that the true inheritors of Romanticism as this study defines it are the novelists who revolutionized the conventions of their genre in the first half of the century.[5] After all, the movement of the Greater Romantic Lyric unfolds through the mind's encounter with the world, the juxtaposition through memory of past and present, the altering of nature through affection, and the mind's projection of hopes for the future; the subtle shifts between levels of experience, external and internal, anticipate the stream of consciousness. The Romantic Quest, which interiorizes the traditional action of the romance and which in Baudelaire and Yeats embodies its events in cityscapes and politics, serves as a prototype for the great journeys through mind and time in the modern novel. In this respect Joyce's grudging but undeniable admiration for Yeats can be understood as the recognition of a younger contemporary for an acknowledged master, but one already relegated to the status of precursor.

The theory of the symbolizing imagination in Romanticism has the peculiar effect of dangerously narrowing the boundaries of poetry in the twentieth century—and Yeats exemplifies this tendency, though he manages to overcome it through resurgent fidelity to his system of symbols—but also of expanding

The Symbolic Method

those ׳of fiction and drama into areas discovered by poets like Coleridge and Baudelaire and therefore considered the domain of poetry. The "psychological" novel and the interiorized stage of the most innovative twentieth-century drama represent developments stemming directly from Romantic poetics. Yeats, who of modern poets understood best the necessity to shape his life's work into unity, is a logical link in a study of the centrality of the symbolizing imagination. He represents both a shattering and a culmination of the continuing enterprise of Coleridgean and Baudelairian Romanticism to redefine man in terms of his mind's powers over the mutable world.

The process of symbolization for all three poets charts the journey through and out of experience into restructured or (as Yeats put it) radical innocence. The two phases of the Quest—involvement with the world and return to the self—coexist and fight for supremacy in the mind. Out of this conflict comes the healing, though qualified triumph, ever in need of renewal, of the imagination: the creation of the symbol. For all three poets, the consciously shaped *oeuvre* unified by a system of symbols provides the coherence needed to stay chaos and restore psychic integrity. But, though he invents the genre of the symbolizing poem, Coleridge abandons his creative ambitions early in life, leaving Wordsworth the task of writing the great philosophical poem of the age and turning to the metaphysical formulations which would sustain Wordsworth's monumental cathedral. In his theoretical writings, Coleridge develops his aesthetic of symbolization by using imagery and terminology derived from the experience and language of his poems. Baudelaire and Yeats succeed in structuring their poetry into an overall design and thus answer, in unique ways, Coleridge's hope for a unified body of lyrics which is to shape the consciousness of an age. Their critical pronouncements, however, draw sometimes upon states of despair in the poetry and express an exasperation with circumstances, an intolerance of life which the Quest's progress overcomes in the course of the poetic work, but they mark lapses from imagination—divisions of the psyche—in the criticism.

Coleridge's use of the word "symbol" in his prose creates generally overlooked connections between the poetry—his Greater Romantic Lyrics and Romantic Quest—and his the-

Introduction

ory of the imagination, which in turn illuminates basic principles of his philosophy. The Lyrics and *The Rime of the Ancient Mariner* anticipate Coleridge's lifelong preoccupation with the dialogue of mind and nature and with the process by which a natural object changes under imaginative perception into symbol. The unachieved symbolizations of some Lyrics and of *The Rime* point to Coleridge's ambivalence about his daring claims and hopes for the imagination as instrument of psychic reintegration. At the climax of *Biographia Literaria,* his orthodoxy makes him retreat from disclosing more than a barely sketched theory of the mind in which the imagination rivals God. From 1817 onward, Coleridge turns to theology in an attempt to obviate the split between subject and object which he earlier tried to heal through the aesthetic of the symbol; he decries the need to render ideas concrete, argues that Reason has access to God without recourse to the senses and understanding, and dispenses with the mediating function of the imagination and its constructs, which become distractions from devotion to God. Yet a glimpse at the private man in the shadow of the "sage of Highgate" reveals a Coleridge acutely aware still of the conflict waged in the mind between dependence upon outward stimuli and reliance upon imaginative vision, but with the difference that the older Coleridge grudgingly acquiesces to nature's victory. That knowledge of the visionary power imprisoned at last by external circumstances explains Coleridge's abandonment of faith in the imagination.

In Coleridge's aesthetic, the word "symbol" designates both the transformation of *natura naturata* into *natura naturans* and artistic creation. Both the primary and secondary imaginations have symbolizing functions. The primary imagination transforms the materials of the senses and the generalizations of the understanding into moments of revelation when external nature becomes coherent. The secondary imagination uses the fixities and definites of memory and fancy to create in art the process by which the imagination triumphs over the flux of the senses. Through its symbolizing power, the imagination reconciles the inner division between intellect and feelings and thus reverses the psychic and artistic decline suffered by civilization after the Renaissance. Coleridge attributes several characteristics to this rec-

The Symbolic Method

onciliation which show its unmistakable identity with the symbol; a swimming sensation, a dimming of the edges of objects, and a diffusion of light accompany the union of thought and feeling. These changes occur in the speaker's perception at the climax of imaginative vision in the Greater Romantic Lyrics and *The Rime* when the process of symbolization is culminated.

Coleridge's metaphors for the symbol and the properties he ascribes to it are at times identical with those he uses in discussing the poetic process and, in particular, its language. Both poem and symbol result from a mediating process that overcomes opposites by synthesizing them. The poem unites the most intense emotion with the highest order; the symbol fuses head and heart. Poetic language and the symbol take on forms that are readily accessible to the senses and understanding. Coleridge argues for a *lingua communis,* a diction without artifice which combines the universal elements of language with a highly individuated articulation. Similarly, the symbol is described as "a translucence . . . of the Universal in the General, . . . of the Eternal through and in the Temporal."[6] Yet neither the language of poetry nor the symbol should distract attention from the revelation they contain. In this they serve as media; like the crystal in Coleridge's famous metaphor,[7] they allow light to pass through while giving it perceptible form. Perhaps the most striking similarity between symbol and poem is their circular form. Coleridge uses the image of the *ouroboros* to express the ever-renewing process of creation and to reject the limitations of finite products. The function of poetic language becomes that of the "self-circling energies of reason" (*Lay Sermons,* p. 29) in the symbol, which govern and order the flux of the senses but which move in a perpetual return upon themselves.

In both the Greater Romantic Lyrics and *The Rime,* Coleridge effects or strives for a circular return, ideally transforming the poem into a portion of eternity which, like the symbol, renders reality intelligible. The Greater Romantic Lyric is a poem of process which ends at its beginning, though with a notable gain in vision. Its setting is in a defined landscape, and its movement centers upon the speaker's mind interiorizing the landscape and then contemplating himself or a loved one within a locus perceptibly changed from a *natura naturata* to a *natura naturans,* from reality to symbol. Apart from its spatial expansion and flux, without/within/without, the locus of the poem becomes the focal point of the speaker's past, present, and future, thus changing from a moment in time to one encompassing eternity.

When the mind incorporates the locus within itself, the speaker ends the contemplation with a restored perception, as in poems like "Frost at Midnight" and "This Lime-Tree Bower My Prison." However, some of Coleridge's greatest poetry, as well as his lesser Lyrics, illustrates an unachieved process of symbolization and a speaker whose imaginative perception is far from being restored. In these poems, the mind, unable to assert its staying hold upon experience, ultimately lets itself be overwhelmed by factors outside the process of imaginative creation. In "The Eolian Harp" the vision of an animated nature in which the mind partakes is censored by guilt about a religious transgression. The twin Lyrics "Reflections on Having Left a Place of Retirement" and "Fears in Solitude" suggest Coleridge's unease with the antagonism between mind and nature; the "undetermined conflict" results in a speaker quaking with fear and rage, unable to perceive and transform nature imaginatively. In *The Rime* the Mariner recants his identification with nature almost immediately after he has achieved it. Finally, in "Dejection: An Ode" the speaker is initially so absorbed in himself that he remains unaware of the external world, only to be overwhelmed and possessed by a natural movement over which he has no control. In a poignant ending, the speaker sets the unattainable beloved into the proper relationship with nature while he remains in the desolate setting that has supplanted his freedom.

Yet Coleridge's ideal extends beyond the privileged moment, the single symbol of the lyric. He understands too well the danger of the imaginative product hardening into the deathlike stasis of the Image,[8] the false idol. Like other Romantic poets, he yearns for epic inclusiveness, for a modern myth to restore and sustain psychic integrity. As poet, Coleridge attempts neither the kind of *oeuvre* shaped out of lyric poems which will appear with Baudelaire and Yeats nor the great philosophical poem of the age. Doomed by the urgency and grandeur of expectations, his enterprise remains unfinished and in that sense fails, but Coleridge's groundwork in a theory of symbolization and poems achieving it

The Symbolic Method

creates the foundation of a nineteenth-century aesthetic that continues to dominate the aims and accomplishments of major poets in the twentieth century.

Unlike Coleridge, who faces the problem of revitalizing an art that had become stultified by the conventions of an established tradition, Baudelaire must contend with the failure of the Romantic revolt, whose aim, in France as in England, was to create an art that answers to the needs of the whole man. The French Romantics' belief in the perfectibility of man through external means such as social institutions proves to be a delusion in terms of the actual historical developments of the nineteenth century.[9] Their adherence to Christian doctrine leads them away from the secularization and internalization of the Christian view of history that occurs in English Romanticism and makes them dependent upon outward signs of dissolution, apocalypse, and regeneration as a basis for their art. Baudelaire's revisionist enterprise consists of a poetry that takes into account the disillusionment stemming from the historical defeats of the Romantic revolution as well as certain failures of the movement itself. Since external solutions to man's problems yield no results, the remedy is an internal regeneration of faculties undertaken by the artists and communicated to others by means of his creation.

For Baudelaire, as for the English Romantics, the imagination reintegrates reason and senses and in turn triumphs over external circumstance. Although not as systematic and consistently defined as Coleridge's theory, Baudelaire's account of the mind parallels it closely in its emphasis on the redemptive power of the imagination.[10] Baudelaire's formulations about the imagination reach their apex during the great creative period between the first and second editions of *Les Fleurs du Mal*, when Baudelaire is not only writing thirty-five new poems to replace the six condemned pieces but is consolidating the structure of the work. This fact weighs more in explaining the similarity of Baudelaire's aesthetic to Coleridge's than the tracing of influences through the circuitous route of Catherine Crowe and Edgar Allan Poe. *Les Fleurs du Mal* fulfills Coleridge's criteria for the great poem of the age. It is an epic formed by short interrelated lyrics sustained by a system of symbols and composed in a pattern of circular returns. It exhibits both the larger structure of the Romantic

Introduction

Quest, with its goal of a recovered inner paradise, and the mind-nature tension of the Greater Romantic Lyric. The cycles of *Les Fleurs du Mal* are, in effect, acts of symbolization, and the outcome—the success or failure of the imagination against passive perception—gauges the mind's progress toward regeneration. It is not surprising that Baudelaire, immersed in such a creation, should reach conclusions in his concurrent criticism which accord with Coleridge's theory of symbolization.

For Baudelaire, who does not adhere to the word "symbol" as faithfully as Coleridge (he occasionally substitutes for it "hieroglyph," "correspondence," "analogy," and even "allegory"), the imaginative act performs the same synthesis of opposites in transmuting the unintelligible flux of experience into coherent wholeness. Baudelaire defines the act in *Salon de 1846* as "the heroism of modern life," which consists of perceiving beauty in the chaos of modern urban life and creating this beauty in art. The enterprise, as the word "heroism" suggests, takes on epic proportions in the cycle of *Les Fleurs du Mal* entitled "Parisian Scenes." While nature in Romantic poetry remains, true to the lyrical tradition, confined to the pastoral, Baudelaire's impinging external world has all the brutality and dissonance of modern city life. That reality dictates metaphors about the act of symbolization different from Coleridge's antitheses of light and opacity in the twilight and moonlight gleams of his poetry. Unlike Coleridge's symbol, which reveals the supernatural through man's highest sense—sight—thus ennobling his perception, Baudelaire's symbol must satisfy a longing that expresses itself in images of hunger and thirst. Beauty, the result of symbolization, is the "Divine Pastry" (*OC*, 2:685)—not the crystal—nourishing man's unceasing appetite for the plenitude of Eden, whose loss and distance are so sharply felt by the urban dweller. The triumph of allaying hunger and thirst through symbolization, out of the very materials offered by the city, belongs to the creative imagination, as "The Swan," the central poem of "Parisian Scenes," magnificently proves.

Baudelaire expands the symbolizing process to include in its phases memory and dream. Unlike Coleridge, he considers symbolization in life and art indistinguishable; his creative imagination (Coleridge's secondary imagination) is not limited to coexisting with the conscious will. Less overwhelmed by the shadow of

The Symbolic Method

the Age of Reason than perhaps was Coleridge, who relegated free association to mechanical functions of the mind, Baudelaire introduces into the theory of imagination the resources of the subconscious and of memory, as Yeats will do in his reliance upon reverie and passion. In *Les Fleurs du Mal* the words "dream" and "recollection" frequently signal the passage from passive to active perception, from description controlled by sensations to vision. Because Baudelaire does not distinguish between imaginative perception and artistic creation, the very means of art, such as poetic language and painting techniques, are themselves a system of symbols which make up the universe and render it intelligible. Baudelaire's claims for art seem more daring because less carefully articulated than Coleridge's: whereas for Coleridge poetry mediates on the linguistic level between ideality and form as the symbol does on the metaphysical, for Baudelaire the universe is a poem in which moral transgressions are faults of prosody and the painting is a world organically composed of successive layers completing and exceeding each other in a progression toward infinity.

Baudelaire's thoughts on the composition of the ideal painting provide an essential clue to the principle of unity in *Les Fleurs du Mal*. Successive cycles build upon one another by renewing and advancing the poet's quest. Instead of appearing only in the individual poem, as in Coleridge's work, the process of symbolization informs the structure of each cycle and indicates the mind's progression through experience, its transformation through each defeat, and its final triumph. Although in its totality the work is affirmative, the three initial cycles conform to the structure of the unachieved symbolization seen in many of Coleridge's poems. Confident at first of its vision, the mind becomes prey to the mutability of experience, to a reality that prevails upon it, and ends in defeat. In the cycle of "Flowers of Evil" the gruesome ending contains a brief, ephemeral triumph of the mind even while devoured by Love in the guise of Venus Genetrix at her most destructive. The last two cycles, "Revolt" and "Death," show the progression of the mind through experience to the point where reality is not only powerless to overwhelm the mind but unable to satisfy it. The Romantic Quest for infinite desire renews itself once more in the concluding poem, "The Voyage."

Baudelaire's warning about the inordinate pursuit of

Introduction

"ideal beauty" or even of perfection of form alone goes unheeded by the two movements that claim their kinship with him and the Romantics and that are most preoccupied with the symbol, namely, the Symbolist and the Aesthete. Their poetics represent the fragmentation of an aesthetic and with it the renouncement of the humanist enterprise implicit in symbolization. Their avowed lack of interest in the world destroys the mind-nature tension that precedes the symbolizing act. On the linguistic level, denotation becomes submerged in favor of connotation and auditory effect.[11] Forced to acknowledge the imagination's inability to restructure the world, these poets refuse to represent reality; they renounce the hope of integrating mental faculties and remain content to specialize in either philosophical, sentimental, or sensory aspects of experience in their poetry. Although this art has its own interest and merit, it fails to measure up to the great achievements by predecessors because it can neither show imagination triumphing over external reality nor represent poignantly and consciously the reason for the mind's failure.

Yeats shapes his poetics out of a strong Romantic heritage and the milieu of the Nineties. He maintains a precarious balance between the two traditions, on the one hand striving to reintegrate the mind and thus redeem civilization and on the other hand banishing the modern world from his art. In the early criticism and poetry, the unappeased desire for a world "made wholly of essences,"[12] which Yeats associates with the enterprise of the Romantics and the Rhymers, exists side by side with a fear of isolation, incommunicability, and untimely death. Even when young, Yeats was too determined an artist not to perceive the danger of destruction inherent in the cult of Beauty; his worship of the Image, the Rose, exhibits a healthy prudence. Yet at the same time his poetic quest of the nineties exhausts itself under the strain of a desire for apocalypse incompatible with life.

Yeats struggles out of the weariness of the Nineties by proclaiming two antidotes for it: passion and the pursuit of Unity of Culture. Passion allows him a subjectivity without solipsism because without self-consciousness. He exalts passionate genres like folk art, which validates the poet's vision by giving it the resonance of ancient myth and simplicity of language, and like heroic poetry, which addresses itself to an audience familiar with its ritual, thus combatting the vulgar naturalism of middle-class art. The political realities of the Abbey Theatre force Yeats to transform his initial ideal of achieving Unity of Culture throughout Ireland by means of ritualistic drama into an art for the keepers of culture, namely, the aristocrats. Yeats's System in *A Vision* further consolidates this enterprise with its account of *primary* and *antithetical* phases of human history when democratic fragmenting impulses or aristocratic and artistic forces dominate in turn. Yeats's search for Unity of Culture, because of its dependence upon a system outside the psyche to sustain it, represents his greatest departure from the humanism of the Romantics. Antihumanist associations intrude occasionally upon the fabric of the poetry and bring with them destructive contexts.

Concurrent with Yeats's attempt to create Unity of Culture is his artistically more successful continuation of the Romantics' pursuit of psychic integrity, which Yeats terms Unity of Being. Identifying Baudelaire's and Coleridge's roles as predecessors provides new insights into Yeats's creation of his poetic heritage and his development of symbolization in criticism and in the cyclical structure of *Collected Poems*. As long as Yeats attempts to escape the dangers of the Romantic Quest, he associates Coleridge and Baudelaire with the doomed figures of the Tragic Generation. When he returns to the Quest, he pays homage to Coleridge by using him for support repeatedly in the criticism of the thirties, and echoes Coleridge's poetry and prose in his own poems throughout his career. Although he is mentioned infrequently in Yeats's prose, and his poetry never reverberates directly in that of Yeats, Baudelaire is given a prominent place in "The Phases of the Moon" (*A Vision*). In conjunction with Plotinus[13] he seems to confirm Yeats's discovery in *Supernatural Poems* and *Last Poems* that sexuality and spirituality lead to the same expansion of the imagination toward infinity. Symbolization through the dialectical movement of cycles structuring the *oeuvre* and appearing in both *Les Fleurs du Mal* and *Collected Poems* represents a striking instance of analogous variation upon the Greater Romantic Lyric and the Romantic Quest by these two post-Romantic poets.

In his pursuit of Unity of Being, Yeats turns to the inner conflict of desires and needs and attempts to find a solution that

Introduction

answers to the whole self. Moments of truce within the being result in luminous symbolizations and unreconciled division in the imagination's defeat. As the true heir of Romanticism Yeats understands that externalized conflict produces fanaticism and fragmentation, whereas the recognition that war begins in the mind precedes the synthesis called Unity of Being. In order to give his early poetry this inwardness and tension, and to cure it of its weariness, Yeats introduces through revisions a sharp emphasis on man and his inner struggle. Occasionally the poetry fairly buckles under the strain of knowledge and experience unavailable to the speaker at that early stage of the Quest. Yet, though lacking the dialectical structure of the later cycles, the early work does contain images of antinomial conflict which Yeats raises to the status of symbols in his mature work.

Yeats, whose insight into Shelley's use of recurring symbols produces a pioneering Romanticist study,[14] manages to create an equally consistent system of symbols in his own work.[15] Certain words and images, such as moments of illumination, birdsong and heart, become associated with the continuing, persistent quest for psychic regeneration. These appear in contexts where the mind is at its most divided. The quester, in danger of embracing abstractions or solutions that fragment the being, is brought back to his full humanity and to his own power, the creative imagination. For Yeats, whose imagination remains less drawn by nature's lure, acts of symbolization are triumphs, not over rival nature, but over antinomies that have become negations, that are in danger of canceling each other out. In the face of potential nothingness, the mind through the supreme effort of the imagination overcomes its divisions and creates.

In his prose as in his poetry, Yeats amply demonstrates that symbolization remains as vital an aesthetic in the twentieth century as it was in the nineteenth. To argue that Romanticism occupies a central position in shaping twentieth-century literature is of course no longer revolutionary, though resistance to such a view of literary history has by no means disappeared and may in fact be gathering momentum. This study undertakes to establish interpenetrations of poetics beyond the English-speaking tradition, delayed and changed enough by a different epoch and language as to affect writers several generations later with the charm of a new discovery. The methodology developed by Romanticist critics in examining the works of British Romantic poets and Yeats applies admirably to Baudelaire,[16] though no critic has yet analyzed the structure of *Les Fleurs du Mal* as a Quest. And, if eminent critics have illuminated in new and profound ways the role of Romanticism in literary tradition, highly praised studies continue to deny Baudelaire's affinity with Coleridgean Romanticism or Yeats's self-made last-Romantic stance by focusing not on Baudelaire's work, which, like Yeats's, culminates and shatters the Romantic formulations of *his* predecessors, but on his critical writings, which are those of an interesting but minor critic.[17] Ironically, critics who concern themselves with Baudelaire's poetry isolate him,[18] either by seeing him as the heir of Racinian classicism and Christianity alienated in the modern world[19] or by placing him at the crossroads of Romanticism and modernism as an anomaly, whose work revolutionized poetics but who came to a spiritual dead end.[20] Like the British Romantic poets, Baudelaire subverts classical diction and traditional Christianity; though it has scandalized some humanists, Baudelaire's Quest for ultimate knowledge, which ends in embracing death, anticipates Yeats's discovery that sexuality and spirituality are antinomies, not contradictions, and that death leads to the most complete knowledge of the self.

Because of Yeats's work on the Blake edition and his original appraisal of Shelley's poetry, critics who argue for Yeats's Romanticism—a fairly recent trend in Yeats studies—have focused on his struggles to forge a poetic identity in relation to these predecessors and in opposition to them.[21] Rarely does anyone mention Yeats's relatively frequent references to Coleridge, his perception of Coleridge's multifaceted genius, and the Coleridgean echoes in his poetry.[22] More significantly, no critic other than Bloom traces Yeats's commitment to the imagination to Coleridge's theory of the mind in perception and creation.[23] This oversight has less to do with the fact that Coleridge is not a "precursor" in the Bloomian sense for Yeats than with the division among Romanticists as to what constitutes Romantic tradition. In identifying three types of Romantic imagination, Donoghue distinguishes between modes of creation of Romantic and post-Romantic poets.[24] Yet the prevailing judgment of scholars

Introduction

settles on one type or another as the imagination that captures the essence of Romantic poetics. The proponents of the poetics of experience view the imagination as secularizing divine love by conferring upon objects of nature supernatural radiance and place Coleridge and Wordsworth at the center of British Romanticism. Experience in Romantic art takes the form of the circuitous quest for the lost paradise, and communion with nature signifies the quest's fulfillment. For these critics, who regard the Romantics' sustained contact with life and their restructuring of experience as the primary aspect of poetics, the reconciliation between subject and object becomes the Romantics' ultimate achievement, indicative of restored perception and of man's potential integration into the universe.

Although Yeats scholars tend to agree that Yeats's discovery of his poetic voice coincided with his deliberate embracing of experience, a movement "downward upon life," they do not hail the shift as a move toward the Coleridgean or Wordsworthian center. They view his changes in diction toward a more direct, conversational language and in subject toward the tangible images of experience as swerves away from "precursors" like Shelley or from the extreme symbolism of figures like Mallarmé. Clearly, if much of Coleridge can be interpreted so as to conform to the poetics of experience (though not without violence, as I propose), Yeats's Quest cannot be so perceived: this Quest is cyclical, not circuitous, and its provisional triumphs rise from resistance to the fragmentation of experience, not out of communion with nature. As a poet Yeats understood better perhaps than literary critics that Coleridge's attitude toward nature was fraught with ambiguities and that the older poet too had embarked upon a quest in nature's spite, a doomed quest in Yeats's judgment.

Regarded by other critics as the true legacy of Romanticism, the poetics of vision concentrates precisely on this power of imagination and vision to free man from the temporal forms of nature and the mutability of experience. For the critics who emphasize the poetics of vision, Blake and Shelley become the central figures since art reflects imagination's fictions created in opposition to the forms of nature and serving as proof that infinite desire, the dream, cannot attach itself to any temporal form, for none is

The Symbolic Method

its analogue. Yeats is the natural descendant to such a version of the Romantic tradition,[25] though so are the French Symbolists and the British Aesthetes and Decadents who fragmented the Romantics' humanist enterprise of reintegrating the psyche. The poetics of vision contains dangers of which Coleridge, when on the verge of articulating a theory of imaginative vision, was all too aware. The pursuit of the dream must be accompanied by a good deal of skepticism lest the quester become so absorbed in his vision that he isolates himself from humanity, especially his own humanity. This danger threatens and occasionally overcomes Yeats's poetry, though Yeats at his greatest recognizes and renounces the schooling of the soul at the expense of the heart.[26]

Both approaches to Romantic poetics deal with the central aspect of symbolization—the mind's relationship to reality—but because of their different emphases on the function of the imagination the proponents of each see less continuity between Coleridge and Yeats than this study will argue for. Although Coleridge has fostered some of the finest exegetes of this century, his poetry and criticism are consistently seen as less daring than those of other Romantics because he has fallen victim to the kind of dissociation he dreaded: he represents reconciliation through experience, other Romantics represent vision. Coleridge, however, proposed a third type of imagination, one that requires a twofold process: restructuring experience through imaginative perception and creating its mental analogue. The world lives only through the mind's concentrated power—imagination. Its quickenings—the wings of the air-sylph—occur in moments that are privileged only because they are created by the supreme effort of the mind which, Coleridge knew, cannot long be sustained. Coleridge's symbolic method, the aesthetic he forged out of his awareness of infinite desire and its dangers, becomes the structuring principle of the poetics of Baudelaire and Yeats. I shall therefore turn to Coleridge, the first English Romantic critic to formulate a theory of the symbol which exceeds both the poetics of experience and vision, and the poet who created the prototypes of the poems of symbolization—the Greater Romantic Lyric and the Romantic Quest.

TWO COLERIDGE

THE SYMBOL AS TRANSLUCENCE

In November 1804, Coleridge records the following entry in his notebook:

> Hard to express that sense of the analogy or likeness of a Thing which enables a Symbol to represent it, so that we think of the Thing itself—& yet knowing that the Thing is not present to us.—Surely, on this universal fact of words & images depends by more or less mediations the *imitation* instead of *copy* which is illustrated in very nature *shakespearianized/*—that Proteus Essence that could assume the very form, but yet known & felt not to be the Thing by that difference of the Substance which made every atom of the Form another thing/—that likeness not identity—an exact web, every line of direction miraculously the same, but the one worsted, the other silk.[1]

This double awareness of the thing as itself and as representation *in absentia* of the metamorphosis from worsted to silken thread presents Coleridge with a difficulty that recurs throughout his writings in the definition of the symbol, namely, that it is

The Symbolic Method

"hard to express that sense." Eleven years later, in *Biographia Literaria,* he adds to the existing difficulty by attributing a conceptual problem to the nature of the symbol: "An IDEA, in the highest sense of that word, cannot be conveyed but by a *symbol*; and, except in geometry, all symbols of necessity involve an apparent contradiction" (*BL,* 1:100). The inability to express the double awareness produced by the symbol and the contradiction apparent, but not inherent, in symbols are problems that Coleridge attempts to resolve in his poetry and criticism.[2] He resolves them magnificently during those periods of his life when the desire to reconcile the contradiction and to communicate the awareness is equal to, "miraculously the same" as, the achievement.

Ideally, the symbol unites intellect and feelings, enabling the whole mind to confront Nature and give coherence and shape to its images.[3] The symbol represents imaginative achievement in both the primary and secondary modes Coleridge distinguishes in his definition. The underlying unity in his theory of Imagination becomes evident when we recognize that he endows the primary Imagination with a regenerative function that alters and redeems the mundane traffic between mind and world via sense impressions and the generalizations induced from them.[4] Coleridge's statements on the symbol, on the function of the Imagination, and on poetic diction are intricately related to the symbolic method of his poetry. The poems of symbolization supplied Coleridge with an ideal for the work of art, psychic unity, and sacramental vision. From the imagery and movement of those poems, Coleridge constructed three major criteria for his literary, philosophical, and theological formulations: translucence, circularity of form, and diffusion of outlines in light. Coleridge recognized the enormous claims he made for symbolization in poetry and criticism and admitted to the inherent possibility of failure in his enterprise. Through the criticisms he leveled either at schools or individual authors whose notions resembled his own dated poetics, he advanced beyond what he came to view as the bankruptcy of some of his earlier positions. This method is evident when he dissociates himself from Wordsworth's theory in the *Preface* to the *Lyrical Ballads* and from some of his poetic practices and those of Bowles, the idol of his youth. More importantly, these shifts in theory indicate Coleridge's revaluations and often distortions of his own poetic achievement.

The words "symbol," "symbolical," and "symbolic" appear in contexts where Coleridge establishes the role of the Imagination as the faculty that mediates between Reason and the Understanding or where he discusses the results of imaginative activity and distinguishes the effects produced by these "symbolical" types—the Scriptures, superior art—from the effects produced by mere copies or allegorical interpretations. The symbol, which is closely tied to Coleridge's definitions of the Imagination and its functions, suffers the same fortune as the Imagination in Coleridge's writings. As long as the Imagination retains its key position as reconciler of human faculties in Coleridge's criticism, the symbol functions as the medium in which the forms of Nature become infused with the spirit of the perceiver. When the Imagination begins to lose its importance and Reason becomes the faculty that generates knowledge, the definition of the symbol also changes to a mere definition of metonymy. Traceable roughly to 1816–17, this gradual shift parallels Coleridge's detachment from a theory of knowledge that uses the dynamic interplay between passive reception of sensory data and active perception to one of inner contemplation of the divine through Reason, the faculty least susceptible to contact with the external world. The ambiguities of Coleridge's attitude toward Nature,[5] present throughout his writings and poetry but coming to the fore in the orthodox phase of his later years, inform these shifts of thought about the Imagination and the symbol. Once he determines that the meeting of mind and external reality leads to disaster, not to knowledge, Imagination, which mediates between the appearances of Nature and self-originating ideas, and its product, the symbol, become unnecessary. But this change itself arises from a series of disappointments, after a lifelong attempt to arrive at an understanding of the interaction between the mind and the external world.

Nowhere does that undertaking succeed so well as in Coleridge's discovery and use of a poetic structure ideally suited to the presentation of the mind's dialogue with Nature and to the transformation of the "Thing" into symbol. The poem of symbolization, which encompasses both the Greater Romantic Lyric and the Romantic Quest, conforms in its diction and movement to Cole-

The Symbolic Method

ridge's theory of the mental process whereby the image—the mind's notion of objects derived from sensations—changes into symbols. The process refutes the associationist view of the mind and mechanical philosophy by transforming external circumstances (the precise locus in time and space in which the speaker finds himself at the beginning of the poem) into vision, where the limitations of experience are broken through by an imaginative perception and reconstruction of Nature. The so-called conversational genre[6] anticipates Coleridge's standards for the ideal poem and poetic language, and his definition of the symbol: circular structure, passion reconciled with order and universality with individuation, and Idea given shape without being obscured or immobilized. Coleridge uses the symbolizing mode begun with the Greater Romantic Lyric in his internalized Quest, *The Rime of the Ancient Mariner*. The mind/Nature dialogue, the moment of vision characterized by illumination, and the circular return establish *The Rime*'s identity with Coleridge's poetry of symbolization.

Coleridge's symbolic method in those poems sets up a contest in the mind between images of the senses—overwhelming in the initial encounter of mind and Nature—and imaginative constructs. Whether symbols win dominance in the mind determines the success of the process. In "This Lime-Tree Bower My Prison" and "Frost at Midnight" the speaker begins in dejection, a state caused by Nature's overwhelming the Imagination and making the speaker aware of the need to resist the intrusive flux of the senses. The moment of symbolization succeeds when the speaker exercises his imaginative power to restructure Nature and thus conquer it, and he returns to his original setting with joy. When the Imagination fails to reconstruct images of the senses, as in "The Eolian Harp," in the parallel Lyrics "Reflections on Having Left a Place of Retirement" and "Fears in Solitude," and in *The Rime,* the poems, which began on a euphoric or contented note indicative of the speaker's misperception of Nature's powers, end in frustration. While the speakers of the earlier poems remain trapped in their limited perception, the poet in "Dejection: An Ode" is acutely aware of both the symbolizing power of the Imagination and its irreparable loss. "Dejection" is a more satisfying work because it articulates the reasons for both the mind's failure—inner division—and the at-

The Symbol as Translucence

tendant despair, whereas the other three Lyrics and *The Rime* end with an uneasy, unenlightened speaker who covers up his failed vision with commonplace orthodoxy.

Does Coleridge recognize the orthodoxy of his speakers as a retreat from vision? Although it is undeniable that strong censors were at work in his mind throughout his life, Coleridge remains a most discerning watcher and judge of self. As a poet he did not remake himself through revisions in the Yeatsian manner. Yet the unsatisfactory resolutions in these poems haunted him, for he emended and added to "The Eolian Harp" throughout his career, and he composed "Fears in Solitude" three years after "Reflections" on the blueprint of the earlier poem. His dissatisfaction with the conclusion of *The Rime* is well known. And, while the elimination of personal details serves to draw the conflict in "Dejection" into sharper focus, the revisions of the poems of failed symbolization attempt to mask the unresolved struggle between mind and Nature. When we consider that two of these—"The Eolian Harp" and "Reflections"—are honeymoon poems and that "Fears in Solitude," though written in the *annus mirabilis,* is an echo of that time, we may wonder whether Coleridge's inability to create a unified psyche stems in the first two from his divided feelings about his wife[7] and in the other from a reluctance to break openly with Wordsworth's views about nature's renovating virtues.[8] Coleridge condemned himself to tell the tale of "Reflections" once more, until he uncovered its meaning in "Dejection"; however, he made his Mariner tell his tale more than ten thousand times since the Mariner remains forever bound to his lame conclusion.

Generally, critics treat separate aspects of Coleridge's activity as a writer: his theory of imagination and symbol, his innovations in poetic diction both in criticism and poetry, and his poems. Although some critics discuss the relationship of these aspects to one another—imagination to symbol and to poetry, imagination to poetic diction and to poetry—there has been little systematic attempt to see Coleridge's theory of the symbol, his theory of poetic diction, and his poetry as part of a larger aesthetic of the symbolizing imagination.[9] The publication of the first volumes of the *Notebooks* (1957–62), which makes available for the first time material about Coleridge's most intimate thoughts, has inspired some critics to use the life as a pattern for the poetry by drawing heavily upon Coleridge's mental struggle with nightmares and fixations in their interpretations of particular poems.[10] The *Notebooks* also offer, in characteristic, tantalizing elliptical entries, occasional illumination for Coleridge's all-too-brief definition of the imagination and his use of the word "symbol" in a variety of contexts—poetical, critical, religious.

While the secondary Imagination, or the poetic imagination, has been called the symbolic or symbol-making power by some critics,[11] there seems to be no general attempt to relate the symbol to the primary Imagination.[12] The secondary Imagination as the poetic faculty responsible for artistic creation is an established notion in Coleridge criticism. The primary Imagination remains, however, subject to debate, ranging from I. A. Richards's functional view of it as the faculty that perceives the world of the senses in its most mundane way—the world of beefsteaks and buses[13]—to Baker's identification of it with the power that "intuits the real forms or the ideas behind the sensuous forms and establishes, in this way, direct contact with the divine."[14] Other opinions about the meaning of the primary Imagination or its function range between these two extremes and occasionally differ from both.[15] What has not, for the most part, been noted, however, is that Coleridge's definition of the primary Imagination carries sacramental meaning by virtue of the vocabulary Coleridge chooses to describe it. But consequently placing the primary Imagination and the symbol in an exclusively religious context or neglecting the relationship between the primary and secondary Imagination because one exists at the religious, the other at the aesthetic, level hardly explains the development of Coleridge's thought. If the secondary Imagination's attributes were limited to art, not to perception and cognition as well, there would have been little need for Coleridge's recantation about the role of the Imagination. If, as J. Robert Barth argues, he did invest the primary Imagination with the power of perceiving "all that man can know,"[16] and if the context were without doubt religious, again there would have been no basis for Coleridge's later uneasiness. If, however, Coleridge attributed to the primary Imagination a power too godlike, too independent in its activity of the orthodox applications of religious faith, then the retreat of the later years becomes understandable,[17] as does the reduced role of the symbol.

This tendency to compartmentalize Coleridge's thought appears in discussions of Coleridge's principles of poetic diction. These have been perceptively analyzed as his application of the ideal of organic unity to works of art, but critics have not seized upon the resemblance of the metaphors Coleridge uses to describe the ideal poetic diction and their frequent direct relevance to the metaphors he develops for the symbol.

In assessments of Coleridge's poetry, particularly of the Conversation Poems and *The Rime,* the majority of critics use specific aspects of the criticism to illuminate their interpretation of the poems. Occasionally, as in M. H. Abrams's "Coleridge's 'A Light in Sound': Science, Metascience, and Poetic Imagination," an exegesis of seven lines becomes a recapitulation of Coleridge's intellectual development and knowledge of science, but more frequently Coleridge's critical terminology is not applied in any systematic way to the poetry. The use of the words "symbol" and "symbolic" recurs in discussions of the poetry, but these words are applied in their general sense rather than with a strictly Coleridgean meaning, as are "imagination" and "nature." Abrams warns that the Greater Romantic Lyric should not be mistaken for a nature poem since the Romantic poets dealt "with the nonhuman only insofar as it is the occasion for the activity which defines man," namely, "the process of intellection." Nonetheless, the Conversation Poems are widely regarded as moments of union between the mind and nature, and the process of achieving the fusion acquires several names, such as "the systolic rhythm," or "the centripetal-centrifugal action."[18] In these interpretations, nature is beneficent, and cognition results from the meeting of mind and nature.[19] In other studies, the success of the fusion or the vision of the Conversation Poems comes into question.[20] These latter studies attribute the failure of the Conversation Poems to the deficiencies of the speaker or of Coleridge himself, who, because of his fear of the imagination or for psychological reasons, is unable to effect the fusion with nature.

The speaker's dejection, "a profound sadness, sometimes bordering on the anguish of terror or despair, at the sense of loss, dereliction, isolation, or inner death," becomes, as Abrams comments, a frequent issue of the Greater Romantic Lyric. Even Abrams, however, only partially accounts for that state, declaring it to be "inherent in the conditions of the speaker's existence."[21] Yet Coleridge's opinion of Nature, of the images received by the senses and generalized into abstract concepts by the Understanding, surely offers a clue that this very Nature is initially the cause of the dejection and that, instead of fusing with Nature, the imagination wars with images of sense in order to impose its constructs upon the mind's ultimate perception of the world.

Critical interpretations of *The Rime,* Coleridge's only complete Romantic Quest, suffer from the same attempt to find psychological causes for Coleridge's inability to create a more rational, more comprehensible universe for the Mariner. Part of the problem is in assigning the poem its true genre, and Fogle's veto of the Romantic Quest as the genre of *The Rime* seems to have discouraged further investigation.[22] Seen as a psychic journey, *The Rime* can be freed from both defenses of and attacks upon its verisimilitude, and the all-too-frequent charges of irrationality[23] arising from many critics' unwillingness to accept the Nature in the poem as the passive perception that dominates the Mariner's experience through most of the journey, including the return. The purpose of the Quest, like that of the Greater Romantic Lyric, is not the desire to fuse with Nature but to transform it into a coherent and meaningful pattern through symbolization. The Mariner succeeds but once in triumphing over Nature; his pitiless fate, the universe of horror he inhabits, results from his refusal to exercise his imagination.

II

Coleridge invests the primary Imagination with a generative, creative power that counteracts ordinary perception. The secondary Imagination supplements this power by consciously striving to sustain the regenerated perception and to reproduce it in works of art, which in turn ideally elicit a similar activity in the mind of the perceiver. The term "symbol" designates the summation of both kinds of imaginative mode. Coleridge alternately ascribes it to the constructs of the primary Imagination which oppose the images of the senses and to the reconstruction of the secondary Imagination in art. The relationship between the two modes of Imagination has often been misperceived because the primary Imagination was defined as the organ of mundane perception.

Perception for Coleridge may be passive or active. He occasionally distinguishes between the two phases by specifying "the receptivity . . . of impressions . . . or . . . the passive perception" (*BL*, 1:70), but he generally looks upon the term as inclusive of both meanings.[24] The phrase "all human Perception" occurs in his famous definition of the primary Imagination: "The primary IMAGINATION I hold to be the living Power and prime Agent of all human Perception, and as a repetition in the finite mind of the eternal act of creation in the infinite I AM" (*BL*, 1: 202). The fact that Coleridge allows for the mind's passivity in perception, as well as the fact that the primary Imagination seems in the definition to coexist with all human perception, has led to a confusion of the primary Imagination with *all* human perception, both passive and active. However, Coleridge drastically limits the participation of the primary Imagination in all perception with the phrase, "living Power and prime Agent," which gives sacramental significance to the primary Imagination's role. The religious connotations of the words chosen by Coleridge have been overlooked, yet they offer a key to the interpretation of the famous passage. The word "agent," defined by the *Oxford English Dictionary* as "one who (or that which) acts or exerts power, as distinguished from the *patient*, and also from the *instrument*," and "of things: the efficient cause," rules out the possibility that passive perception, the mind acted upon by sensory impressions, is one with the "prime Agent." Coleridge's choice of modifiers, "living" and "prime," increases the meaning of the phrase beyond even active perception to a special kind of mental activity, whose function is no less than redemptive. The word "prime" derives from *prima*, as in *prima hora,* the first hour, which "in ecclesiastical and connected senses" means the canonical hour of the divine office, appointed for the first hour of the day. Figuratively, it means the beginning or first age of anything, and, in that respect, its relation to "the eternal act of creation in the infinite I AM" is evident.

The Symbolic Method

Perception, when imaginative, creates within human limitations the universe in an action analogous with the divine.

The second adjective, "living," has an equally religious significance: "that lives or has life," "said of the Deity (after Biblical use)" (*OED*). In the context of Coleridge's own writings, "living" is a key word, signalizing vitalism and organicism, opposed to the "dead" philosophy of mechanism and used with the full import of its religious meaning.[25] Since the "living Power" is the primary Imagination, all human perception has the potential to become alive and to act, rather than to be acted upon by impressions. This potential, though common to all,[26] is not commonly realized. It awaits those moments when, in Coleridge's analogy of the water-insect, the mind has gathered "strength and a momentary *fulcrum* for a further propulsion" (*BL*, 1:86) and successfully resists the river current, the pressure of reality.

The primary Imagination overcomes the flux of sensations assailing the receptive senses by transforming Nature into itself and infusing it with the coherence and unity of being.[27] However, this process remains indistinct and intuitive and cannot be contemplated outside the moment of union except by a renewed separation into self and object. The function of the secondary Imagination is to reconstruct that identity without objectifying it: "the secondary Imagination . . . dissolves, diffuses, dissipates, in order to re-create; or where this process is rendered impossible, yet still at all events it struggles to idealize and to unify" (*BL*, 1:202). Coleridge's definition does not explain what it is that the secondary Imagination dissolves, nor why the process is at times impossible. The suggestion has been made repeatedly that the primary Imagination supplies the secondary Imagination with the materials of the external world, which the secondary Imagination idealizes and unifies. But the primary Imagination also dissolves the distinctness of the object; and, since the secondary Imagination "struggles," apparently against some odds, to idealize only when it can no longer re-create by dissolving, the materials themselves must be in need of ideation, that is, be truly material. Given Coleridge's definition of the primary Imagination, it becomes incompatible for its sacramental agency to furnish the secondary Imagination fixities and definites.

Several passages in Coleridge's *Notebooks* and in the

Biographia elucidate the famous definition by clarifying the secondary Imagination's agency and the odds against which it struggles. In 1811, Coleridge has the following entry in his notebook:

> The image-forming or rather re-forming power, the imagination in its passive sense, which I would rather call Fancy . . . this, the Fetisch & Talisman of all modern Philosophers (the Germans excepted) may not inaptly be compared to the Gorgon Head, which *looked* death into every thing—and this not by accident, but from the nature of the faculty itself, the province of which is to give consciousness to the Subject by presenting to it its conceptions *objectively* but the Soul differences itself from any other Soul for the purposes of symbolical knowledge by *form* or body only—but all form as body, i.e. as shape, & not as forma efformans, is dead—Life may be *inferred*, even as intelligence is from black marks on white paper—but the black marks themselves *are truly "the dead* letter." Here then is the error—not in the faculty itself, without which there would be no *fixation,* consequently, no distinct perception or conception, but in the gross idolatry of those who abuse it, & make that the goal & end which should be only a means of arriving at it. Is it any excuse to him who treats a living being as inanimate Body, that ~~he~~ we cannot arrive at the knowledge of the living Being but thro' the Body which is its Symbol & outward & visible Sign?—
>
> From the above deduce the worth & dignity of poetic Imagination, of the fusing power, that fixing unfixes & while it melts & bedims the Image, still leaves in the Soul its living meaning—[28]

Through the passage Coleridge gropes for a clearer expression of the difference between death as the mechanical faculty Fancy and the living power of Imagination, although he will adhere to the distinction between Fancy and Imagination much more rigidly in subsequent published writings. In the passage, the materials to be dissolved by the poetic Imagination are those fixities and definites provided by the Fancy, whose too distinct outlines cut them off from each other and from the perceiving self. The Image becomes symbol by losing its separateness, changing from mere object to a union of Body, "the outward & visible Sign," and the "living Being," the Soul.

Coleridge's note anticipates some dissatisfaction with the proposed solution. His rhetorical question "Is it any excuse" concludes in an apology for a state of affairs in which knowledge begins with the soul's symbol—the form that literally embodies the spirit—for, as he remarks, that process leads many to stop at the form. This uneasiness with the outward form will grow in his later writings. The proposed agency of the poetic Imagination, on the other hand, because of the "worth & dignity" with which Coleridge invests it, performs two contrary actions. "The fusing power, that fixing unfixes" must dissolve the image of the senses, and, at the same time, create a symbol that itself fixes or stays the interpenetration of soul and body, and that, moreover, has a communicable form.

In the *Biographia* and especially in a marginal note to Schelling's *Letters on Dogmatism and Criticism,* Coleridge expresses even more sharply his sense of the inadequacy of outward forms and the necessity of going beyond them, even against them, fully aware of the seductive power of these forms and of the ease of succumbing to them. In distinguishing between men of talent and of genius, Coleridge writes: "The former rest content between thought and reality, as it were in an intermundium of which their own living spirit supplies the *substance,* and their imagination the ever-varying *form*; the latter must impress their preconceptions on the world without, in order to present them back to their own view with the satisfying degree of clearness, distinctness, and individuality" (*BL,* 1:20). The effort to idealize and unify mental constructs in order to oppose the too-vivid images of the senses appears in the note on Schelling as well, where Coleridge recognizes the difficulty of making the mind independent of Nature: "the continual warfare [against the "vividness of worldly impressions"] . . . calls forth every energy, both of act and endurance."[29]

Before his conversion Coleridge proclaims his faith in the power of the imagination. The head and the heart, thought and

The Symbol as Translucence

feeling, are the antinomies Coleridge strives to unite in his theory of the imagination and the symbol. The reconciliation of these opposites results not in clear and vivid concepts or perceptions, but in an indefiniteness that recalls the melting and dimming of the Image by the secondary Imagination and that in poetry is rendered as a swimming sensation. Coleridge refuses to associate the moment of cognition with the clarity of Reason alone. He insists on including the heart in the processes of the mind, from which, he argues, it has too often been excluded. Criticizing Hartley's philosophy in a letter to Southey (1803), Coleridge declares that associationism is based more on "the recurrence of resembling states of feeling, than on trains of Idea."[30] He objects to the very principle of mechanism when he states: "A metaphysical Solution, that does not instantly *tell* for something in the Heart, is grievously to be suspected as apocry[p]hal. I almost think, that Ideas *never* recall Ideas, as far as they are Ideas—any more than Leaves in a forest create each other's motion—The Breeze it is that runs thro' them / it is the Soul, the state of Feeling—. If I had said, no *one* Idea ever recalls another, I am confident that I could support the assertion." Significantly, Coleridge associates the soul with feelings rather than ideas and affirms the need to include feelings in any philosophic account of mental functions. Seven years later, he will assert that a philosophy that does not include the heart exerts the "mere understanding," "without exciting or wakening any interest, any tremulous feeling of the heart, as if it heard or began to *glimpse* something which had once belonged to it, its Lord or its Beloved" (*Nb*, 3:3935). The emotional response, the "tremulous feeling," occurs simultaneously with the intellectual awakening, and both result in an awareness which is by no means distinct, but rather a glimpse of "something." The imagery of the glimpse and of the tremulous feeling finds its way both in the poetry at moments of symbolization when thought and feeling are unified and the distinctness of objects dissolves, and in the prose when Coleridge explains the outline and consistency of the symbol.

The language in which Coleridge describes the symbol suggests, as in the case of the imagination, that the symbol requires a cluster of metaphors and images to describe its properties and functions. Moreover, although its nature and origin

The Symbolic Method

make it a much more profound medium than any of those Coleridge associates with mechanical philosophy, the symbol itself leads to an impatience with forms, which still remain the only means of communicating imaginative vision. Ideally, for Coleridge, the symbol is a construct that incorporates the essence of Reason with the forms of the Understanding. In it the mind, able to grasp at first the familiar forms, arrives at the truths of Reason that cannot be deduced from the experience of the senses. One of Coleridge's best articulations on the symbol occurs in the well-known passage of *The Statesman's Manual* (*Lay Sermons*, p. 29). Here, the "birth" of symbols happens whenever the imagination incorporates "the reason in images of the senses, and organi[zes] the flux of the senses by the permanence and self-circling energies of the reason." The symbol is both medium—a conductor allowing the passage of energy through it—and embodiment, circular in shape, but with no fixed boundaries, as suggested by the phrase "self-circling energies," in which the self-generated and self-directed motion of Reason opposes the flux of the senses and gives them shape. Although Coleridge warns of the bankruptcy of forms that, unlike the symbol, embody no meaning,[31] it is with the idea of embodiment that his dissatisfaction will begin.

The symbol as conductor transmits light, which, in Coleridge, as in the European Platonic tradition, can mean truth, ideas, God, beauty. These seemingly disparate concepts are metaphorically above the world of the senses, hence their identity with light. At the other end of the scale, opacity represents for Coleridge materialistic perception or matter itself. As early as 1801, he writes: "Materialists unwilling to admit the mysterious of our nature make it all mysterious— . . . Stir up the sediment into the transparent water, & so make all opaque" (*Nb*, 1:920). The world of forms can be both empty and dense, and Coleridge contrasts it to "that eternal reason whose fulness hath no opacity, whose transparency hath no vacuum."[32]

The symbol differs from both matter and the eternal reason in that *it* is translucent. Unlike matter, it allows the passage of light, but, unlike the divine Reason, it is only semitransparent and diffuses the light "so as not to render bodies lying beyond clearly visible."[33] The swimming sensation and the dimming of the image connected with the moment of imaginative perception and creation relate to the translucent quality of the symbol. The indistinct boundaries of the symbol exemplify the dissolving and diffusing of the secondary Imagination. When religious concerns take precedence and the Imagination loses its place as the indispensable mediating faculty, the symbol, too, falls short of the ideal medium since it distorts the light or, at least, interferes with its transmission. The two years that separate *The Statesman's Manual* from the *Essays on Method* produce a significant change in Coleridge's thought about the need for mediating forms between ideas and the senses. In *The Statesman's Manual* Coleridge compares Fancy and the senses to air because, while they are the medium "between heaven and earth," they function best when recognized as passive faculties and relegated to an inferior position: "for that very cause [sense and Fancy] stand in a desirable relation to spiritual truth then only, when, as a mere and passive medium, they yield a free passage to its light" (*Lay Sermons*, p. 10). The same work contains the second famous description of the symbol as characterized by translucence, "above all by the translucence of the Eternal through and in the Temporal" (p. 30). The diffusion and embodiment of a truth otherwise not perceptible represent positive functions of the symbol in *The Statesman's Manual*. In the *Essays on Method,* however, the human imagination is reduced to measuring its limits "as the foot measures itself on the snow." Since reality—"finite things"—ceases to exist altogether except in terms of substance or light, transparency becomes vastly more important than translucence, the light of Reason more important than the mediating constructs of the Imagination (*Friend*, 1:520).

The idea of translucence is far more fruitful aesthetically than that of absolute transparency, and, when less preoccupied with thorny theological problems like pantheism, Coleridge elaborates on its meaning. In the essay *On the Principles of Genial Criticism Concerning the Fine Arts,* Coleridge discusses beauty in music and painting. Here, properties of the form, such as "smoothness, richness of sound," play a role similar to the Fancy and the senses in *The Statesman's Manual* in that they, too, remain passive and do not interfere with the transmission of light: "Something there must be to realize the form, something in and by which the *forma informans* reveals itself: and these, less than any that could be substi-

The Symbolic Method

tuted, and in the least possible degree, distract the attention, in the least possible degree obscure the idea, of which they (composed into outline and surface) are the symbol."[34] The "illustrative hint" that follows represents Coleridge's most specific statement about his optical metaphors. He distinguishes between the forms of Nature and of art by pointing to the difference between the role of Fancy and sense, and the function of outlines and surfaces in the symbol: "An illustrative hint may be taken from a pure crystal, as compared with an opaque, semi-opaque or clouded mass, on the one hand, and with a perfectly transparent body, such as the air, on the other. The crystal is lost in the light, which yet it contains, embodies, and gives a shape to; but which passes shapeless through the air, and, in the ruder body, is either quenched or dissipated."[35] In contrast to the metaphors in the *Essays on Method,* the air serves light ill since it lets the light pass through without giving it perceptible form, so that the *forma informans* cannot be apprehended. If the surface and outline become the ends rather than the means of achieving beauty, they cannot transmit light and become like the images of the senses, *forma formata*—matter quenching or dissipating meaning. The crystal, however, shapes without fixing, embodies without immobilizing. The indistinct boundaries of symbolic forms, lost in light, exemplify the dissolving and diffusing of the secondary Imagination, a process parallel to the union of thought and feeling which produces the swimming sensation in moments of imaginative perception.

Coleridge's dissatisfaction with forms of Nature appears most clearly when the symbol is discussed not as conductor but as the potential working in the actual. As early as 1805, Coleridge records his thoughts about the correspondence of natural forms to states of mind,[36] and he concludes that the phenomena observed rarely strike him as new except that, in perceiving them, he discovers unknown aspects of his mind. They seem rather to be external manifestations "of a forgotten or hidden truth of [his] inner nature," "a symbolical language for something within," which has yet to be articulated. The symbolic expression for the power of the mind working within forms of Nature achieves that articulation in the *Biographia,* where Coleridge explains through imagery conditions under which form becomes symbol. Coleridge uses a favorite image, the metamorphosis of a butterfly, and con-

The Symbol as Translucence

trasts the beauty of the potential with the unattractiveness of the natural form: "They and they only can acquire the philosophic imagination, the sacred power of self-intuition, who within themselves can interpret and understand the symbol, that the wings of the air-sylph are forming within the skin of the caterpillar. . . . They know and feel, that the *potential* works *in* them, even as the *actual* works on them" (*BL,* 1:167). He explains, however, that "all the organs of sense are framed for a corresponding world of sense" and all organs of spirit for their corresponding world, so that the senses seem doomed to perceive the skin of the caterpillar, while the spirit intuits the presence of wings. Coleridge already begins to emphasize the difference between spirit and sense rather than their reconciliation.

The Philosophical Lectures of 1818 exposes even more clearly Coleridge's growing impatience with the impotence of forms in satisfying the spirit. Although he begins his illustration with Italian Renaissance art, he ends it with a look into infinitude not prompted by any form, but by a vast and shapeless expanse:

> There [at the court of the Medici] the mighty spirit still coming from within had succeeded in taming the untractable matter and in reducing external form to a symbol of the inward and imaginable beauty. . . . We feel it for this reason, because we look at the forms after we have long satisfied all curiosity concerning the mere outline; yet still we look and look and feel that these are but symbols. . . . Why, having seen their outlines, why having determined what they appeared to the eye, do we still continue to muse on them, but that there is a divine something corresponding to ⟨*something*⟩ within, which no image can exhaust but which we are reminded of when in the south of Europe we look at the deep blue sky? The same unwearied form presents itself, yet we still look on, sinking deeper and deeper, and therein offering homage to the infinity of our souls which no mere form can satisfy.[37]

In the phrase "these are but symbols," the adverb "but" expresses the writer's desire to move beyond even the embodiment of the "divine something" to the corresponding infinity of the

The Symbolic Method

souls, which, as he declares, "no mere form can satisfy." Even the symbol can become a mere form in the quest for the spirit, and though its function as medium between the world of the senses and the world of ideas still remains important at this point in Coleridge's writings, the impatience with the solution the symbol offers appears more pressing.[38]

Despite his growing dissatisfaction, which parallels his increasing orthodoxy, Coleridge does not abandon the symbol as distinguishing mark of the highest form of art even in this later phase of his thought. Some time after March 1819, he jots in his notebook: "the conversion of an *Idea* into a *Fact* by an imagined first Instance. 'In Adam we all die.' This constitutes Symbolic Poesy. . . . Symbols evince the *Fact* of the Poet."[39] His symbol and process of symbolization inform the criteria he applies to poetry and poetic theory—especially to the problem of poetic diction. The *Biographia* sets out to define poetic character and to settle once and for all the controversies about poetic diction raised by the *Preface* of 1800 to the *Lyrical Ballads*. However, Coleridge's enterprise is burdened by attempts to dissociate his poetics from Wordsworth's and his poetry from that of the Lake School. Before the 1800 *Preface,* Wordsworth and Coleridge collaborated closely. Coleridge's objections to Wordsworth's attitude toward nature can therefore be applied to a great extent to Coleridge's own youthful thoughts and practices, and Coleridge's unease about the pantheism in Wordsworth's work arises out of his all-too-intimate understanding of a position he shared and now rejects. Second, since the *Biographia* was prompted by a need for a preface to his first volume of collected poetry, Coleridge justifies his work before the world by trying to anticipate hostile charges against it as representative of the Lake School and by dissociating himself from the no longer congenial *Preface* of 1800.

Coleridge's somewhat altered opinion of Wordsworth's genius is evident in the change from unconditional to qualified praise in the course of eleven years. In a letter of 1804 Coleridge asserts that Wordsworth "has effected a compleat and constant synthesis of Thought & Feeling and combined them with Poetic Forms" (*CL,* 2:1034). The synthesis of thought and feeling, which for Coleridge signalizes the integration of faculties, should produce the great philosophical poem in the language, and Coleridge prophesies Wordsworth's composition of it repeatedly throughout his life until 1832, when he speaks of the promise in the past tense.[40] In a letter of 1801 Coleridge announces his goal of establishing a philosophical system that will reform metaphysics by the same means through which Wordsworth, the acknowledged superior artist, will reform poetry. Coleridge's hopes are grand indeed; he envisions not only overthrowing mechanic philosophy but solving "the process of Life & Consciousness" (*CL*, 2:706), just as Wordsworth is to overthrow the poetics dominated by eighteenth-century rationalism and to reproduce that process in his great work. In the *Biographia*, however, that hope is somewhat curtailed. Wordsworth's gift is limited to "the fine balance of truth in observing, with the imaginative faculty in modifying the objects observed" (*BL*, 1:59).[41] Coleridge's escalating criticism of Wordsworth in the *Biographia* relies upon the notion of Wordsworth's dependence on observation rather than meditation for his art.

Coleridge's disengagement from what he perceives to be Wordsworth's *cause célèbre*, reform in poetry, begins with some hesitation and retreat but develops into precise critical formulation, although some of the motives for Coleridge's objections remain unstated in the *Biographia*. In March 1801, Coleridge writes his approval of the *Lyrical Ballads* and, implicitly, of the *Preface:* "I should judge of a man's Heart, and Intellect precisely according to the degree & intensity of the admiration, with which he read those poems."[42] A little over a year later, in letters to Southeby and Southey, he writes of his suspicion that there may be a "*radical* Difference" (*CL*, 2:812, 830) between himself and Wordsworth on the subject of poetry, stemming from Wordsworth's statements in the *Preface* and even from practices in his poetry. He admits that the *Preface* is half a child of his own brain, but insists that he and Wordsworth differ, especially when it comes to poetic diction. "Metre," he writes, "*itself* implies a passion"; Wordsworth, he claims, has not done justice to that concept in the *Preface*. The distinction of poetic diction from any other has not been observed by Wordsworth either in his "system" or in his practice.[43] In the *Biographia* this difference yields

The Symbolic Method

fruitful results in Coleridge's formulation of a counter-system of poetic diction, which arises out of the different poetic interests of the two men. The very division into types of poems to be written by Coleridge and Wordsworth for the *Lyrical Ballads* indicates a divergence of interests which grew with the passage of time. Coleridge's poems were to deal with the psychology of characters, with the inner experience produced by an agency not in Nature, while Wordsworth would portray the emotion elicited as a result of actual events and observations of Nature.

The root of the controversy consists of Coleridge's and Wordsworth's diverging attitudes toward nature. The *Biographia*, Coleridge's first and last attempt to deal systematically with the theory of the creative imagination, contains his most daring affirmation about the mind's powers and, at the same time, his retreat from that position, exemplified most clearly in some of his major corrections of Wordsworth. Coleridge never shared completely, and in 1815 certainly no longer shares, Wordsworth's belief in the redemptive power of nature. In his own theory, however, the primary Imagination as agent and the symbol as conductor mediate between that world and the higher consciousness of man. The Imagination controls the fluctuating images of the senses by reshaping them and reading in them the eternal meaning of the divine creator. These assertions are apt to make the Coleridge of 1815 uneasy, since they verge on what he regards as pantheism,[44] and, as the conclusion to the *Biographia* attests, he is already moving toward a more orthodox position. In the orthodox scheme, salvation is reached through faith in Christ, not through the mind's own powers or the redemptive power of Nature.

In his applied criticism of Wordsworth, Coleridge objects to Wordsworth's description of poetic language as the language of real men and to his choice of characters from low life; the assumptions, implicit in Wordsworth's statements, are that what is natural is morally good and artistically superior. For Coleridge, Wordsworth's strength, his truth of observation, develops into a reliance upon Nature to provide the regenerative forms of art. Coleridge calls this tendency "*matter-of-factness,*" defining it as "a laborious minuteness and fidelity in the representation of objects . . . as they appeared to the poet," and as "the insertion of accidental circumstances" for the sake of establishing a verisimilitude unnecessary in poetry (*BL*, 2:101). Coleridge argues that closeness to nature in real life leads neither to the development of a better language nor to more humane values. Poetic language is subject to the rules of the imagination, and these rules the poet discovers by meditation, not observation of nature (*BL*, 2:32, 39–40, 64–65).

Coleridge defines poetic character and poetic diction in *Biographia* in part because of the controversy with Wordsworth, but in much larger part through the application of terminology dealing with the imagination and symbol to the area of poetry. Coleridge's requirements for the language of poetry closely resemble the characteristics of the symbol. The symbol unites thought and feeling. Poetic language unites similar opposites, passion and logic. These pairs of antinomies have in common the fact that one of the members provides intensity while the other imposes order and form. A notebook entry of 1807 suggests that Coleridge sees poetry as a synthesis of elements that combine to create symbols: "Pleasure the shadow & sacramental Type of that Joy (which by union fit and et facit et creat et creatur) or is it rather, that its essence being a divine synthesis of highest order reason—and passion vehementest Impulse, it must needs the soul in its two faculties, or perhaps of the two souls, vital power of Heat, & Light of Intellect—attract & combine with poesy, whose essence is passionate order" (*Nb*, 2:3092). The light of the intellect and its formative laws give shape to the heat of the impulse or passion in the creation of poesy. The account of the origin of meter in the *Biographia* emphasizes the same reconciliation of opposite forces at work in poetic creation. "The *elements* of metre owe their existence to a state of increased excitement," but their communication can be achieved only when these elements "are formed into metre *artificially*, by a *voluntary* act." The result of the two contrary forces at work, Coleridge specifies, is "not only a partnership, but a union; an interpenetration of passion and of will, of *spontaneous* impulse and of *voluntary* purpose" (*BL*, 2:50). The voluntary purpose that Coleridge insists upon in the metrical composition represents that conscious will at work in the agency of the secondary Imagination; the secondary Imagination strives to retain the intensity of imaginative perception by creating constructs embodying that vision. The diffuse nature of passions, that "vehementest Impulse" Coleridge describes as Heat, which in itself is disordered and serves as a stimulus rather than an agent of creation,[45] is retained but channeled into a communicable artistic construct, namely, meter.

The tension generated by the opposing forces of poetic composition is a requirement for imaginative creation, just as the opposition of mind and Nature produces the symbolizing perception. Coleridge calls works in which the conscious will and the intellect engage in composing without the stimulus of passion "a species of *wit,*" and contrasts the process of their creation with that of imaginative poetry: "a leisure and self-possession both of thought and of feeling [is] incompatible with the steady fervor of a mind possessed and filled with the grandeur of its subject" (*BL,* 2:68).

Poetic language, like the symbol, functions as a medium through which truths of a universal nature are transmitted. In the poem, the presence of the imaginative process reveals itself in "the balance or reconciliation" of opposites, which Coleridge lists: "of sameness, with difference; of the general, with the concrete; the idea, with the image; the individual, with the representative" (*BL,* 2:12). A comparison of this passage with the well-known definition of the symbol in *The Statesman's Manual* shows the striking similarity of poem and symbol: "A Symbol . . . is characterized by a translucence of the Special in the Individual or of the General in the Special or of the Universal in the General" (p. 30). Both symbol and poem have a concrete, individualized, perceptible form; both embody something that pertains to the class to which the form belongs. More importantly, both embody an idea that requires form in order to be communicated since it cannot be abstracted from images of the senses; its origin is in Reason, not in the Understanding.

Like the form of the symbol, which must not identify too closely with the distinct and fixed image of sense, poetic language must also sever matter-of-fact connections in order to renew perception in the reader. In a notebook entry of 1801, Coleridge speculates on the nature of such a language: "Whether or no the too great definiteness of Terms in any language may not consume too much of the vital & idea-creating force in distinct, clear, full made Images & so prevent originality—*original* thought as distinguished from positive thought" (*Nb*, 1:1016). Coleridge objects to the "full made Images," the total connection between term and meaning, which prevents the "idea-creating force" from combining terms in original ways and severing associations with those images. Like the secondary Imagination, which diffuses and bedims the image, poetic language works against the fixity of everyday usage. Much later, in his essay on *Logic,* Coleridge sets out to establish the criteria for a language of philosophy, and, though this differs from poetic language since it excludes the passions, it, too, requires a dissociation from the commonplace: "to emancipate the mind from the despotism of the eye" by tracing words to their origin will enable the philosopher "to use the language of sight without being enslaved by its affections."[46] Common usage of language, like the images of everyday perception, must be altered and reshaped before it can become a medium for ideas that originate in the mind, not in the experience of the external world.

As for the form itself, the equivalent of the crystal in transmitting beauty, Coleridge demands qualities parallel to those described as the symbol's in *On the Principles of Genial Criticism.* Smoothness and richness of sound, like translucence, do not attract attention to themselves, but allow the form to conduct the light. About verse, Coleridge writes: "The words, the *media,* must be beautiful, and ought to attract your notice—yet not so much and so perpetually as to destroy the unity which ought to result from the whole poem . . . the great thing in poetry is . . . to effect a unity of impression upon the whole; and a too great fulness and profusion of point in the parts will prevent this" (*MC,* p. 423). The language of imaginative vision must not impede its communication, and Coleridge argues for the need to express moments of great emotional intensity or of vision in plain language: "the more purely imaginative they [the works of the imagination] are the more necessary it is to be plain" (*MC,* p. 406). In this instance, Coleridge has established a criterion for poetic diction which describes his own experiments with the conversational mode.

The metaphors of form and movement used by Coleridge for both symbol and poem indicate further connections between the two imaginative products and illuminate Coleridge's poetic

The Symbolic Method

practice in the Greater Romantic Lyrics and *The Rime*. The "self-circling energies" of Reason which give the symbol its circular shape and suggest continuous movement, yet stay the flux of the senses, have their parallel in the ideal form of the poem, the snake with its tail in its mouth, which Coleridge describes to Cottle in a letter of 1815:

> The common end of all . . . Poems is to convert a *series* into a *Whole:* to make those events, which in real or imagined History move on in a *strait* Line, assume to our Understandings a *circular* motion—the snake with it's Tail in it's Mouth. Hence indeed the almost flattering and yet appropriate Term, Poesy—i.e. poiésis = *making.* Doubtless, to *his* eye, which alone comprehends all Past and all Future in one eternal Present, what to our short sight appears strait is but a part of the great Cycle—just as the calm Sea to us *appears* level, tho' it be indeed only a part of a *globe.* [*CL,* 4:545]⁴⁷

The poem, like the symbol, is not merely a circle but a self-circling motion, containing in its circumference events of experience in time and transforming them into representations of eternity. These two products, symbol and poem, retain within themselves the creative process, reflected in the movement within the stabilizing form. The past, present, and future experienced in daily living become "the great Cycle" by being embodied in a moment of vision which transcends the temporal so that both poem and symbol are a translucence of the eternal through and in the temporal.

Coleridge's enormous claims for the symbol and the poem make him acutely aware of the difficulty of his enterprise. He writes in the *Biographia:* "it is possible, and barely possible, to attain that ultimatum which I have ventured to propose as the infallible test of a blameless style; its *untranslatableness* in words of the same language without injury to the meaning" (2:115). The symbol, the blameless style, and the ideal poem remain ideals, and, although he strives to identify and define them in his criticism, Coleridge realizes the actual insufficiency of means at the disposal of even the most gifted poet in the practice of his art.

The Symbol as Translucence

In writing about "Intimations of Immortality," Coleridge recognizes the disparity between the poet's subject and the limited ways in which he can communicate his vision: "But the ode was intended for such readers only as had been accustomed to watch the flux and reflux of their inmost nature, to venture at times into the twilight realms of consciousness, and to feel a deep interest in modes of inmost being, to which they know that the attributes of time and space are inapplicable and alien, but which yet can not be conveyed save in symbols of time and space" (*BL*, 2:120). The symbols, ideally translucent with the light of eternity, remain nevertheless in time and space in order to be intelligible, and so they inevitably distort "those modes of inmost being" which are extratemporal.

III

In the structure of the Greater Romantic Lyric, Coleridge discovers the poetic mode that parallels the mental process of symbolization. Whether the images of sense or the imaginative constructs will win dominance in the mind determines the success of the symbolization. The question is, in Coleridge's terminology, Will reality become intelligible, translucent, or will it remain opaque? The question has equal relevance to *The Rime*, where the process of symbolization informs the overall quest pattern. The success of the Quest, and the outcome of the Greater Romantic Lyrics, depends upon the victory between two warring modes of perception. The relationship between the Conversation Poems and *The Rime* is much closer than has been previously established, and *The Rime* will appear less a miraculous departure from Coleridge's other poetry than an exploration of the symbolizing process in another typically Romantic genre.

In Coleridge's Lyrics of successful symbolization, "Frost at Midnight" and "This Lime-Tree Bower My Prison," the localized landscape perceived by the speaker at the beginning contains elements inimical to him. He finds himself trapped in circumstances that exert strong pressure on his mind. "This Lime-Tree Bower" includes a prose introduction with precise details of the

The Symbolic Method

poet's situation. Although the passage cannot legitimately be considered a part of the poem, it functions as emotional foundation for the speaker's bitterness in the first lines. The conversational "well" with which the poem begins sums up his helplessness. "This Lime-Tree Bower" starts with a conclusion: "they are gone, and here must I remain" (l. 1).[48] The garden bower with its lime tree imprisons the poet both because of its shape and because he is forced to remain in it. However, the juxtaposition between "lime-tree bower" and "prison" suggests that the natural setting, with its normally pastoral associations, turns inimical when it forces itself unsought upon the mind. The natural prison contrasts with the "beauties and feelings" contained in a landscape chosen by the poet and shared with friends; these not only would have provided momentary pleasure but also would have extended past and present associations into the future and compensated the poet for the loss of youth and its keen senses. Imprisoned by circumstances, he sees himself abandoned to a setting that fixes him to the present.

"Frost at Midnight" begins with a speaker less obviously at odds with his position vis-à-vis nature. Yet, as the description of the natural scene extends to include the speaker, the uneasy contention between his mind and Nature becomes pronounced. The poet, as in "This Lime-Tree Bower," is passive. He has been left to "that solitude, which suits / Abstruser musings" (ll. 5–6), yet he does not avail himself of it. Nature, all that is not human, intrudes upon him and destroys his chance for imaginative activity; the calm "disturbs / And vexes meditation with its strange / And extreme silentness" (ll. 8–10). "Meditation" for Coleridge is a word charged with significance. It denotes the act of creation by which an artist discovers the *forma informans*, the spirit in things. But the intruding Nature of "Frost," devoid of movement, of wind, imposes a similar lack of inspiration on the poet. The spirit of Nature is "inaudible as dreams" and as imperceptible to the poet as the ministry of frost. The point of departure of both Lyrics is not the descriptive "out" of a speaker in a particularized landscape, but the inimical "out" of the senses establishing itself as the mode of perception. Both poems represent successful symbolizations precisely because Coleridge identifies the problem between mind and Nature at the outset, whereas in "The Eolian

Harp," "Reflections," and "Fears," the initial confusion as to the role of Nature and mind prepares for the failure of their speakers to interpret the vision correctly.

"Frost at Midnight" and "This Lime-Tree Bower" move from the disturbing setting to the speaker's long-held desire for a comprehension of the world which cannot be satisfied by any natural form. In "Frost at Midnight," outward forms betray the speaker because he mistakenly places his faith in them as they are, without a creative transformation by the imagination. Left with his sleeping child, the speaker chooses instead the film on the grate (rightly called "*stranger*" as his remembrance reveals) as a "companionable form" because its motion resembles life. He admits that to identify the film with himself is an idle association. The lines are replete with references to the mind's passivity and to the triviality of its endeavor. The film mirrors the spirit in movements described as "puny flaps and freaks" (l. 20); the spirit (changed, from an earlier version, from "living" to "idling") and its search for itself in this form of Nature are reduced to "a toy of Thought." Vexed by stillness, the mind chooses to focus on the film, though its desire for companionship can hardly be satisfied by it.

As it moves from film of present contemplation to "*stranger*" of childhood reverie, the poet's consciousness follows a train of free association instead of imaginative activity.[49] The speaker's indulgence in a mechanical process of mind, combined with his misplaced faith in the natural form, anticipates the terrible disappointment inherent in this course of thought. Coleridge deletes lines contrasting the present playful mood with the child's earnest hope and changes "most believing superstitious wish" to "most believing mind" in order to give more weight to the betrayal of faith inherent in both idle thinking and superstitious wishing. The ardency of the child's desire makes him create from memory dreams of his home to the point where the intensity of his feeling dissolves the reality of his surroundings: "And so I brooded . . . / . . . mine eye / Fixed with mock study on my swimming book" (ll. 36–38). The speaker's initial unease, which made him turn his attention to the "companionable" film, has grown in the course of the reverie occasioned by the film to outright anguish, the anguish of the orphan child who vainly hopes for signs of familial affection. The faith the poet as child placed in the portent of the *stranger* remained unfulfilled, and he grew "pent 'mid cloisters dim, / And saw nought lovely but the sky and stars" (ll. 52–53). The warning from his unrequited feelings, which violently contradicts and awakens his spirit out of idleness, frees the poet from both the oppressive calm of Nature and his passive fancies. His search for a kindred being turns from the film to the child beside him when he understands that dead forms betrayed his yearning.

"This Lime-Tree Bower" establishes as great a disparity between desire and Nature's power to answer it. Trapped in his prison, the poet feels the frustration of desire as keenly as the child in "Frost at Midnight." While he broods on blindness and an old age bereft of consoling memories, his friends "wander in gladness." In his isolation he focuses on forms of Nature recalled from past experience, thus mistakenly and uncertainly paralleling the others' journey. Not until he abandons a landscape recalled through memory and revives his feelings for his friends does the poet break free of his prison and create. Imagining from a shared past the intensity of Charles's desire—Charles who has "pined / And hunger'd after Nature"—he reconstructs Nature in order to satisfy both his present longing for the beauties and feelings he misses in his bower prison and for those he and Charles lost as children. The poet invokes those powers in himself which can transform Nature so that experience becomes vision, sense perception becomes imagination.

The poet's invocation restructures his perception and unites him with his friends, particularly with Charles. It begins with an apostrophe to the sun, in which the poet asks for a prolonged sunset, in the course of which all of Nature becomes infused with light. The flowers are to "shine," the clouds "richlier burn," the groves "live in the yellow light," and the ocean "kindle." The images of sense change to symbols as the poet, through the imaginative process, dissolves and diffuses the precise outlines of natural images and makes them translucent. The swimming sensation associated with the union of thought and feeling overcomes the poet and, imaginatively, the friend, as they gaze on a landscape where "all doth seem / Less gross than bodily," since the imagination, not the physical eye, perceives it.

The Symbol as Translucence

Coleridge combines lines 41 and 42 by dropping the description of the "all" as a "living thing / Which acts upon the mind," thereby eliminating any passivity of the mind at this moment of perception. Moreover, the act renders reality intelligible by being sacramental, since the "all" it sees is "of such hues / As veil the Almighty Spirit, when yet he makes / Spirits perceive his presence" (ll. 41–43). The transformation of Nature results in a union in gladness of the poet and his friends. Whereas before the vision the word "gladness" indicated the separation of the desolate speaker from his fortunate friends, the words "delight" and "glad" apply now to the poet, who has been able to break through the prison of his senses; spatial limitations disappear as he imaginatively joins his friends, and those beauties and feelings to be stored for use against temporal decay become his as he declares, "I am glad / As I myself were there!"

The same process of transforming Nature into symbols activates the speaker's perception in "Frost at Midnight" when he turns from the fluttering *stranger* to his sleeping son. Just as the identification with Charles serves to break Nature's hold on the mind in "This Lime-Tree Bower," so the speaker's corrected thought frees itself from the overpowering calm when he chooses life instead of its seeming counterpart. The child's breathings, "heard in this deep calm" for the first time by the speaker, who had complained that the life around him was inaudible before, "Fill up the interspersèd vacancies / And momentary pauses of the thought." The idling intellect unites with feeling as the poet watches the child: "it thrills my heart / With tender gladness, thus to look at thee" (ll. 48–49). His hopes for the child disperse the imprisoning solitude of the poet's own childhood and of the initial setting. He reconstructs Nature for his son as he does for Charles from "nought lovely" to "lovely shapes and sounds intelligible." This Nature cannot betray because the mind is independent of images of sense. The verbs of sense "see" and "hear" in Hartley's unconfined wanderings (l. 58) refer to imaginative perception since through its agency he will find intelligible reality and read the meaning that informs images, the idea embodied in the symbol. The poet's misplaced faith, righted in his son, will enable the child to perceive the divine presence in symbolic forms, not vest mere images like the *stranger* with life and power.

The Symbolic Method

Abbreviated from the original version so as to create a circular structure characteristic of the Greater Romantic Lyric and of much of Coleridge's poetry, as well as of his symbol, the conclusion of "Frost at Midnight" consists of the intelligible Nature the poet offers his son. The exceptionless "all seasons" announces Hartley's freedom from temporal circumstances. The last three lines, which constitute the return, express the poet's freedom as well, this time a freedom from an encroaching, unintelligible, and inimical Nature. Although the ministry of frost remains secret, the quiet, dead Nature[50] preceding the vision gives way to the translucent icicles "shining" and to a vision of the only light in the poem other than the "thin blue flame" of the fire—the imagined moon. The icicles' natural formation may have remained a mystery, but their reshaping by the poet's imagination creates them anew, changing them from mere matter to a sort of crystal, transmitting a light bestowed upon the landscape by the poet's mind.

The return in "This Lime-Tree Bower" is more strained. The tortuous diction of the double negative, "nor in this bower, / . . . have I not mark'd / Much that has sooth'd me," suggests the poet's reluctance to leave the imaginative union with his friends for the bower that overwhelmed his mind. Light, with which he infused the Nature of the imaginative vision, again becomes a manifestation of a mind active in perception as the poet restructures his setting in terms of radiance and sunshine. But a subtle irony underlies the moral drawn from vision—"Nature ne'er deserts the wise and pure":[51] when the self maintains its integrity, Nature does not betray it because it does not give anything the mind does not already possess. Nature stands, rather, as a gauge of the mind's wholeness and of the dominant mode of perception. In terms of diction and structure, the imperfect return indicates how fragile the triumph of symbolization is since it depends upon an undivided sensibility. The bower seems to remind the poet of the circumstances that robbed him of "promis'd good," leaving him in need of soothing, and vision contracts a little as it takes stock of its pastoral prison.

Although the structures of "Frost at Midnight" and "This Lime-Tree Bower" are not identical, the symbolization in both follows the same pattern of an initial setting in which the mind falls prey to the unintelligible flux of the senses and remains imprisoned in the limits of time and space. In both, the turning away from Nature and the identification with a living being through feelings save the speaker by reactivating his perception and giving him the impetus to seek for forms, opposed to those of the senses, which correspond to his desire. When the imagination reconstructs Nature, the speaker breaks free of the original limitations. He unites with other beings and uses his regenerated perception to reclaim a meaning for the universe in his name and theirs. The forms of Nature become infused with light, sound, and spirit.

Much of the phraseology and imagery used by Coleridge to describe and define the symbol in his critical and religious writings borrows from the transformed Nature of the Lyrics, and the function he assigns to the symbol derives from the healing and liberating role of symbolization upon the speakers who create them. Coleridge's speakers, however, do not always identify the conflict between the senses and imaginative perception in their encounter with Nature; if they do not break the thrall of Nature and passivity, symbolization fails, as "The Eolian Harp," "Reflections on Having Left a Place of Retirement," and "Fears in Solitude" demonstrate through landscape and *The Rime* through the journey. The speakers in the first three poems and the quester in *The Rime* face an unintelligible Nature, at times obviously inimical, and have to recognize that Nature as the product of their own perception. They must either move to regenerate the imaginative powers through which they can oppose the images of sense with their own constructs—their system of symbols—or continue to be ruled by everyday experience and imprisoned in it.

"The Eolian Harp" and "Reflections" antecede "This Lime-Tree Bower" and "Frost at Midnight" by two and three years respectively, and their failed symbolization could easily be attributed to the poet's uncertainty in the genre he initiated with these poems. However, with "The Eolian Harp" a major problem of interpretation arises from Coleridge's insertions, the central one being the passage on "the one Life" (ll. 26–29), published twenty-two years after the original composition, although he added it to the poem in the *Errata* of 1817. As for "Reflections," one could argue that "Fears in Solitude" represents its revision.

The Symbolic Method

From the viewpoint of symbolization, the more important addition to "The Eolian Harp" is the little-discussed insertion of lines 30–33, made in 1803 and 1817, in which Coleridge sets up the assertions about Nature which lead to its rejection at the end of the poem. Coleridge's revision of the whole central section (ll. 26–33) may represent, as Abrams argues, his intellectual development,[52] but it obviates the mind/Nature conflict introduced in 1803, thus making the retreat seem arbitrary. In the 1803 lines Coleridge sets up assertions about Nature which need to be defeated either by affirmations of the imagination's greater powers or through religious arguments. The speaker, who moves from a conventional perception of Nature toward an imaginative one, grants images of sense so much independence that he surrenders his autonomy at the visionary moment. Symbolization fails in "The Eolian Harp" when, instead of restructuring Nature's randomness, he replies to the question What if? with orthodox responses, beating a safe retreat into convention from the awesome specter, raised by his speculations, of an inanimate Nature more powerful than the mind.

The poem begins with a description of a particularized landscape that lacks the inimical aspects of the locus in "Frost at Midnight" and "This Lime-Tree Bower" and from which the speaker draws moral parallels. Coleridge later observed that this "perpetual trick of *moralizing* every thing," of connecting descriptions of Nature "by dim analogies to the moral world," shows a divided psyche unable to meet the challenge of Nature's vividness and "proves faintness of Impression." The "formal Similes" evince not a transformation of Nature through unified thought and feeling but a "solution & loose mixture" with it (*CL*, 2:864). The intrusion of these devices into the initial description shows an emotional distancing on the part of the poet whose causes one could trace to biography, but which remain unexplained in the context of a setting that presents no threat.

The similes of the second part—"like some coy maid," "as twilight Elfins make," "like birds of Paradise"—move the speaker beyond the physical setting and emotional distance toward vision. Yet the problem is that the vision does not arise out of the experience of the speaker. Rather, the famous "one Life" passage functions as a theological justification for loving a world to which Coleridge grew reluctant to attribute power and which he became weary of opposing imaginatively:

> Methinks, it should have been impossible
> Not to love all things in a world so fill'd;
> Where the breeze warbles, and the mute still air
> Is Music slumbering on her instrument.

Despite the beauty of the metaphor in line 33, without the preceding four lines (ll. 26–29), there is no imperative reason to love a world because the breeze warbles and the still air has the potential for music. Admittedly, this paraphrase is a reduction, but the fact remains that Coleridge's text of 1803 and 1817 shows a decidedly greater claim for the world:

> Methinks it should have been impossible
> Not to love all things in a world like this,
> Where even the breezes, and the common air,
> Contain the power and spirit of Harmony.[53]

The phrase "even the breezes, and the common air" intimates that even the most insubstantial of the world's elements have forces equal to the mind's highest powers. These lines, censored from 1817 on, make up the genuine attempt at vision in "The Eolian Harp" and contain the explanation for the failure to symbolize. The magnificent and complex addition of "the one Life," on the other hand, does not rest upon the experience of the speaker and remains an insertion of Coleridge's philosophical thought, as well as a theologically sound justification for loving a world to which he is reluctant to attribute power.[54] In the earlier version, moving from the realm of experience toward vision, the speaker sees the potential inherent in natural forms as "the spirit of Harmony." But instead of recognizing his own power in transforming the initial conventional perception of Nature into this vision of the spirit in even lowly aspects of Nature, he attributes that power to Nature itself. This error anticipates his discovery of the deceptiveness of the senses and his subsequent rejection of it.

The poet's experience away from Sara turns the second section of the poem into a simile for the process of the mind. The tranquility of the setting provokes the same response in the mind as does the silence in "Frost at Midnight." The speaker's physical indolence parallels his mental passivity. Associations and fancies come and go like the wind and play upon his mind, while the conscious will of creation lies dormant. The accumulation of words denoting passivity is impressive: "thought uncall'd and undetain'd," "idle flitting phantasies," "indolent and passive brain." The simile between mind and "this subject Lute" pointedly reverses the meaning of "subject" from center of action and interest to subject subservient, in this case, to the randomness of Nature.

The second vision (ll. 44–48) resembles the first in that, again, the poet attributes power to external factors. The mind, instead of creating a construct that opposes the flux of Nature, extends the simile in a disastrous fashion from itself to "all of animated nature," which becomes the subject Lute, while the random gales have their counterpart in the "intellectual breeze." The answer to What if? is that animated Nature would then surrender its freedom, trembling "into thought" only at the will of the breeze. Similarly, the intellectual breeze—and Coleridge's qualifier limits the breeze to only one aspect of mental activity—would become God. The poet's reconstruction of Nature remains idle intellectual speculation rather than vision. The union of thought and feeling and the passion of an unsatisfied desire are absent from this central section of the poem, as are the symbols that could transform the randomness of Nature into coherence.

The return in "The Eolian Harp" can only ironically be termed so since, instead of identifying the problem of the unachieved vision, the poet retreats, in fear of pantheism and blasphemy, to the conventionality of the initial setting and goes so far as to denigrate the powers he failed to use. The word "shapings," used by the speaker to describe the mental process away from Sara, gives the unachieved vision undeserved strength; the problem with the vision has been precisely a failure to shape. The uneasy retreat serves to distort the real conflict and to suppress its solution.

In the end, left with an incomprehensible world that threatens to distract him from God and with an equally incomprehensible God, the poet is reduced to enumerating his possessions, equating the cot with peace and Sara. Even this curious counting of blessings is done under constraint, without the "tremulous feeling of the heart" or "the swimming sense" that dissolves the separateness of objects and unites him with life. Of "Peace, and this Cot, and thee, heart-honour'd Maid," the poet indisputably possesses only the cot. The strained return and the unachieved symbolization do not provide a peaceful solution to the vision of Nature subjecting the mind; and, though the poem was composed before Coleridge's marriage, he added the return later, so that notwithstanding chronology Sara remains the maid instead of becoming the wife. The poet's unconsummated marriage stands as a parallel of sorts to the unachieved union of intellect and feeling in "The Eolian Harp."

Written in the same year as the first version of "The Eolian Harp," "Reflections on Having Left a Place of Retirement" remains a minor poem among Coleridge's Greater Romantic Lyrics. Coleridge himself gibed at the subtitle of "Reflections"—*Sermoni propriora*"—and disparagingly called such poetry "properer for a sermon" (*CL*, 2:864). Yet "Reflections" serves as a blueprint for the longer, but more severely marred, "Fears in Solitude," written in the *annus mirabilis*. Since Coleridge had reached virtuosity in the symbolizing mode with "Frost at Midnight" and "This Lime-Tree Bower," one is left to wonder why he returned to the unsatisfactory pattern of "Reflections" in order to create another poem less unified and less even in tone than the first. Moreover, one may puzzle over the fact that the contraries of passivity and action, which are set up with almost Blakean clarity in "Reflections," become blurred and threaten the already diffused focus of "Fears in Solitude."

The problem of Nature's power which appeared in the censored section of "The Eolian Harp" haunts these more neglected poems of Coleridge's canon. Here, the speaker disguises problems of perception and creation with the veils of orthodoxy and patriotism. A mysterious crisis occurs in these lesser Lyrics.[55] In the context of Coleridge's theory of symbolization, "Reflections" and "Fears in Solitude" reveal the creative failure that gives rise to the unusually strident expression of feelings and to the fear and rage of the speaker. Despite his knowledge as poet by 1798 of the dangers of Nature's vividness, Coleridge feels impelled to extol the low and silent dell in both the earlier and later poem. Hence, the movement from dejection in nature to

The Symbolic Method

vision and back to a Nature corrected by visionary gain undergoes major changes in these poems, as it did in "The Eolian Harp." The inner vision here concerns itself with matters unrelated to the seemingly blameless setting, and the return undermines both the experience of Nature with which the poems began and the notion of any gain from the vision itself. With greater violence than in "The Eolian Harp," the speaker disrupts the initial calm and makes us question the healing virtues of his beloved dell.

A curious mixture of explicit praise and implicit emotional shrinking appears in the opening descriptions. And, whereas "Reflections" presents a lovers' retreat, the speaker addressing his beloved, in "Fears in Solitude" Coleridge intensifies the seclusion by having the speaker alone in the dell. Moreover, the dell, seen from the larger prospect of the hilltop, appears as a sort of bower-prison, keeping the speaker from communion with other human beings in the landscape. Small wonder that eleven years later Coleridge will reprint parts of the poem in *The Friend* under the title "Fears *of* Solitude" (italics mine).

In both poems the setting has a stupefying effect on the speaker's mind. The refuge it provides becomes in large doses an opiate. The speaker's mind is not fully engaged with *visibilia*, with what Coleridge calls in an 1802 letter "the great appearances in Nature." In the letter in which he reevaluates his admiration for Bowles and his own earlier poetry, specifically "Reflections," Coleridge insists that both "A Poet's *Heart & Intellect* should be *combined . . . & unified*" in perceiving Nature (*CL,* 2:864). Coleridge finds fault with Bowles's lack of "Passion," due not to a defective sensibility but to a weak intellect. The speaker of "Reflections" is a weak poet vulnerable to similar criticism for his view of Nature. The first two stanzas, like the opening of "The Eolian Harp," suffer from moral summations punctuating description; the most intrusive of these is the appearance of Bristowa's citizen, itself interrupted by the parenthetical "(Hallowing his Sabbath-day by quietness)." Even the masterful lines on the skylark turn to "dim analogies" as the speaker instructs his beloved, " 'Such, sweet Girl! / The inobtrusive song of Happiness.' "

Does the poet of "Reflections" also lack passion? He

professes that he, his beloved, the place, the hour are blessed. His survey of the two natural scenes, the "low Dell" and the "stony Mount," concludes with nature's effect on his heart: "all is hush'd, / And the Heart listens!"; "No *wish* profan'd my overwhelmèd heart." Apart from the personal happiness found in the dell—though that, too, has the religious function of quenching the merchant's thirst for gold—the poet recounts the greater joy of apprehending (or is it *seeming* to apprehend?) God's design in the wide prospect. Yet the poet has described without restructuring the landscape before him. He has performed no imaginative act, no fusion of heart and intellect with the appearances of nature. His most arduous toil, his climb, can hardly be taken as metaphorical since it remains an entirely external event. Before the vividness of nature and the despotism of the eye, the intellect is in abeyance and the heart is overwhelmed; "It was a luxury,—to be!" exclaims the speaker—to be, without wishes, with a mind overcome by images of the senses. The setting of "Reflections" affirms Nature's virtues but implies Nature's dangerous powers.

"Fears in Solitude" opens with one of Coleridge's most beautiful descriptions, and his summation (l. 12), his parenthetical aside (ll. 18–19), indicate the growth of his poetic mastery in the three years separating the poems. The man in need of Nature's healing virtues is not a chance passerby but the speaker himself. Nature's effect on him, however, contains ambiguities already expressed in "Reflections." The conditionals "would love" and "might lie" suggest the speaker's precarious situation vis-à-vis Nature. The speaker's physical position parallels his mental one: he is passive, "his frame" another subject Lute to sense impressions from the scene—skylark song, sun, "breezy air." As in "Reflections," the speaker might or might not apprehend "Religious meanings in the forms of Nature," since the clause containing that action is dependent upon the principal clause with the conditional tense "might lie." When the tense changes to the present, we know with certainty only that the man's whole soul is anything but roused into activity: "his senses gradually wrapt / In a half sleep, he dreams . . . / And dreaming hears / . . ." Coleridge, who presents the effect of nature on the mind so masterfully in "Fears in Solitude," multiplies the ambiguities. Nature can play upon the

The Symbolic Method

passive mind and at the same time supply it with the "materials ready made" for revelation of God's meaning, or it can play upon the mind until it lulls it into ineffectual dreams. The subtle manipulation of tenses in the first stanza leaves us with a speaker half-dozing.

Although the poet of "Reflections" and "Fears in Solitude" lacks the despair, regret, or frustration of the man in nature in "Dejection," "This Lime-Tree Bower," and "Frost at Midnight," Nature for him is neither consoling nor overwhelming enough to prevent him from attempting to overthrow it. But because he does not recognize his unease, his visionary flight displaces Nature's presence in his mind and disrupts the low-key conversational diction of the opening with bursts of rhetorical bombast which account in large part for these poems' minor status in assessments of Coleridge's canon. This second movement of the Greater Romantic Lyric, toward vision, begins with an alacrity on the part of the speaker belying his protests in both poems that he is "constrained" to leave the scene of his psychic indolence. The pretext is a pang of conscience at being so comfortable while others endure oppression or face war, and the speaker goes to great lengths in "Fears in Solitude" to conjure up images of battle and suffering. In both poems Coleridge gives us powerful versions of Blake's Human Abstract with "sluggard Pity's vision-weaving tribe" and the metamorphosis of "fratricide" into "mere abstractions." But how do these visions relate to the natural setting? The speaker told of a heart overwhelmed by a landscape and seascape that "seem'd like Omnipresence," of a mind finding religious meanings in Nature. Are such activities of the mind to be dismissed as "feelings all too delicate for use"? The speaker admits, in denunciations of his "coward heart," to attempts to "preserve / His soul in calmness," the uncomfortable passivity of his mind in the critical encounter with Nature.

"Reflections" contains a franker, clearer break with the pretense of Nature's beneficence. Since the claims for Nature are more qualified by the carefully repeated "seem'd" (ll. 38, 40), the vision is less vengeful against the localized scene than that of "Fears in Solitude." Nevertheless, the speaker mounts an unmistakable attack against the "Valley of Seclusion," which, with its "rose-leaf beds" and dream-enmeshed hero, harks back to the

The Symbol as Translucence

Bower of Bliss, whose enchantments must be broken for the hero's spiritual progress. The problem with the vision in "Reflections" is an obvious imbalance in sheer number of lines, as well as artistry, between description and denunciation of setting, and the alternative the speaker proposes. The resolution "I therefore go . . ." (ll. 60–62) dissipates its energy in the grand abstractions of "Science, Freedom, and the Truth of Christ." Renouncing his passivity, the speaker turns to a life of action but leaves behind, unsolved, his inability to respond imaginatively, to combat and restructure the images of the senses so that they reveal, rather than just seem like, Omnipresence.

If there is an imbalance in "Fears in Solitude," surely it is in the length and occasional bombast of the central section (ll. 29–202), where the poet constructs an imagery at odds with that of the first stanza and superimposes it upon the initial description in an attempt to obliterate the latter. The tortuous, often-interrupted sentence that begins the vision (ll. 29–40) becomes much clearer if one substitutes "imagine" for "think" in the construction "that he must think / What uproar and what strife may now be stirring" (ll. 33–34). But the speaker, who indeed imagines the French invasion, the near-defeat of the English, and their ultimate victory, disguises his creative activity under the cover of dutiful concern. The "small and silent dell," the "spirit-healing nook," like the film in "Frost at Midnight" and the lime-tree bower, inspires images of loss whose very violence cancels the dell's virtues—"uproar," "strife," "thunder," "shout," "fear," "rage," "conflict," "carnage," "groans." In his poetry as well as his life, Coleridge, far from being restored by the contemplation of natural forms, is often driven to violent imaginings. In a notebook entry written approximately a year and a half after the composition of "Fears in Solitude," Coleridge records his impressions of the landscape during a tour with Wordsworth and associates curiously, but repeatedly, aspects of landscape with human disasters, imagined or recollected: "The chasm thro' which it flows, is stupendous—so wildly wooded that the mosses & wet weeds & perilous Tree increase the ~~Hill~~ Horror of the rocks which *ledge* only enough to interrupt not stop your fall—& the Tree—O God! to think of a poor Wretch hanging with one arm from it / The lower Fall i.e. from the Brook is broader" (for additional disasters see complete entry, *Nb*, 1:540). "My eyes fatigued," writes Coleridge in the middle of the entry, leading one to speculate whether the imagined "Wretch" does not serve as a rebuke, a recalcitrance of the imagination against the all-too-vivid impressions from nature. A similar resistance appears in "Fears in Solitude," with a speaker inflicting imagined horror upon the landscape, from soldiers being gored to fleeing women "Fainting beneath the burthen of their babes."And when the speaker envisions the victorious return of the English, "with fear, / Repenting of the wrongs with which we stung / So fierce a foe to frenzy," it is not too far-fetched to suggest that the overwhelmed imagination is the fierce foe and the images of destruction its frenzy. As in "Reflections," the imagination fails in this poem, not because it is held in abeyance, but because it creates images of war divorced from the Heart to superimpose upon sense impressions instead of creating symbols with which to transform and give permanence to the vivid flux of natural forms.

The superimposition of violence upon the initial setting (carnage in "Fears," the "brethren" who "toil'd and bled" in "Reflections") leads to a peculiarly inconclusive return. The speaker has regained peace of mind but maintains the same ambiguity toward Nature exhibited in the opening lines of the poems and resulting in vehement denunciations and fearful imaginings. The fears that, with their tumult, noise, and carnage, have destroyed the quiet solitary presence of the dell in the speaker's mind appear in the conclusion to have remained a completely separate experience like the gust of wind which "bowed not the delicate grass." The heart and intellect have failed to meet the appearances of Nature, and the "undetermined conflict" that rages in the speaker's mind is powerless to move a blade of grass. In "Reflections" the site condemned as a bower of luxury reverts once more to the "sweet Abode" of the beginning, and, although the speaker attributes to it its proper function as a repose from mental toil (ll. 63–65), not a permanent dwelling place, in the concluding lines he elevates it to the status of a lost Eden.

This wavering between extremes—the claims made for Nature's power to save the morally corrupt and the denunciation of Nature as a lure to the senses which blocks moral progress—suggests that the failure of imagination in "Reflections" stems from the refusal on the poet's part to face the problem of his passivity and to resolve it internally. His turning to a life of action on behalf of the oppressed is morally commendable but poetically irrelevant. In the larger terms of Coleridge's enterprise, the failure becomes a betrayal of the mind's symbolizing power, of that which makes us human and thus able to perceive the divine reality sustaining natural forms.

"Fears in Solitude," the later poem, achieves in its concluding stanza an almost satisfactory resolution of ambiguities, only to turn again in the very last lines (228–32) away from the recognition needed for the breakthrough. As he is leaving the dell, the speaker experiences weariness from his fatiguing, groundless efforts at vision and from the oppressive setting. This latter thought, that Nature itself might have caused his fears and rage, breaks upon him as here he ascends both physically and psychically the "heathy hill":

> I find myself upon the brow, and pause
> Startled! And after lonely sojourning
> In such a quiet and surrounded nook,
> This burst of prospect . . .
> . . . . .
> . . . seems like society. [Ll. 212–18]

The "surrounded nook," like the lime-tree bower, turns out to have kept the speaker from the affective presences in the landscape—his friend, his child, and his wife—who would have made him perceive, and create for them, "The lovely shapes and sounds intelligible / Of that eternal language" found neither in the silence of the dell nor in the "thunder and the shout" of his besieged imagination. But, unlike the vision and return of "This Lime-Tree Bower" and "Frost at Midnight" where images of the senses are suffused by the light of the imagination, the final lines of "Fears in Solitude" once more extol the "quietness" and solitude that initiated such vividly imagined cruelty, yet that, the speaker insists, really softened his heart.

Nature's revenge in "Reflections" and "Fears in Solitude" is not simply imaginative failure. Coleridge creates the moving "Dejection" out of the same powerlessness of the mind. The revenge is the failure to recognize and articulate, as Cole-

The Symbolic Method

ridge is capable of doing brilliantly in "Dejection" and in his later poems of despair, the true state of a mind trapped in passivity. That suppression of recognition undoubtedly preoccupied Coleridge, who tried to solve the problem in "The Eolian Harp" through substantial and contradictory revisions, and in "Fears in Solitude" by correcting the glaring flaw of "Reflections," only to achieve complex, fascinating, yet deeply marred poems.

The Rime is a journey away from everyday perceptions and possessions toward vision, and the success of the hero, like that of the speakers of the Lyrics, depends upon his ability and willingness to forego the comfortable world of the familiar. The pattern of the quest generally consists of a youth embarking on a journey that has a definite object; the journey itself becomes a rite of initiation into manhood. The Romantic Quest maintains within its pattern the youth and the journey, not the specified goal, internalizing not only the adventures but even the landscape or seascape of the narrative to the point where it expresses the hero's psychic vision rather than an outer natural existence. Although the Romantic Quest comprises elements of the initiation rite,[56] the hero as a rule fails to become a man either in the ordinary sense of the word—successful integration into the procreative and societal life—or sometimes in the sense intended by the internalized Quest, namely, psychic awakening. The youth commits a transgression not against the natural order, but against his own progress, and retreats from imaginative perception into common beliefs and modes of behavior inadequate to his situation. He then finds himself in another plane of existence, which is even more removed from the norm than the original one, and becomes an object of horror or desolation, a premature old man who has not known manhood. The change following the transgression is rarely understood by the hero so that when he narrates his adventures, we must not expect direct enlightenment from him as to the nature of his act or his present condition. His quest may be termed "unending" in that the hero cannot return to human society. He remains forlorn, doomed to wander or loiter, seeking a pretransgressive state instead of an imaginative resurrection. He may, as the poet in *Alastor,* die, but, like the bewildered heroes of eternal quests, he would do so without reaching the goal.

The Symbol as Translucence

The Rime's uniqueness, its deviation from the general pattern, consists of Coleridge's inclusion of two transgressions instead of one on the part of a hero who at the same time comes extremely close to fulfilling the Quest's purpose: imaginative growth.[57] Moreover, Coleridge's Quest derives its uniqueness from the obvious, but not trivial, fact that it belongs to his *oeuvre*. It contains similarities of structure and content with the Greater Romantic Lyrics and, like them, lends clarity and force to Coleridge's theory of symbolization. Just as the specific locus of the Greater Romantic Lyric was used as a measure of the mind's success in symbolizing the evidence of sense, so the seascape of *The Rime* serves as a gauge of the speaker's progress and regression. Translucence signalizes the moment of symbolization here as in the Greater Romantic Lyrics, and *The Rime* has the distinct circular return of the *ouroboros*—a tale within a tale repeated eternally.

The voyage begins as a collective experience for the youth and his companions. Conforming to the genre of the Romantic Quest, it has no specific destination or purpose. The departure establishes the contrast between the sailors' expectations and the unfamiliar world they enter, and it foreshadows the inadequacy of their responses. They set out "merrily," oblivious to the portents of the ship's drop "below the kirk" and of the sinister sunrise. Beyond the range of familiar protections such as religion, community, and the watchful eye of the lighthouse, the sailors nevertheless cling to the conventions of the world they left. They judge seascape and events according to Christian superstitions when clearly these do not explain their predicament. The universe perceived by their limited modes of thinking remains threatening and incomprehensible. A measure of the narrator's lack of psychic progress is his unchanged perspective in the retelling. For the Mariner the terrors of the journey retain their full power. The storm that drives the sailors toward the unknown is still "tyrannous and strong" (l. 42), the ship still a victim pursued so closely that it "treads the shadow of his foe" (l. 47).

The descent into experience (and "descent" describes the movement of *The Rime*—"below the kirk") shows the hero as a naive youth unprepared to meet Nature at its most delusory, either in its seductive or in its threatening guise. Like other he-

The Symbolic Method

roes, the Romantic Questers are young, and the Mariner is no exception. Struck by the incongruity of an illustration of the Mariner as an old man during the voyage, Coleridge writes: "It is an enormous blunder in these engravings of De Serte . . . , brought here by Dr. Aitken, to represent the An. M. as an old man on board ship. He was in my mind the everlasting wandering Jew— had told this story ten thousand times since the voyage, which was in his *early youth* and 50 years before" (*Nb,* 1:n.45, italics mine).

The arrival of the albatross represents the chance to break out of limited perception. The bird, like the sailors, is a sign of life in the desolate seascape, and as such it could mediate between them and the unfamiliar world, since it belongs to that world and has ties with the Polar Spirit that loves it. A careful reading of the lines, "As if it had been a Christian soul, / We hailed it in God's name" (ll. 65–66), indicates, however, that the sailors remain trapped within their conventional responses. The subjunctive clause, instead of equating the albatross with a kindred being, contrasts it with one by means of the doubtful "if" of the simile. The lines point to the sailors' isolation, their willingness to accept companionship, and at the same time their refusal to acknowledge kinship. With his revision of line 67 from "The Mariners gave it biscuit-worm" to "It ate the food it ne'er had eat," Coleridge changes the albatross's status from pet to unfamiliar visitor in order to make clear the sailors' continued perception of the bird as an alien presence. Moreover, the association of the bird with navigational weather shows the trivialization undergone by the albatross in the sailors' minds. Their correct assessment of the bird's function is accidental rather than prophetic; they change their minds three times about the meaning of the albatross's death, each time basing their conclusions on whether the wind blows. In a journey whose purpose is the growth of the psyche, the sailors' death represents their refusal to develop so that they condemn themselves to the Coleridgean limbo of dead forms where the mind remains passive before the universe.[58]

The crime differentiates the Mariner from his companions. Serving as the turning point of the poem, it occurs just after the hero confronts a dimension of life, a possibility hitherto undreamed of in his limited knowledge. It appears as a response so

The Symbol as Translucence

wrong, a resistance so stubborn to the vision, that it brings devastation, blasting the hero and consequently the universe he perceives, transforming youth's early paradise into a nightmarish entrapment in experience. This aspect of the Quest presages the cyclical passage from innocence to the horror of experience in Baudelaire's and Yeats's poetry. As for the Mariner's act, Coleridge's comment about a real incident of bird-shooting from a ship, "It is not cruelty / it is mere non-feeling from non-thinking" (*Nb*, 2:2090), damns minds that commit such acts to living death. The absence of Heart in the Mariner's crime reaches its greatest limit since the Mariner transfixes the albatross to the irreversible definiteness of death. Starting with the confession "With my cross-bow / I shot the albatross" (ll. 81–82), the narrative shifts from collective experience to the Quest pattern of personal agony. The psychic killing of the albatross by the sailors, who feed it but refuse to see it as part of their world, discloses its full meaning in the Mariner's act, in the violently destructive retreat from vision which kills the only link of sympathy with an unknown that, perceived solely through the bodily eye—without feeling or thinking—remains a fearful universe of death.

Fittingly, then, the Mariner's punishment is life-in-death. Unlike the others, however, he accepts the responsibility for his crime and the added guilt of having caused the death of his companions. He hears his crime amplified two hundred times— "and every soul, it passed me by, / Like the whizz of my crossbow" (ll. 222–23)—and sees it mirrored in the undecaying corpses' eyes. The sailors' presence serves as a sort of affective center which, however grotesque, forces him to acknowledge that the outer corruption has an inner source, that the fearful unknown reflects the undreamed-of possibilities within. As he surveys his state, the Mariner finds that the rotting sea and ship and the curse in the dead men's eyes correspond to inner desiccation—"heart dry as dust"—and malevolence—"wicked whisper" instead of prayer. When he tries to shut out the horror by closing his eyes, he sees the same images pursuing him even in that radical retreat from experience.

After his dark night of the soul, the Mariner almost atones for his crime. He briefly frees himself from the mechanical modes of thinking Coleridge associates with death, namely, the

The Symbolic Method

senses, memory, superstitious fancy—"loneliness and fixedness"—in order to endow the images of horror created by such thinking with life, light, and beauty. The Mariner's imagination changes the sea and snakes from multiple mirrorings of his inner desolation to symbols, translucent with the mind's light.

Clouded by the delusion of believing itself "under supernatural agency," the Mariner's mind perceives only the strangeness, horror, and threat of the unknown:

> The very deep did rot: O Christ!
> That ever this should be!
> Yea, slimy things did crawl with legs
> Upon the slimy sea.
>
> About, about, in reel and rout
> The death-fires danced at night;
> The water, like a witch's oils,
> Burnt green, and blue and white. [Ll. 123-30]

The movement toward symbolization begins gradually, with sense perception, "The moving Moon" (l. 263); then sympathetic identification (l. 265 is the first place in the poem where the moon is personified); then recognition of familiar and therefore endearing aspects of the alien seascape, "April hoar-frost," "hoary flakes" (ll. 268, 276); and finally transformation of a fearful world into intelligibility:

> Within the shadow of the ship
> I watched their rich attire;
> Blue, glossy green, and velvet black,
> They coiled and swam; and every track
> Was a flash of golden fire. [Ll. 277-81]

In the absence of beneficent moonlight—"within the shadow of the ship"—but by the light of the imagination sliminess changes to "rich attire" and the "death-fires," "still and awful red," to "a flash of golden fire."

The spontaneous release of feeling occurs in *The Rime* at the symbolizing moment as explicitly as it does in the Lyrics. The Mariner declares, "A spring of love gushed from my heart, / And I blessed them [the water snakes] unaware" (ll. 284-85). By means

74

The Symbol as Translucence

of parallels to previous events and perceptions, as in the description of the sea and snakes, Coleridge contrasts the deathlike faculties with the Imagination. The image of love gushing like blood[59] recalls the earlier painful and ultimately destructive bloodletting, in which the Mariner bites his arm in order to find voice to herald the specter-bark. The spring of feeling fed by imaginative vision washes away the despair of a heart "dry as dust."

The regenerated perception is only a near-atonement for, immediately after the Mariner exerts the power of his mind over images of sense, he lapses into unregenerate modes of thought, namely superstitious delusion. Since "never a saint took pity" on the Mariner during his crisis, he attributes his release to an external source, a kind saint who takes pity at last, as he later attributes his continued punishment to the Polar Spirit. The intervention of the saint and the Virgin free the Mariner from accepting the implications of vision. He knows he can dispel the charm through imaginative vision and the inner spring of feeling, but the responsibility for a world full of horror and death is too great, and he withdraws, as does the speaker in "The Eolian Harp," to a conventional morality that dooms him to life-in-death.

Fear of the unknown, isolation from other men, and submission to supernatural control dominate the Mariner for the rest of his existence. While still at sea, the Mariner finds himself in the midst of a grotesquely ironic reviving of the dead bodies of the sailors, temporarily inhabited by spirits. This mechanical animation magnificently contrasts with Coleridge's principle of cognition, the fusion of subject and object, and becomes an effective image of a world abandoned by imaginative perception, devoid of a union of flesh and soul. On the voyage home he expresses nostalgia for the earthly paradise through similes that compare supernatural events on the high seas and the pastoral beauty of skylarks' songs and hidden brooks. His perception, however, remains essentially unchanged; Coleridge measures his lack of growth through parallel passages of the departure and return, in which the ship is and remains a victim pursued by "a frightful fiend" (l. 450). The Mariner's homecoming shows the impossibility of his reintegration. Although his mind longs for innocence, his experienced eye detects corruption in natural forms (ll. 520–22, 534–37). His presence devastates (ll. 560–61, 564–65), and

75

The Symbolic Method

despite his professed holiness, he negates the one sacrament, marriage, which in "Dejection" becomes the chief metaphor for the mind's redemption of nature.

The Mariner's conclusion to his rime reveals his doomed state and his own responsibility for continued loneliness. His paltry consolation for being shut out of the marriage-feast—after all, *he* is not a guest—contains disturbingly disjunctive language that stands in contrast to the imaginative moments in *The Rime* and in other Coleridge poems. Although the Mariner turns his back on the wedding for the sweetness of walking "together to the kirk / With a goodly company" (ll. 603-4), once there his company sunders into "each" who prays "to his great Father" (l. 607), so that the sense of community dissolves. The Mariner lists and catalogs humans and other creatures of God into distinct groups. This process reminds us of his predilection for fixing the infinite into dead forms and the dire outcome. Yet one could argue that what sustains these categories is the Mariner's awareness of God's love. The notion, however, that one is constrained to love because God does, which may make respectable orthodox doctrine, negates the Mariner's only moment of genuine vision. Love, joy, gladness of the heart come spontaneously when the Imagination symbolizes, creates a beauty hitherto nonexistent in Nature. Small wonder, then, that the Mariner's hypnotic constraint, which keeps the Wedding Guest from the marriage-feast, renders the Guest "of sense forlorn: / A sadder and a wiser man" (ll. 623-24). Like the Mariner, the Wedding Guest falls from innocence into experience without reaching the joy of Imagination. The Mariner's inadequate explanation of his voyage accounts for the nature of his punishment. He dooms himself to repeat his tale more than ten thousand times until he understands its meaning, until he sees that freedom from life-in-death lies in his power to symbolize and thus transform death into life.

Separated by four years from the *annus mirabilis*, "Dejection: An Ode" represents a significant departure from Coleridge's earlier poetry of symbolization. In "This Lime-Tree Bower" and "Frost at Midnight" the speaker discovers his power over the images of the senses which imprison him and delights in exercising it, and in *The Rime* and the failed Lyrics he retreats

The Symbol as Translucence

from the implications of that power. The poet in "Dejection" begins fully cognizant of the symbolization essential to his psychic survival and yet remains unable to achieve it. This double awareness of the need for vision and the inability to attain it gives the lament its poignancy, for here the speaker does not rationalize the failure and cannot reconcile himself to his state. Ironically, the knowledge of the vision and the recognition of its importance render the speaker's situation more intolerable than even the Mariner's compulsive retelling of his tale.

Coleridge's diction in "Dejection" is free from the defects in earlier poems (double negatives, parenthetical moral parallels, and the bombast of the moral views of "Reflections on Having Left a Place of Retirement" and "Fears in Solitude"). It gains a clarity of expression and a communicability attested by Coleridge's habit of quoting from this poem in letters, notebooks, and essays. The plainness of the language looks forward to Coleridge's requirements for a diction that can shape without distorting the "more than usual state of emotion" contained in the poem, does not attract attention to itself, and yet represents that order and logic necessary for transmitting the emotion.

"Dejection" begins with the word "well," surprising here as in the beginning of "The Lime-Tree Bower" because of its conversational and concluding quality. In both cases, Coleridge establishes that the poet's situation precedes its expression in the poem, and he amplifies this sense of stage-setting through a prose introduction in one and an epigraph in the other. The speaker in both poems finds himself in a pleasant natural setting—the bower and the balmy night—which is nonetheless inimical to him. Yet in "Dejection" the disharmony of mind and Nature is so great that, while ostensibly calling for relief, the poet calls for external forces to equalize the imbalance by destroying the serenity of Nature in order to make it consonant with his troubled mind. Rather than opposing imaginative vision, as in the successful Lyrics, Nature taunts the poet with images of sense which he can no longer render intelligible since the fusion of thought and feeling is denied him. The "swimming phantom light," usually indicative of the symbolizing moment, is enclosed in rigid boundaries, "rimmed and circled by a silver thread," just as the poet's grief stays imprisoned within.

The Symbolic Method

The poet's dejection shows the psychic ill responsible for his sense of irremediable loss and indicates the enormous distance traveled by Coleridge in the years that separate "This Lime-Tree Bower" from "Dejection." Whereas in "This Lime-Tree Bower" the poet suffers a disability (a lame foot) possible to overcome because it belongs to his physical being, the ill besetting the poet in "Dejection" results from an inner division he cannot hope to cure. His "unimpassioned" grief and "heartless" mood (ll. 22, 25) are symptoms of a deliberate suppression of feeling which has become automatic: "For not to think of what I needs must feel, / . . . / This was my sole resource, my only plan" (ll. 87, 91). The first version of the poem (the more clearly autobiographical verse letter to Sara Hutchinson) suggests Coleridge's personal dilemma, portrayed in the poem: a continual denial of emotion and passion for a woman forbidden to him until the mechanism of repression dominates his mind and becomes the "habit of my soul" (l. 93). The poet's inability to find that spontaneous union of thought and feeling which characterizes symbolization shows the continued division of his faculties.

Unlike the successful symbolizers, the speaker of "Dejection" is perfectly conscious from the beginning of both his ill and the uselessness of expecting relief from external sources such as the storm he invokes at the outset. He contrasts his state with that of his beloved, and here the lesson of "This Lime-Tree Bower" takes on an added dimension. The knowledge of the fall from the harmony with Nature granted to the wise and pure separates the poet from his own earlier and the beloved's present state of grace. She remains "pure of heart" (l. 59), and her psychic integrity leads her to see her life in Nature and to endow Nature with spirit.

The imagery and metaphors connected with symbolization in the earlier poetry and in the criticism appear in "Dejection" when the speaker distinguishes between modes of perception which decide the mind's life or death. In a poem whose emotional center is hopeless love the marriage metaphor effectively points out the contrast between the speaker and the beloved in terms of their power to structure Nature into intelligibility. The "ever-anxious crowd," unable to love, perceives reality as "that inanimate cold world" (ll. 51, 50) of death resulting from

The Symbol as Translucence

unimaginative perception. Lack of life and love becomes the "shroud" of daily images mechanically perceived and associated. To these images of death, Coleridge opposes the emotion "whose fountains are within"—joy—and whose release, like the spring of love in the Mariner's heart, transforms the whole universe of sense. The wedding of the self and Nature through the power of joy creates "a new Earth and new Heaven," so that the self weds an imaginative construct—a Nature that has become symbolical and thus meaningful. The marriage metaphor of "Dejection" illuminates the problem of the unconsummated marriage in "The Eolian Harp" and of the rejection of marriage in *The Rime* by suggesting that the failure to symbolize stems from a rift between the emotional and the intellectual being.

The imagery of light and translucence connects the "passion and the life" of the self with the forms of Nature. The transforming power emanates from the soul as "a light, a glory, a fair luminous cloud" (l. 54) and permeates the "cold world" so that Nature receives its life from a "suffusion from that light" (l. 75). Similarly, sounds (such as the sounds of life expected vainly in "Frost at Midnight") are echoes of the "sweet and potent voice" (l. 57) of the soul. The spirit, the life, the light of natural forms, the poet tells us, originate in the mind, which reconstructs mere images into symbols.

The lucid and explicit statements on symbolization present a contrast to the very process occurring in "Dejection." The poet's awareness about the relation of mind to Nature produces no transformations of images of the senses. No landscape suffused in the imagined light of a setting sun, no icicles translucent with moonlight modify Nature in "Dejection." As the poet surveys his past and measures his losses, and as he turns to the storm he invoked in the beginning, he remains imprisoned in a mode of unimaginative perception which cannot transform his circumstances, but rather delivers his mind to the play of Nature's images.

The imagery of stanza 6 suggests that the poet has subconsciously succumbed to the mood evoked by the changing weather, even though he consciously acknowledges the wind "which long has raved unnoticed" (l. 97) only when his lament is over. Of the past, he says, "hope grew round me, like the twining vine, / And fruits, and foliage, not my own, seemed mine" (ll.

The Symbolic Method

80–81); at present "afflictions bow me down to earth" (l. 82). The image of the poet as tree, especially a tree bent by gales of affliction, suggests that he has incorporated the wind's movement in his recollection and has allowed it to shape his thoughts. The lament for the loss of his "shaping spirit of Imagination" (l. 86) is thus not an idle cry of self-pity, but a painful realization of an actual state.

The speaker's conscious response to the wind reinforces the storm's dominance over the mind. The initial welcome of the approaching storm as a force capable of rousing his psyche from lethargy proves false. Here, as in "The Eolian Harp" and "Fears in Solitude," the poet is being played upon, but from passive instrument he becomes accomplice. He takes upon himself the role of interpreter of the wind, who is the "mighty Poet," a "mad lutanist," and whose proper instruments are the lonely, deserted, wrecked pieces of nature, or even unholy habitations. The poet associates himself with these, especially with the "blasted tree," when he becomes the agent of the wind's voice, and his office takes on unholy duties as he conjures up images of massacres and battles. The destructiveness of the fragmented psyche, suggested in the beginning by the poet's desire to bring the storm upon the balmy night, reveals itself undisguised. Unlike the powerless wind of "Fears in Solitude," which could not bow a blade of grass, the wind here, out of step with the season, wreaks wintry destruction upon the spring garden, and the poet translates that havoc in human terms instead of opposing it.

The wind's last tale, though of "less affright" for the listener, contains images of abandonment countered by a hope the poet himself no longer has. His own lament, explicitly expressed in the "Letter to Asra," is a cry for love which will not be answered.[60] Unlike the child who placed his hope in outside intercessors, the poet of "Dejection" has learned that deliverance comes only from within.

In the conclusion of "Dejection," the imaginative union with another being, which frees the poet from the prison of the senses in "This Lime-Tree Bower" and "Frost at Midnight," remains unachieved. His wishes for the beloved are a prayer for a state of grace in which he cannot share. To emphasize the hopelessness of the union, Coleridge discards the line "And sing his

The Symbol as Translucence

lofty song and teach me to rejoyce" (in his revision of the address from William to "Lady").

"Dejection" represents Coleridge's most conscious poetic statement on symbolization. Because of the crisis of his psyche—the fragmentation of intellect and feeling—though he faces by turn a calm and peaceful Nature and a stormy one, the poet is unable to give it coherence and meaning. Conscious of the mind's powers and of the need to regenerate the inanimate world, he can no longer perform the symbolizing act and lets himself fall prey to the images of death and hopelessness which threaten those bereft of imagination.

IV

With "Dejection," Coleridge reaches a final impasse in his poetry of symbolization, though the poem by no means represents his poetic last testament.[61] The biographical events, expressed more directly in the letter to Sara, indicate Coleridge's crisis of confidence in his powers as poet and as man. The problem of psychic fragmentation, unresolved in the poetry, compels Coleridge to seek solutions in a system of metaphysics in which the theory of imagination and of the symbol play a major role. However, after having proclaimed the ascendancy of the mind over phenomena, he begins to turn more and more to religion and inward contemplation as the means of discovering God and the divine order of the universe.

Coleridge's uneasiness with his faith in the creative imagination is evident as early as 1795, in the unsuccessful symbolization of "The Eolian Harp" and "Reflections," but it becomes more powerful in his transitional work, the *Biographia,* where marginal notes and revisions show Coleridge's gradual retreat from his daring theory of the imagination. That he invents the excuse of the letter from a friend in order to avoid an extended definition of the imagination, the elucidation of which stands at the apex of the *Biographia,* suggests that he had strong second thoughts about a theory in which the mind, unaided by faith, can formulate the meaning of the universe. Sara Coleridge's note

The Symbolic Method

about an edition of the *Biographia* emended by Coleridge confirms the speculation that he did, indeed, fear he affirmed too much about the power of imagination. She writes that the last clause of the definition of the primary Imagination—"as a repetition in the finite mind of the eternal act of creation in the infinite I AM"—is "stroked out."[62] The cancellation of the phrase that likens the finite mind with God in the act of imaginative creation indicates to what extent the *Biographia* represents the climax and the end of Coleridge's faith in the mind's independent powers.

The most striking difference between Coleridge's view of the imagination and symbol up to approximately 1817 and his later orthodoxy appears in the dethroning of the Imagination as the essential mediating faculty in favor of Reason. In the earlier works, Coleridge without hesitation equates the Imagination with the discovery of the divine order in the universe. In *Lectures on Politics and Religion* (1795) he calls the Imagination the power of discerning the Cause in the Effect, which enables men to "see . . . God everywhere—the Universe in the most literal Sense is his written Language."[63] Similarly, in *The Friend*, Coleridge ascribes the deterioration of the world to the fact that the Imagination has been excluded from poetry, the result being "the eclipse of the ideal by the mere shadow of the sensible" (1:447). *Aids to Reflection* emphasizes Coleridge's change of thought. He pairs Reason and Understanding in the same way as he does Imagination and Fancy in the *Biographia;* Reason serves as the supreme faculty, with no mediator between the opposites of the pair. He writes: "Understanding in its highest form of experience remains commensurate with the experimental notices of the senses from which it is generalized. Reason, on the other hand, either predetermines experience, or avails itself of a past experience to supersede its necessity in all future time; and affirms truths which no sense could perceive, nor experiment verify, nor experience confirm."[64] The mediating Imagination has no function to perform here. The separation of the senses and Reason obviates the role of the Imagination. Nature in *Aids to Reflection* remains unregenerate as the mind seeks for the light of God through a process that obviates the need for symbolization.

Coleridge's argument on immortality sets an equally sharp contrast between human nature and "animated [living things] or inanimate nature." He dismisses those "things in visible nature" which "endure amid continual flux unchanged," such as beauty, harmony, order, as "*congenera* of mind and will, without which indeed they would not only exist in vain . . . but actually not exist at all." The process of symbolization—the regeneration of Nature through imaginative perception—becomes the "*peculia* of humanity" as that process is supplanted by thoughts of immortality. Even when he desires to prove the soul's immortality by observing that Nature fulfills her prophecies, he apologizes to the reader for turning to Nature for his proofs: "The Reader will . . . understand, that I am here speaking in the assumed character of a mere naturalist, to whom no light of revelation has been vouchsafed" (*AR*, p. 329).

This new sort of *contemptus mundi*, which dismisses altogether the relevance of the world of senses, necessarily diminishes the status of the symbol together with that of the imagination. While Coleridge insists on the distinction of symbols and metaphors, he describes the process of analogy which goes into the making of a symbol as "a principle in a higher dignity . . . expressed by a principle in a lower but more known form" (*AR*, p. 235). His symbol is no longer the light in crystal, the imaginative construct embodying the idea, but two separate principles, one of which descends to the general level of men by adopting a lower form. From the symbol in *The Statesman's Manual*, which, "while it enunciates the whole, abides itself as a living part of that Unity, of which it is the representative" (p. 30), Coleridge moves to simple metonymy in *Aids to Reflection:* "The word symbol, rightly defined;—[is] a sign included in the idea which it represents;—that is, an actual part chosen to represent the whole, as a lip with a chin prominent is a symbol of man" (p. 270n). The part chosen to represent the whole, the lip with the chin prominent, can hardly bear the burden assigned to the symbol in the earlier work, namely, that of rendering the reality it represents intelligible.

In *Aids to Reflection*, it becomes apparent that Coleridge wants to curtail sharply the power of the mind over the world of sense whenever that power threatens to act independently of faith. In a passage on discursive thinking, Coleridge warns against transforming the products of such thinking into "real ob-

The Symbolic Method

jects, by aid of the imagination." Such embodiment results in superstition, since "these substantiated notions were . . . expressed by the same terms as the objects of religious faith" (*AR*, p. 210). However, the imagination in Coleridge's aesthetic theory does not transform ideas into images of the senses, into objects that are real in the sense of belonging to the external world. Coleridge's fear that the constructs of the imagination may be mistaken for the objects of faith determines his retreat from the affirmations of the mind's power. The role of the imagination in *Aids to Reflection* becomes the same as that of Nature in his poems, deluding the mind with its constructs and distracting it from finding God.

In his famous letter to Gillman, Coleridge gives a highly spirited account of his disappointment with the failing power of his imagination and his losing battle against the psychic fragmentation that disabled him from supplanting the images of the senses with those of his creation:

> In youth and early manhood the mind and nature are, as it were, two rival artists both potent magicians, and engaged, like the King's daughter and the rebel genii in the Arabian Nights' Entertainments, in sharp conflict of conjuration, each having for its object to turn the other into canvas to paint on, clay to mould, or cabinet to contain. For a while the mind seems to have the better in the contest, and makes of Nature what it likes . . . transforms her summer gales into harps and harpers, lovers; sighs and sighing lovers, and her winter blasts into Pindaric Odes, Christabels, and Ancient Mariners set to music by Beethoven, and in the insolence of triumph conjures her clouds into whales, and walruses with palanquins on their backs, and chases the dodging stars in a sky-hunt! But alas! alas! that Nature is a wary wily long-breathed old witch, tough-lived as a turtle and divisible as the polyp, repullulative in a thousand snips and cuttings, *integra et in'toto*. She is sure to get the better of Lady *Mind* in the long run and to take her revenge too; transforms our to-day into a canvas dead-coloured to receive the dull, featureless portrait of yesterday; not alone turns the ci-divant sculptress with all her

The Symbol as Translucence

kaleidoscopic freaks and symmetries! into clay, but *leaves* it such a *clay* as to cast dumps or bullets in; and lastly (to end with that which suggested the beginning) she mocks the mind with its own metaphor, metamorphosing the memory into a *lignum vitae* escritoire to keep unpaid bills and dun's letters in, with outlines that had never been filled up, *MSS.* that never went further than the title-pages, and proof-sheets, and foul copies of Watchmen, Friends, Aids to Reflection, and other *stationary* wares that have kissed the publishers' shelf with all the tender intimacy of inosculation![65]

In a losing battle against circumstances, Coleridge turns to inward contemplation and searches for meaning in religion rather than art. Yet he possesses the self-knowledge to list his artistic triumphs with the imaginative, youthful phase of his mental life, and other works (among which is *Aids to Reflection*) with the unpaid dues, the unfulfilled potential serving as mocking mirror to the promise of his early years.[66]

While it was his orthodoxy that earned him his reputation as the "sage of Highgate," Coleridge's continuing influence on the latter half of the nineteenth century and the early part of the twentieth rests on his theory of the symbolizing imagination and on his poetry of symbolization. The Greater Romantic Lyric, adopted by Wordsworth for some of his most important poems and later by the younger generation of the Great Romantics, continues to be used by modern poets like Yeats, Eliot, and Stevens, and survives as a genre because it successfully embodies the dialogue of mind and nature leading to symbolization. Its adaptability to low-key descriptions of the everyday and to the passionate language of vision represents a peculiarly modern development in which private vision becomes universal; vision begins with the strife between passive faculties, ruled by sense impressions, and active ones, and ends with the mind's freedom from the constraints of daily circumstances and with its creation of an intelligible, coherent reality. The Mariner's journey provides one of the Romantic prototypes for the structuring of an *oeuvre* along the patterns of the mental event and mental progress.

The Symbolic Method

Coming to France via the circuitous route of Edgar Allan Poe and lesser intermediaries, Coleridge's ideas of the mind active in perception and at war with nature strike a responsive chord in Baudelaire and continue to reverberate in their literary heirs. Coleridge's aesthetics reach England via Symbolism and in turn influence the young Yeats. Symbolism, a system of symbols, the reintegration of the mind as prelude to imaginative creation, and the search for a communicable diction are major concerns in Yeats's poetry and aesthetic formulations.

As a result of its widespread—though often diffuse and distorted—influence, Coleridge's criticism remains a source of critical theories and debates in the twentieth century as well, both because of the issues it raises about the human psyche and the process of creation and because so many poets and writers with whom criticism deals have been influenced by Coleridge's ideas and reflect them in their writings. Words like "imagination" and "symbol," for example, adopted into the language of criticism, have become almost always synonymous with successful artistic creation. Some critics feel that, like his symbol, Coleridge frustrates his readers with a potential, a glimmer of possibilities never fulfilled. His enterprise, however, is one which of necessity requires a continual renewal of the mind's powers, an effort difficult to sustain in the face of inevitable distractions and defeats suffered because of those very circumstances against which the imagination tries to score its triumphs.

Coleridge's legacy to our age, in criticism and in poetry, contradicts T. S. Eliot's influential assertion of a dissociation of sensibility in the English Romantics. Coleridge decried that dissociation and remained conscious of its dangers at all times, attempting to heal it by a union of the faculties, of head and heart. The dissociated sensibility as the tyranny of one faculty to the exclusion of the others becomes fatal to humanity in Coleridge's view, resulting in the mass madness and derangement that in his age was exemplified by the aftermath of the French Revolution (see *Lay Sermons*, pp. 63–64). Unlike his imperfect quester, the Mariner, Coleridge continued his search fully conscious of the probability of failure and of the ever-present need to renew the struggle toward constructing one's humanity.

THREE BAUDELAIRE
HUNGER FOR THE TRUE PARADISE

> As light to the eye, even such is beauty to the mind, which cannot but have complacency in whatever is perceived as pre-configured to its living faculties.
>
> Coleridge,
> "On the Principles of Genial Criticism Concerning the Fine Arts"

> Beauty is made up of an eternal, unchanging element, whose quantity is extremely difficult to determine, and of a variable, incidental element, which might be . . . a given period or fashion, a set of morals or passions. Without this second element, which serves as the pleasing, tingling, appetizing glaze on the Divine Pastry, the first element would be indigestible and imperceptible as well as unsuitable and unfit for human nature.
>
> Baudelaire,
> "The Painter of Modern Life"

Like Coleridge's symbol, Baudelaire's beauty embodies eternity in the particulars of time in order to give perceptible form to the divine. Yet Coleridge's metaphors about beauty and the symbol emphasize without exception the divine component—

The Symbolic Method

light. Appealing to man's highest sense, his sight, the symbol activates man's "living faculties" and effects his regeneration. Baudelaire shows more skepticism about mankind's attraction to the divine. His "eternal element" appeals to man's "immortal appetite" (*OC*, 2:685) by becoming firmly grounded in tantalizing temporal forms. Yet both the word "Pastry," that superfluity of culinary art, and the word "Divine" strongly suggest that beauty fulfills psychic, not bodily, needs, and that its temporal shape encloses the promise of inexhaustible plenitude. Baudelaire's creative and critical work expresses a consciousness of the Fall and a longing for the lost paradise which appropriately manifest themselves through the same senses that caused the Fall—thirst, hunger for knowledge and completion. For Coleridge, "living faculties" recognize beauty as their own divine origin in a spontaneous and instantaneous act. He therefore relegates memory, which is not related to spontaneous perception, to mechanical functions of the mind. Baudelaire, on the contrary, elevates the role of memory and reverie to imaginative creation since they become the means of restructuring reality according to prelapsarian models within the mind.

Despite these divergences of focus and emphasis in Coleridge's and Baudelaire's views of man's relationship with the divine, Baudelaire's work represents a continuation of Coleridge's theory of creativity and poetic practice. Both men concentrate on the nature of the symbol, on the imaginative process that produces it, and on the redemptive role of an art that embodies this process. For Baudelaire, as for Coleridge, the transformation of nature into symbol begins with the mind/nature tension and ends with the imagination creating coherent structures out of the oppressive chaos of sense impressions. These triumphs stand as evidence of a mind made whole through symbolization. Baudelaire's search for psychic integration in his criticism and particularly in the quest structure of *Les Fleurs du Mal* emphasizes his commitment to the humanism of the Romantics.

First published in 1857, twenty-three years after Coleridge's death, *Les Fleurs du Mal* clearly belongs to the European tradition of lyrics composed according to a central theme and having as narrator a quester. At the same time, *Les Fleurs du Mal* adopts the characteristics of the internalized Romantic

Quest. In Christian works, such as Dante's *Vita Nuova* and Petrarch's *Canzoniere*, the overt theme of the lyrics is love, but the awakening of the soul provides the true impetus for the quest. Both the English and French Renaissance sonnet sequences explore more temporal aspects of love, sometimes relating them, as in Ronsard's *Amours*,[1] to the physical growth and decline of man, and, inversely, to increased poetic prowess. The Romantics fuse the Christian and the more secularized Renaissance version of man by internalizing the emblematic journey of the soul. The poet as private being and as representative of mankind becomes the controlling myth of the quest romance. Blake's *Songs of Innocence and Experience*, Wordsworth's and Coleridge's *Lyrical Ballads*, Keats's *Poems* (1817),[2] all represent the effort to create the vaster movement of the epic through the personal genre of the lyric. The word "architecture" itself,[3] encountered so frequently in exegeses of *Les Fleurs du Mal*, finds a striking precedent in Wordsworth's conception of the body of his work: "The two works [*The Prelude* and *The Recluse*] have the same kind of relation to each other . . . as the ante-chapel has to the body of a gothic church . . . his [the author's] minor Pieces, which have been long before the Public, when they shall be properly arranged, will be found by the attentive Reader to have such connection with the main Work as may give them claim to be likened to the little cells, oratories, and sepulchral recesses, ordinarily included in those edifices."[4] Disappointing Coleridge's hope for the great philosophical poem of the century, Wordsworth did not finish *The Recluse* and left his monument incomplete. Wordsworth's desire for a unified body of lifetime production will be fulfilled by Yeats's *Collected Poems*, where, despite the contradiction of the word "collected," Yeats uses poems not as individual summings-up of experience but as stones for the larger structure of the *oeuvre*.

Conscious of the importance of its arrangement, Baudelaire, like Wordsworth, attempts to give cohesion to his poetry throughout his life. Moreover, he considers *Les Fleurs du Mal* his original work. He refers to *Spleen de Paris* as a variant of *Les Fleurs du Mal*, written with greater freedom.[5] He continues to add to the work, at first constrained by the necessity of replacing the six pieces condemned in 1857, then relishing the addition of thirty-five new poems in 1861, and referring repeatedly in the year before his death to the *Nouvelles Fleurs du Mal* (*Corr.*, 2:521-23, 591), which was to incorporate new poems into the overall design. Unlike Yeats, Baudelaire refines and strengthens the structure of the already existing cycles instead of writing new ones. Like Wordsworth and Coleridge, he leaves his own vision unachieved, but, with the definitive edition of 1861, he leaves his readers that specifically Romantic work, a lyrical epic, with stages of the journey exemplified by the successive cycles of symbolization of *Les Fleurs du Mal.*

Since Baudelaire parallels closely the English Romantic experience rather than the French, a number of studies deal with the question of influence. However, these tend to center on Poe more than on any other figure. Clearly, Baudelaire's involvement with Poe's life and work, his reading of Catherine Crowe, and his general awareness of the contemporary English literary world[6] immerse him in a post-Romantic atmosphere; here, the aesthetic and philosophy of German Romanticism and of Coleridge find their way even in works on spiritualism like Crowe's *The Night-Side of Nature,* where terms such as "imagination," "fancy," and "symbol" become diluted without Coleridge's fastidiousness for precision and consistency in definitions. Baudelaire's use of a quotation from Crowe illustrates the thorny problem of determining indebtedness. Baudelaire goes much farther than Crowe in delegating powers to the imagination, while seemingly depending on her definition. Remarkably, he manages to seize upon a passage on imagination and fancy in the midst of a discussion in Crowe about the powers of the dead over the living. One can only speculate what might have happened had Baudelaire read Coleridge.[7] By means of a creative distortion generally unnoticed by commentators,[8] Baudelaire changes Crowe's timid terms into pre-1817 Coleridgean affirmations. He writes, "since imagination created the world, it governs the world" (*OC,* 2:623), a statement even bolder than Coleridge's definition of the primary Imagination as "a repetition in the finite mind of the eternal act of creation in the infinite I AM" (*BL,* 1:202) because Baudelaire does not distinguish between the divine and the finite powers of imagination. Perhaps anxious about having gone too far, Baudelaire then uses Crowe's definition, "*the* CONSTRUCTIVE *imagina-*

tion, which . . . bears a distant relation to that sublime power by which the Creator projects, creates, and upholds his universe," to back up his assertion and declares that he has found a passage that justifies him. He shamefacedly defends Crowe's authority— "I am not at all ashamed—on the contrary I am very happy— to find myself in agreement with the excellent Mrs. Crowe"—and uses her watered-down definition as a buffer, permitting him to maintain his much more powerful version in the face of possible public outrage.

The more substantive problem of Poe's influence still causes lively controversy and remains of interest to students of Baudelaire's brand of Romanticism. L. J. Austin affirms that Baudelaire became aware of the theory of the imagination through his reading of Crowe and Poe and his acquaintance with Delacroix. Yet Baudelaire's contact with Poe begins in 1847, and the crystallization of Baudelaire's ideas about imagination appears eleven years later in the *Salon de 1859*, after the publication of the first edition of *Les Fleurs du Mal*. Indeed, Poe seems to hold a more exalted place in Baudelaire's personal religion than he does in the formulation of his critical opinions, being for Baudelaire the prototype of the genius unrecognized and even vilified by his contemporaries (see *OC*, 1:673).[9]

Certain issues central to Romanticism and closely related to Coleridge's theoretical work appear in studies of Baudelaire's aesthetics. In fact, Baudelaire by his own assessment is a Romantic.[10] Discussions of imagination in his critical writings, of subjectivity, of the opposition of mental constructs to the external world, and of his evolving attitude toward nature—from pantheism to repudiation—suggest, whether directly stated or not, his kinship with the Romantics. A relevant point in Baudelaire's aesthetics is his terminology regarding imagination and symbol. His definitions of the imagination parallel those of Coleridge, yet Baudelaire uses a number of terms, including *symbole*, to refer to the result of the imaginative process. Although he shows less partiality to the word "symbol," Baudelaire's view of the imaginative construct as the embodiment of the eternal in coherent form and his commitment to the creative process that arrives at the symbol show the unmistakable relationship between his aesthetic and Coleridge's symbolization.

The Symbolic Method

Baudelaire's contribution to the aesthetic of symbolization and hence his Romanticism, like Yeats's, depend on the assessment of his poetic achievement. The disputes regarding Baudelaire's criticism pale in comparison to the divergent opinions generated by *Les Fleurs du Mal*. On the essential subject of the work's unity, some critics agree that *Les Fleurs du Mal* has a structure, but many qualify their admission, and others reject altogether the idea of unity.[11] There are studies of themes,[12] of archetypes,[13] of the overall moral effect,[14] which point to the unity of the work but which do not analyze its incorporation of process and progression. Moreover, critics disagree about the comparative unity of the 1857 and the 1861 editions.[15] Some critics insist on the unity of *Les Fleurs du Mal* as a coherent body of poetry revealing the structure of the psyche,[16] but, along with others, they qualify the work as a triumph in despair, an exhilaration that rises out of the very subject of tragedy of the work.[17] Most critics concentrate, however, on the nihilism of *Les Fleurs du Mal* rather than its success. They see it as a failed enterprise of desperate attempts to come to terms with life.[18]

As Benjamin Fondane acutely articulates it in his *Baudelaire et l'expérience du gouffre*,[19] the problem of ethics resides in the feeling of *malaise* that Baudelaire's work inspires in some readers, particularly when they realize the extent of Baudelaire's fame and influence in the twentieth century. A work of poetry titled "Death," in which the fulfillment is in its last cycle and which seemingly descends with each cycle in a spiral movement toward despair and perversity, understandably generates the outraged indignation of some readers. However, evil in *Les Fleurs du Mal* opens the door to the sacred, prelapsarian thinking that allows the poet to reconstruct his paradise through his identification with the dispossessed of life. Baudelaire's identification of the poet with the pariah and the damned gives him the power to claim their rights.[20]

The question of ethics in *Les Fleurs du Mal* would prove less thorny if ethics were perceived as linked to and dependent upon the unity and sense of progression in the work. The last cycle, the cycle of death, which is largely responsible for the charge of pessimism,[21] indicates neither escape from human concerns nor an aesthete's refusal to deal with them, but the final step in the "identification of and with reality" which "may be or at least include death."[22] Death as the ultimate knowledge appears in the second generation of Romantic poets, Byron and Shelley, with whose works Baudelaire was acquainted, and it will also appear in Yeats.

Baudelaire's experiments with language come closer to Coleridge's goals of bringing the supernatural, romantic element into poetry, even to the extent of showing psychological states produced by superstitious delusion, than to Wordsworth's language of real men. In the context of French tradition, however, Baudelaire's inclusion of colloquialisms, conversational phrases, and subjects from the seamiest side of city life into the stately measures of alexandrines caused an outrage at the work and a vilification of the poet unprecedented even by the reaction to *Lyrical Ballads* and its *Preface*. Critical appproaches to Baudelaire's diction do not link it to the deliberate expansion of poetic subjects and the attendant reform of diction initiated by Romanticism.[23] Critics generally divide into two camps: one holds that the sublime, elevated diction transforms or at least attempts to transform gruesome subjects; the other contends that Baudelaire mixes prosaisms in a usually traditional poetic context and thus ends up with a diction approaching realism, which fails him since its concreteness is unconvincing in articulating a movement of ascent.[24]

Baudelaire's poetry exemplifies the internalized quest of a man in a setting and circumstances that continually undermine heroic affirmations. Baudelaire consciously undertakes to discover the supernatural element in the great metropolis, among the most fragmented and fragmentary experiences of modern man. In its movement from innocence to experience and resurgence into restructured innocence, *Les Fleurs du Mal* exhibits the characteristics of the Romantic Quest seen in *The Rime of the Ancient Mariner*, where radical innocence vanishes so quickly, giving way to a redescent into experience. The cycles of *Les Fleurs du Mal*—all but the last, which succeeds—reach or attempt only this tenuous triumph of the imagination. "Parisian Scenes," the most public, most outwardly directed of the cycles, parallels the structure of the Greater Romantic Lyric, where the imagination, assaulted by inimical reality, fights against being overpowered and occasionally wins, applying the mind's corrective order to chaotic *spectacle*. For Baudelaire the affective centers that trigger the union of Head and Heart appear not as friend, child, or beloved who brings to life the overwhelmingly beautiful landscape but as the dispossessed, the exiles from life's feast, who haunt urban scenes and wake the hero from his superstitious delusion about good and evil, making him able to redirect his quest toward the true Eden, the Eden of the mind.

Baudelaire criticism reveals disconcertingly that the creative process and much of scholarship have grown farther and farther apart in the decades following World War II. Two of the most suggestive, poetically attentive studies of Baudelaire, Benjamin's and Fondane's, were written before and during the war. Ingenious and often brilliant analyses add to the understanding of individual poems, or themes, or imagery, but they do so by isolating the work in the intellectual equivalent of a jar filled with formaldehyde solution, killing its vital connections to literary tradition. We find an eminent critic like Bersani summing up Baudelaire's enterprise as if he were talking of an amusement park: "Baudelaire's excitingly playful, if risky, adventure in self-scattering and self-displacement."[25] The point is that many of these exegeses, admirable and serious as they are, throw into shadow the larger issue of Baudelaire's extraordinarily strong and lasting influence on poets (I use the term in its Coleridgean sense) and hence on the modern sensibility shaped by the arts. I shall discuss Baudelaire's aesthetic criteria, which, like Coleridge's, stem from a poet's habit of mind, and shall endeavor to reveal how three movements of consciousness which give shape to the hitherto secret architecture of *Les Fleurs du Mal* transform—symbolize—the fleeting sensory impressions of "modern life" into the epic, heroic dimensions of art.

II

Baudelaire's hope for recovery of Eden through art appears in his statements on the nature and use of poetic language, in the role he ascribes to memory and reverie in imaginative creation, and in his views of the opposition of mind and external reality in symbolization. Baudelaire's activity as critic reaches an apex during the fertile period between the publication of the first and second editions of *Les Fleurs du Mal*. As in Coleridge's work, one detects in Baudelaire's subsequent work an increasing disillusionment with external solutions to man's condition, such as societal progress or the possibility of a reconciliation with nature. The stridency of *Intimate Journals,* which provides critics with evidence of Baudelaire's antihumanism, results from the bitterness of disappointed hopes; as the artist's isolation increases throughout the latter half of the nineteenth century, psychic and cultural regeneration through imaginative works becomes more and more remote.

Baudelaire's theory of poetic language, even more than Coleridge's, relates language to the system of symbols connecting transcendent and earthly reality. Elevating poetic language to a species of revelation entails severe criteria; Baudelaire, who in 1851 still shows some tolerance for imprecision of language,[26] becomes increasingly exacting about prosodic technique and the use of images and metaphors. In *Théophile Gautier* and *Thoughts about Several of My Contemporaries,* written during the interval between the publication of the first and second editions of *Les Fleurs du Mal,* Baudelaire develops his theory of language as revelation and of the poet as supremely conscious of his power. He writes: "There is something sacred in words, in the *Word,* which forbids us from turning it into a game of chance. To handle language expertly is to exercise a kind of evocative sorcery. It's at that point that color speaks . . . that perfume calls forth corresponding thoughts and memories" (*OC,* 2:117–18). Poetry reveals the symbolic relationship between fragments of sense experience, and these correspondences tend toward the initial unity of the universe so ardently desired by Baudelaire. Through his use of language, the poet can effect that return because poetry does not merely recreate the system of symbols linking transcendent reality with daily circumstance but literally belongs to it:

> If we consider that Gautier unites with this marvelous faculty an immense innate knowledge of universal correspondences and symbolism—that storehouse of all metaphors—then we understand that he is capable . . . of

defining the mysterious attitude which all created things maintain before man's gaze. [*OC*, 2:117]

For the best poets, there is no metaphor, comparison, or name whose fitness is not mathematically precise for the occasion, because these comparisons, these metaphors and epithets, are drawn from the inexhaustible depths of *Universal Analogy*, and cannot be drawn elsewhere. [*OC*, 2:133]

Baudelaire identifies the act of perceiving universal analogies with the creative act; poetic language provides the immediacy of an imaginative perception of the world. The elements of poetry and the symbols that order the experience of the senses into foci of intelligibility become one. The universe itself, in its harmonious manifestation, appears as a gigantic poem in Baudelaire's treatment of morality in art. Vice, he writes, is "a kind of sin against the rhythm and prosody of the universe" (*OC*, 2:113). Ethics and aesthetics merge as the flaws in poetic language contribute to fragmentation and thus to the distance between man and his hope for a recovered Eden. On the ethical level, vice disturbs the harmony of a universe created by the same means as poetry.

Whereas Coleridge is tentative about the claims he makes for the secondary Imagination re-creating a higher reality and for ideal diction,[27] Baudelaire seems confident that such diction is within the reach of poets. In letters to publishers, Baudelaire defends the precision of words and constructions, even of details of punctuation in his work. In explaining the use of the word "gouge" in "The Dance of Death," he writes: "color, antithesis, metaphor, everything is precise" (*Corr.*, 1:547). The word "precise" recalls the mathematical relation of poetic language to its context based on the universal analogy out of which language originates. In 1863, four years later, Baudelaire admonishes another publisher: "I spent my whole life learning how to construct sentences, and I can say, without fear of being ridiculous, that whatever I deliver to a printer is *perfectly completed*" (*Corr.*, 2:307). Baudelaire's conviction that language belongs to a unifying system underlying the structure of the universe gives him the assurance to see art as an actual means of redeeming man from an increasingly fragmented world.

Poetic diction, despite such phrases as "mathematically precise" and "*perfectly completed,*" which out of context might indicate a static perfection—a mechanism of mathematical formulae—tends ideally toward embodying an integrated sensibility and a sense of progression. For Baudelaire, poetry is expansion: "horror," "suffering," "the lyrical impulses of the soul," "eternal conjectures," "life's infinite spectacle." These terms suggest a metaphorical expansion in time and space. Prosody orders the directionless movement of poetic emotion; horror becomes beauty; pain, "rhythmic and cadenced," turns to calm joy (*OC*, 2:39, 123). Like Coleridge, Baudelaire knows that, though composed of emotion and order, poetry can be created neither by an extreme sensitivity of heart nor by mere adherence to form.[28] The imagination, which contains both the creative expansion and the critical check, reconciles these opposites. Moreover, the imagination "contains the knowledge of all methods and the desire to acquire them" (*OC*, 2:627). Hence, Baudelaire finds a psychological justification for the elements of poetry: "The arts of prose and poetry are not tyrannies invented arbitrarily but rather a collection of rules called for by the very structure of the spiritual being. And these arts have never hindered originality from clearly manifesting itself. On the contrary, to say that they help originality to unfold would be infinitely more true" (*OC*, 2:626–27). They represent the order necessary to express genius and belong to the faculty indispensable to genius—imagination.

In addition to revealing "the spiritual being," language for Baudelaire exists in a system of dynamic interrelationships. Baudelaire's thoughts on the composition of sentences give an important clue about the architecture of his own work and illuminate a key passage on artistic creation in his criticism of painting. In the notes for an article on Villemain, Baudelaire comments on the writer's method of composition, contrasting it with the correct method: "His sentences are made by accumulation, like a city added to over the centuries, whereas every sentence should be a harmonious monument in itself, the whole of these monuments then forming the city which is the Book" (*OC*, 2:197). With its metaphors of the work as city and its opposition of

The Symbolic Method

fragmented random parts and a unified whole, the passage recalls one of Baudelaire's most suggestive and yet difficult statements on imaginative versus mechanical creation in painting. The difficulty of the second passage arises out of Baudelaire's habit of expressing himself in metaphors that are more applicable to literary than to artistic processes of composition: "A good painting, faithful to and identical with the dream [this is the 'generating idea' which gives the painting its organic unity] which gave it birth, must be created like a world. Just as the world, such as we see it, is the result of several creations in which the following always complete the preceding ones, so, too, a painting harmoniously executed consists of a series of superimposed paintings, each new layer giving more substance to the dream and raising it one degree closer to perfection" (*OC*, 2:626). The mechanically executed painting resembles "a long journey divided into many stages. When one stage is over, it is done with, and when the entire journey is finished, the artist is rid of his painting." If the book is a city, the painting is a world. Although it is difficult to conceive of a painting consisting of successive layers that maintain individual integrity while continuing one another, Baudelaire's statement becomes relevant in terms of his own process of composition in *Les Fleurs du Mal*. The cycles of *Les Fleurs du Mal* complete one another in successive movements that advance metaphorically in a spiral rather than a linear pattern. The sentence, poem, or layer of painting exists in dynamic interplay with other entities, which together form a city, a world.

The identification of "dream" with the "generating idea" that unifies organically the work of art indicates the importance Baudelaire gives to reverie. Together with the role assigned to memory, it introduces a new dimension to the theory of the imagination as expounded by Coleridge. Whereas Coleridge relegates fancy, memory, and the law of association to the inferior level of mechanical functions of the mind, Baudelaire brings memory and reverie up into the imaginative process of creation. At the same time, Baudelaire recognizes the dangers of giving oneself to unchecked reverie, to a mental operation uncontrolled by the will.

For Baudelaire, both reverie and memory oppose external reality, its slavish copy in art, and the fixity of reason. The phantoms of reason are equations, he writes in his critique of *Prometheus Unbound,* while those of imagination are "beings and memories" (*OC,* 2:11). Remembrance, the product of the imagination, becomes the great criterion of art for Baudelaire as early as the *Salon de 1846,* written in the same year as the literary critique (*OC,* 2:455). In a distinction reminiscent of Coleridge's on copy and imitation, Baudelaire writes that a too close reproduction of nature spoils its reconstruction by memory, and, since "art is a mnemonics of beauty," the copying painting presents nature, not its re-created ideal. The later works, the *Salon de 1859* and *The Painter of Modern Life,* show no change in the high value Baudelaire places on memory and in his emphatic association of it with the Imagination. In the latter work, particularly in the subdivision titled "Mnemonic Art," memory appears as a visionary power, capable of infusing life into Lazarus's corpse (*OC,* 2:699). Yet its vision does not depend on conscious effort. The artist must use all the technical means available to him in order to capture the essence of the fleeting vision that fades like Shelley's coal. Undeniably related to imagination, memory remains a capricious, despotic operation of the mind which requires the highest exercise of conscious control on the part of the artist for the creation of art. Its visitation, as *Les Fleurs du Mal* shows, represents a moment of grace.

While Baudelaire often uses "dream" as a synonym for the product of the imagination, the act of dreaming, which is an initial step toward creation, can become an impediment to it. Around 1854, following a long diatribe against nature poems solicited from him by a publisher, Baudelaire sends instead two poems that result from his reveries (*Corr.,* 1:248). This statement of faith, in which Baudelaire renounces pantheism, contrasts sharply the worship of nature with the internal source of creation. In the *Salon de 1859,* Baudelaire will make the same distinction between an art totally dependent on reality and the art that has its source in the inner being: "Day by day, art makes itself less respected, prostrates itself before external reality, and the painter becomes more and more inclined to paint not what he dreams, but what he sees" (*OC,* 2:619). Here Baudelaire distinguishes two steps toward the finished product, the dream and its expression.

In the essay on Hugo, reverie and creation oppose each

The Symbolic Method

other since reverie represents an abandonment of the directing will. The poet translates the fruits of the reverie, "the infinite spectacle of life," into art (*OC*, 2:139). The danger of reverie makes itself poignantly felt in a self-revelatory passage of criticism: "Those whose soul since childhood has been *touched with pensiveness;* always in opposition, action and intention, dream and reality; one always harming the other, one always usurping the other's place" (*OC*, 2:87). The intruding sense of loss marks Baudelaire's weariness and disillusionment and his increasing belief that beauty and the poetic enterprise in the modern world are haunted by misfortune and fatality. Reverie, which leads to creation, saps the will.

Baudelaire's gradual disenchantment embraces his perception of nature, society, and the role of the arts. His attitude toward nature remains full of ambivalence throughout his career. Statements from his writings which at first glance appear as outright contradictions represent the complex working out of one of the most persistent problems of nineteenth-century aesthetics, namely, the creating mind opposing external reality. Always less scrupulous in defining his critical vocabulary than is Coleridge, Baudelaire uses the word "nature" in two opposing senses without formally distinguishing between them; one (which for the remainder of this chapter will be capitalized) is the great Nature, unified in its laws and logic and presenting itself as a key to a higher world for those who imaginatively perceive its totality; the second is the nature of everyday experience, the fragmented data in complicity with man's limited perception, his "vegetable" eye. It impedes wholeness of perception, and, worse still, it produces in those who cannot free themselves a brutish contentment with their limitations. Baudelaire contrasts this ignorant innocence with the quest for knowledge. As in his poetry, the risks involved in the quest are enormous, as are the losses, but the quest, compared to the fate of those who stay behind, affirms the triumph of the mind over the entrapment of nature.

From his earliest essays to the last, spanning at least fourteen years, Baudelaire explores the idea of Nature as a dictionary, a system of signs to be perceived and translated by the artist. In the *Salon de 1846,* Baudelaire follows Heine's lead in declaring that the true artist creates works without analogue in nature. Yet Nature proves indispensable as a reference for Delacroix, Baudelaire's prototype of the modern genius: "For E. Delacroix, nature is an immense dictionary whose leaves he turns and consults with a sure and penetrating eye" (*OC*, 2:433). When seen as a system rather than as random matter, Nature plays a redemptive role as Baudelaire emphasizes through his use of religious terminology in his address to the Pagan School: "To surround oneself solely with the seductions of physical art is to risk damnation. . . . The world will appear only in its material form. The springs that animate it will remain hidden for a long time" (*OC*, 2:46). Warning against the exclusiveness of an art totally committed to the worship of material form, Baudelaire writes: "excessive specialization of one faculty ends in nothingness" (*OC*, 2:49), linking that worship to a limited, fragmented sensibility and to a metaphysical dead end. In the case of a painter like Ingres, incapable of translating Nature "in its totality and its logic" (*OC*, 2:587), the result is also an unconvincing art, a Nature interpreted not by imagination but by a sleight of hand designed to please the eye.

Nature appears "in its totality" to some men. Although in *Artificial Paradises* Baudelaire admits he cannot account for such privileged moments by means of any spiritual diet or exercise, he nevertheless associates these moments of "true grace" (*OC*, 1:402) with the most imaginative artists of his time. Passages on an imaginative vision of Nature appear in his treatment of Delacroix in *L'Exposition universelle de 1855* and in his essay on Théophile Gautier. The highest compliment he can pay Delacroix is that his art translates "these admirable moments, true holy days of the mind" (*OC*, 2:596), in which the specialized data of the senses merge into unity and synesthesia. Art, like the moment of vision, signifies not only an intensity and unity of sensation but revelation: "it reveals the supernatural." As in the passage on Delacroix, Baudelaire's account of perception in *Théophile Gautier* includes Nature, which becomes "Heaven's correspondence" (*OC*, 2:114), affirming man's immortality and his insatiable desire for paradise. Baudelaire, however, admits the limited access to this regenerative perception of the universe. He declares, "everything is hieroglyphic," yet the symbols remain obscure for those devoid of "purity, good will, or the innate

The Symbolic Method

clairvoyance of the soul,"[29] excepting the poet, who relies on imagination to perceive and translate.

Instead of leading the mind toward a coherent view of universal patterns, external nature traps it in the everyday. Unlike the Nature revealed in privileged moments, nature persistently and powerfully attracts the mind only to betray it by trapping it in fixities and definites of the fallen universe. As early as 1846, Baudelaire expresses his view of nature as the great adversary when he conceives of artistic creation as a duel in which the mind must triumph over its opponent in order to arrive at the higher coherence of art. Baudelaire defines three categories of drawing in which ascendancy is based on the ability to master external nature, to the point where the superior artist creates a vision without analogue except to his inner being. Baudelaire emphasizes that this power derives from knowledge of the adversary, not from ignorance: "Drawing is a battle between nature and the artist—the more the artist understands nature's intentions, the easier his triumph. It isn't a matter of copying, but of interpreting nature in a simpler and more luminous language" (*OC*, 2:457).

In later works, Baudelaire will continually remind readers that hierarchy in art depends upon the artist's triumph over the flux of sense experience, over the passivity of his own response to nature. Nature provides the "notes," not the shaping idea, he writes in *De l'essence du rire*. In his study of Delacroix in 1863, Baudelaire concisely defines nature's role in the creative process: "It [external nature] is nothing but an incoherent heap of stuff which the artist is invited to combine and to set in order, an *incitamentum*, an awakening of sleeping faculties. Accurately stated, there are neither lines nor colors in nature. Man creates the lines and the colors" (*OC*, 2:752).

Yet few artists wake to the challenge and few emerge triumphant from the battle with nature.[30] Those who do so suffer the hostility or indifference of a society enslaved by limited perception, by the worship of art which copies and celebrates its daily existence. Much of Baudelaire's hostility toward nature and toward the lives of the "multitudes" derives from the connection he sees between the worship of fixities and definites and the conquering materialism of his age.

Hunger for the True Paradise

The contest between mind and nature informs even Baudelaire's rejection of the use of hashish. Dreams and hallucinations, which are sometimes free from external stimuli and therefore capable of being "supernatural," become under the drug's influence oppressed by an excessive dependence on reality (*OC*, 1:409). The manufactured ecstasy fails because the mind is delivered to sense experience: "The word 'rhapsodic,' which so neatly defines a train of thought suggested and ordered by the external world and chance circumstance, has a truer and more terrible meaning when it comes to the use of hashish"(*OC*, 1:428). Man's delusion of reaching godhead proves to be a cruel and ironic deception as he lets himself be enslaved by a fallen nature.

Despite his feeling of defeat, stemming from the masses' and even many artists' worship of external nature, Baudelaire does not advocate retreat from reality, nor does he wait passively for privileged moments of vision to provide an alternative to the fragmentation of the everyday. He argues for a modern art that can seize the heroic and the eternal in daily life, even in the transitoriness of fashion and the disjointed bustle of the city. Because of its inclusiveness and at the same time its power of transformation, this art triumphs over the circumstances that trap man and heals his psyche. While still full of youthful hopes, Baudelaire talks in 1851 of poetry's "divine utopian nature": "It unrelentingly contradicts facts, or ceases to be poetry. In the dungeon, it becomes revolt; at the hospital window, it becomes the ardent hope of recovery; . . . not only does it ascertain, it also mends. Everywhere, it makes itself the negation of iniquity" (*OC*, 2:35). He prophesies that poetry—imaginative creation—can overturn the oppressiveness of daily circumstances.

Yet when the possibility of external changes appears doomed in a world committed to industry and materialism instead of art, Baudelaire maintains that poetry alone discloses the corruption of the human heart and hence can trigger the inner awakening needed to restore the mind's wholeness. In his analysis of Banville in *Thoughts about Several of My Contemporaries*, Baudelaire discusses Romanticism in order to contrast Banville's escapism with this movement in which art, for the first time in Baudelaire's view, takes account of "the horrible life of contention and strife in which we are immersed" and of the demonic depths in man (*OC*, 2:168). Full of discordance and irony, this art represents the "revenge of the vanquished" (*OC*, 2:168), that revolt of the imprisoned and hope for health of the sick which Baudelaire heralded in his youth as the regeneration of human life. It portrays revolt by means of "splendid, dazzling rays" (*OC*, 2:168) that illuminate the hidden depths of the psyche.

Like Coleridge, Baudelaire recognizes that the initial pressure of reality activates the mind and forces it to oppose chaos with its constructs. Far from retreating into the isolation and safety of the cult of beauty divorced from reality, Baudelaire insists that modern life includes an epic, heroic dimension that artists too often neglect in favor of classical subjects. He reminds them, "Parisian life is teeming with wonderful, poetic subjects. Wonders enwrap us and flood us as does the air; but we do not notice them" (*OC*, 2:496). As in his definition of beauty, Baudelaire regards the eternal contained in the forms of modernity as a source that can assuage man's thirst, if only he perceives it. Artists like Hugo and Constantin Guys extract from history (in Guys's case, from that most transitory history—fashion) "eternity" (*OC*, 2:694), "the legend, the myth" (*OC*, 2:140), and succeed in creating "pure art according to modern thought," namely, "a suggestive magic containing at the same time the subject and object, the artist himself and the world external to him" (*OC*, 2:598). Baudelaire's theory of art strives for the Romantic inclusiveness of an eternal perceived in temporal forms and of a disjointed temporal made coherent and whole in its embodiment of eternity. Baudelaire's ideal, an art containing "the heroism of modern life," imperfectly realized by even Hugo and Guys, awaits fulfillment in his own *oeuvre*.

III

From the earliest records of the inception of *Les Fleurs du Mal* to the projected edition of 1868, Baudelaire conceives of his work as a unity with thematic coherence rather than a collection of lyrics arranged according to reasons extrinsic to the poetic subjects.

In contrast with contemporary titles such as *Emaux et Camées* and *Les Stalactites*, Baudelaire's tentative titles indicate his dissociation from the poetics of art as immobile perfection and his interest in shocking and intriguing his readers with the sensational *Lesbians* and the mystifying *Limbo*. Both titles have legitimacy in light of the completed work. Written eleven years before the publication of *Les Fleurs du Mal*, the first represents Baudelaire's preoccupation with perversion in a metaphysical, rather than sexual or religious, sense, that is, the exploration of sexual deviance as a means to an absolute. The second shows Baudelaire's attempt to find modern man's position in a universal scheme.

The work that finally appears under the title of *Les Fleurs du Mal* has obvious unity even in its first form, comprising eighteen poems and published in the *Revue des Deux Mondes* in 1855. This initial version begins with the famous opening, "To the Reader," and ends with the poem that retains its significant position as an endpiece even in the 1861 edition, namely, "Love and the Skull." Baudelaire expresses repeatedly his concern that the work be perceived as a totality in his letters to his publishers, to friends, and to the men he admires as well as to those who were to judge in a court of law the moral effects of the book.[31] His assessment of his achievement, of whether the work will be sold or will be remembered, always refers to the book, never to individual poems. And, despite the advice to abandon *Les Fleurs du Mal* from his few sympathetic reviewers like Edouard Thierry and Barbey D'Aurevilly, who see it as a dead end, as the utterances of a poet adopting the dramatic mask of an unregenerate character,[32] Baudelaire continues to work at *Les Fleurs du Mal* as Wordsworth planned to work on his cathedral, as Yeats will consolidate the body of his poetry. The original eighteen lyrics grow into the 1857 edition, which is enlarged considerably in 1861, and has yet to be increased in the posthumous edition of 1868, published according to Baudelaire's plans but without his outline for the order of the new *Les Fleurs du Mal*.

The 1868 edition is generally regarded as fairly unreliable, particularly in studies of the architecture of *Les Fleurs du Mal*. Due to the forced removal of the six condemned poems from the 1857 edition, debates as to whether the 1857 or 1861 edition comes closest to the poet's intentions, inspiration, or

The Symbolic Method

sense of unity will no doubt continue. Obviously, Baudelaire undertook to revise *Les Fleurs du Mal* at first out of necessity rather than aesthetic considerations. However, as he did so, he overcame the lassitude and discouragement reported initially in his letters and found a new élan. The doubt expressed in his letter to Poulet-Malassis at the end of 1857, "but when will the poetic mood return to me," disappears in subsequent announcements, and only the exultant tone of the artist, accepting the conditions of life in society and yet subverting them, remains: "I have resolved to submit completely to the verdict, and to write six new poems even more beautiful than the censored ones" (*Corr.*, 1:441). When he finally adds thirty-five instead of the six, he writes to Vigny, supremely conscious of the work's unity, "All the new poems have been written to fit into a particular framework which I had chosen" (*Corr.*, 2:196). Baudelaire's progression from the 1857 to the 1861 work represents his development as a poet, his changed awareness of man's condition, and the 1861 edition incorporates that growth. Had Baudelaire lived to finish the third edition of his poems, that work would have been chosen for this study, for, to continue Wordsworth's simile, while one may have a preference for the perfection of the antechapel or a sepulchral recess, the church as a whole will contain the success or failure of the architectural design. As it is, the 1861 edition represents the farthest completed stage of Baudelaire's poetry, and its text will be the one used here.

Like the Greater Romantic Lyric and the Romantic Quest, the structure of *Les Fleurs du Mal* depicts process rather than product. The quest of the poet-hero centers around achieving a psychic wholeness that perceives reality as coherent and intelligible. In *Rockets* (*Fusées*), Baudelaire describes this state of mind: "In certain nearly supernatural states of the soul, life's meaning reveals itself in its entirety in the spectacle—no matter how commonplace—before one's eyes. That scene becomes its symbol" (*OC*, 1:659). The cycles of *Les Fleurs du Mal* represent attempts to transform the *spectacle* into symbol, and the stage of the poet's growth in each cycle determines its success.

Unified by the poet's consciousness, the cycles show his development as he moves from one to the next and within each one. Baudelaire frames each cycle, as he does the whole work, with poems indicative of the initial state and final progress of the quester and also connects the last poem of each cycle with the beginning of the other in order to create a distanced comment from a new stage of consciousness upon the preceding phase. Those repetitions, for which critics fault Baudelaire's imaginative abundance, produce echoes, foreshadowings, and spiral movements that weave the texture of the work into cohesive patterns.

Three closely interwoven movements inform the structure of *Les Fleurs du Mal,* and the cycle "Revolt" serves as their intersection. The first movement, from innocence to experience, concerns primarily the first cycle, "Bile and the Ideal," but has its conclusion in "Revolt." The second, the mind's confrontation with external reality in the *spectacle* of the everyday, appears mostly in "Parisian Scenes," although it, too, concludes in "Revolt." The last has its origins in the other two, but it encompasses the whole work, appearing most clearly in the false starts of "Wine" and "Flowers of Evil" and in the concluding cycle of "Death"; this movement goes beyond experience to reconstructed innocence—a supernatural state of mind—and sees life in its totality. It, too, intersects with the other movements in "Revolt," but it begins with "To the Reader," if not with the very title and dedication of the book.

The change from innocence to experience contains both a vertical movement—the poet's psyche, above humanity, descends into temporality and mortality—and a horizontal movement following the chronology of the poet's life from youth to age. The contrast between "The Blessing" and "The Clock," the first and last poems in "Bile and the Ideal," shows most emphatically the change in the hero's consciousness, but the reader follows the gradual process of change through poems and groups of poems that mark the mind's descent into experience. "The Blessing" itself contrasts with "To the Reader," where the poet implicates the reader in the common fate and guilt of modern man with the use of the first-person-plural voice and the memorable apostrophe "—Hypocrite lecteur, —mon semblable, —mon frère" (l. 40; "You—hypocrite reader—my double—my brother").

Whereas "To the Reader" represents an assessment of the status quo of civilization, "The Blessing" offers a glorious but naive reinterpretation of the poet's existence in society. Human-

The Symbolic Method

ity itself is little changed from "To the Reader" to the introductory poem of "Bile and the Ideal." "The Blessing" echoes the sins already depicted in the opening address: the monster "Ennui" ("Boredom") possesses "ce monde ennuyé" ("a bored world"), particularly the poet's harpylike wife, and the ferocity and hypocrisy that accompany this nontheological sin count as the chief attributes of mankind (ll. 32, 35). Although born to a vicious mother and married to a monstrous wife, the poet is emphatically not the brother of the human race. He is "gai," "serein," "lucide," even when confronted with unprovoked acts of cruelty. These do not touch him, nor does any terrestrial matter, even in the form of nourishment: "dans tout ce qu'il boit et dans tout ce qu'il mange / [il] Retrouve l'ambroisie et le nectar vermeil" (ll. 23-24; "All that he eats and drinks can fill / Him with memories of the food that was heaven's"). His stay on earth is temporary and insignificant; he remembers his former state in the food he eats and looks forward to his apotheosis after death, when he will return to the "éternelle fête" (l. 63; "heaven's festival"). Although he thanks God for suffering and pain—the "divin remède à nos impuretés" (l. 58; "divine remedy for our folly")—he hardly suffers and cannot be tainted. Contrary to his bitch-wife's boasts, his sexuality does not betray him; he remains inwardly unmoved by the rising hysteria of brutality and debauchery around him.

As for his mission as poet, the hero, supremely confident of his power, his unfailing vision, his harmonious relationship with nature and God, places himself above the limits of time and space and extracts their essence: "il faut pour tresser ma couronne mystique / Imposer tous les temps et tous les univers" (ll. 67-68; "all the universe and all time's length / Must be wound into the mystic crown for my brows"). He asserts that pain is the way to God, but that it remains untouched by earthly or hellish passion: "la noblesse unique / Où ne mordent jamais la terre et les enfers" (ll. 65-66; "the one human strength / On which neither earth nor hell can impose"). He conceives of heavenly triumph without experience and without the descent into the dark night of the soul known by heroes and wise men. Like the Mariner, he is ready to drop serenely, if not "merrily," not knowing what awaits him.

Hunger for the True Paradise

In contrast to the fairly conventional religious terminology and imagery of "The Blessing," "The Clock" presents a vocabulary and an imagery dominated by the consciousness of temporality. The clock, "dieu sinistre" ("calm evil god"), has replaced the Christian God, and the heavenly orientation of the poet has changed to an inevitable journey into night, into the abyss. Instead of undergoing an apotheosis, the poet, now old and identifying with the rest of humanity through his first-person-plural point of view, becomes the victim of the inexorable fate expressed by the clock's imperative "Meurs, vieux lâche! il est trop tard" (l. 24; "Die, old Coward. It's too late!"). His power of forging his crown out of the mastery of time and space has been dissipated, and Time now wins the rich essence of the life wasted by the "mortel folâtre" ("foolish mortal"). Suffering, "la noblesse unique," becomes fragmented into "douleurs" ("woes"), which in turn tear open the heart. Fragmentation appears most strikingly in the breakdown of time into "trois mille six cent fois . . . par heure" (l. 9; "three thousand times . . . each hour").

The ironic refrain "Souviens-toi" ("Remember") summarizes the defeat suffered by the mind in its descent into reality. Whereas in the last poem of the cycle, "Souviens-toi," spoken by the very emblem of time—the clock—reminds the poet of his mortal being, his own recollections in his journey through "Bile and the Ideal" represent the triumph of the imagination over mortality, over the destruction of time. But that victory is absent both from "The Blessing," where the naive poet foresees an all-too-easy access to eternity, and in "The Clock," where he has become hopelessly trapped in time. Rising out of experience, "recollection" means life, continuance, even immortality, and "forgetting" signifies destruction, decay and death. The imaginative process of transformation begins with the poet's contact with external reality.

Generally interpreted as Baudelaire's aesthetic credo and as a fundamental statement for the Symbolist movement, "Correspondances" occupies a key role in "Bile and the Ideal" in charting the poet's movement into experience. The poet for the first time acknowledges his kinship with mankind, his separation from nature, the fragmentation of the natural world, and finally his penchant for knowledge through sexuality, through eroticism.

The Symbolic Method

"Correspondances" breaks with the initial assessment of the poet's role in its response to the last lines of the preceding poem, "Elévation": "Heureux celui . . . / . . . / —Qui plane sur la vie, et comprend sans effort / Le langage des fleurs et des choses muettes" (ll. 15–20; "Happy is he . . . who . . . / Skims over life, and understands with ease / The speech of flowers and other voiceless things"). In "Correspondances" nature rarely speaks, and when it does its language consists of "confuses paroles" (indistinct words) as man passes through, instead of hovering over, reality. A fatal separation takes place in the poet's perception, despite the synesthesia of colors, perfumes, and sounds. The innocent, pastoral side of nature evoked by the "parfums frais" ("perfumes sweet") stands apart from the world of the "parfums corrompus" ("corrupt") which overwhelms it. The source of these perfumes—sex glands and decomposition in the case of "ambre" and "musc"—indicates their closeness to sexuality, generation, and inevitable mortality and announces the poet's search for infinity through the senses as much as the spirit. The poet ecstatically succumbs to his fragmented vision, which will later ripen into states of unrelieved dejection unparalleled even by Coleridge's later poems of despair.

The attraction and power of the "parfums corrompus" plunges the poet into experience. "J'aime le souvenir" ("I love the thought"), immediately following "Correspondances," contrasts subtly the state of man in a pre-Christian world resembling Eden with his present condition, in which he must earn his bread by the sweat of his brow—Cybèle having withdrawn her generosity—and in which women exhibit the marks of their painful childbearing.

After establishing the omnipresence of postlapsarian signs, the poet explores the role of art and his own position from the perspective of the fallen world. The group VI to IX shows the germination of doubts about the self and the power of the creative imagination which foreshadow the dissolution in the great poems at the end of "Bile and the Ideal." Even "Beacons," the positive tribute to great art, portrays imaginative achievement as falling just short of the goal: "cet ardent sanglot qui roule d'âge en âge" (ll. 43–44; "This tide of tears which age after age gathers / To fail and fall on the shore of Your eternity") dies

110

Hunger for the True Paradise

while reaching eternity. Yet at this point in the poet's journey, the doubts of "The Wicked Monk" and "L'Ennemi" ("The Ruined Garden"), however fierce, end in self-questioning that is by no means rhetorical and that allows hope for the recovery of the imagination temporarily defeated in its first contact with reality.

But can the poet, pursued by unrelenting time, create something more enduring than a wave of sobs? In "A Former Life," "Gypsies on the Road," and "Man and the Sea," Baudelaire shows the unsatisfied desire that spurs the quester on in his journey toward exploring those unsounded depths of the soul resembling the sea. In "Don Juan in Hell" and "The Punishment of Pride," he presents the dangers of pursuing fulfillment in earthly forms such as love or science. In poems XVII to XXI, the hero makes his choice, thereupon rushing into the worship of matter and the science of love which will furnish him with the materials needed to counter time and the dissolution of earthly things but which subtly enslave his will and sap his creative power.

Poems XVII to XXI mark the poet's movement from contemplation of outward forms to the descent into the depths of the unknown for a glimpse at the organizing power behind matter. "Beauty," generally interpreted as Baudelaire's Parnassian homage to static beauty, represents rather the monologue of nature. Baudelaire warns against nature's siren song by relating this beauty to the most inert matter—stone: "rêve de pierre" ("a dream in stone"), "éternel et muet ainsi que la matière" ("as lone / As everlasting clay, and as taciturn"), "sphinx," "monuments." Although her eyes appear to contain eternity, they mirror it only (in an earlier version of l. 13, the connection of beauty with nature is clearer since her eyes reflect the stars, as do lakes), and her breast is hard and implacable. The sonnet, with its quiet undercutting of beauty's claims, recalls Baudelaire's criticism of the Pagan School and its worship of forms.

In "The Ideal," "Giantess," and "The Mask," the poet opposes types of dynamic unnaturalness to the unchanging form of "Beauty." Abysses, perverse growths, the "monstre bicéphale" (XX, l. 19; "two-headed monster"), references to earth in its primitive births—giantesses, Titans—all contradict the ideal of static beauty. The poet's penchant for dynamic oppositions and

The Symbolic Method

his sympathy for the true face in "The Mask," who is in despair over her entrapment in time, leads him to choose the type of beauty by means of which he hopes to escape human limitations. Again, his choice divides rather than fuses, avoids rather than confronts the inimical in nature. "Hymn to Beauty," with its series of seemingly rhetorical questions, represents the culmination of the attraction toward the corrupt perfumes of "Correspondances" and contradicts the heavenly orientation of "The Blessing." The accoutrements of beauty in this poem clearly indicate which one of the antinomies that Baudelaire gives as the source of beauty prevails in the poet's consciousness:

> Tu marches sur des morts, Beauté, dont tu te moques;
> De tes bijoux l'Horreur n'est pas le moins charmant,
> Et le Meurtre, parmi tes plus chères breloques,
> Sur ton ventre orgueilleux danse amoureusement.
> [Ll.13–16][33]

While the "bienfait" ("beneficence") and the "joie" spread by beauty remain abstractions, the "désastres" (disasters) become striking images of instantaneous or prolonged annihilation (ll. 17–20). In this context, then, the poet, who cries "Qu'importe" (What does it matter), chooses the abyss over heaven for the sake of escaping the weight of time and the hideousness of the world but does not dare at this point to admit his choice and desperately feigns ignorance. The journey into experience begins thus with a flaw in the hero's consciousness and is doomed to fail unless he rectifies it.

In the groups of poems centering on women, the poet, still misguided in his search for beauty, attributes magical qualities to his human muses. He creates a dependence upon external forms and upon beings who will not be ruled by him which explodes in desperate attempts to wrestle free of the idols, to have them at the mercy of his remembrance and his art. The *Black Venus* subcycle centers on carnal knowledge and passion, a logical development of choices made in "Correspondances" and "Hymn." At first, in "Exotic Perfume" and "Her Hair," the poet seems indeed able to escape space and time. He traverses matter and reaches the port—the point of embarkment toward eter-

Hunger for the True Paradise

nity—through the odor of the beloved's breast and hair. Yet the tropical islands, the exotic continents, "tout un monde lointain, absent, presque défunt" ("Her Hair," l. 7; "a far world, defunct, almost absent") untainted by sin depends, in his subjugated view, upon physical contact with the beloved. The recollections coming to life and the dream taking shape through the poet's imaginative reconstruction of the beloved's tresses, projected by him onto the woman, become indistinguishable from her being, so that he is forced to ransom his moments of imaginative vision with precious stones, with matter that in "Bile and the Ideal" signifies the petrification of forgetting. The woman, his "oasis," quickly changes to a creature reminiscent of the poet's wife in "The Blessing," corrupted by Boredom and its attendant trait, cruelty. This time, far from remaining serene and lucid, the poet feels himself chained, manipulated by a worship both ignominious and sublime (XXV, l. 18), the worship of nature in the form of woman.

During the poet's experience with love, as he loses his freedom along with his innocence, he reaches moments of self-knowledge which lead him to defeat the very limits of the human condition. The triumph depends upon experience and yet rises above and against it. "A Carrion" is the first of these summations of love, which include "The Balcony," "A Phantom," "Je te donne ces vers" ("If by Some Freak of Fortune"), "The Spiritual Dawn," "Evening Harmony," "The Flask," and "To a Madonna." In it, the poet spies a human body in the process of decomposition:

> Les formes s'effaçaient et n'étaient plus qu'un rêve,
> Une ébauche lente à venir,
> Sur la toile oubliée, et que l'artiste achève
> Seulement par le souvenir. [Ll. 29–32][34]

The metaphor announces the ending of the poem, in which the lover tells the beloved of her inevitable fate, the corruption of bodily form in death. She, too, will be an unfinished, forgotten sketch, without the artist's dream and remembrance, which rescue from corruption and the oblivion of death "la forme et l'essence divine" (l. 47) of love and the beloved. The concluding

The Symbolic Method

lines, "la forme et l'essence divine / De mes amours décomposés" ("the divine form and the essence / Of my festered loves"), should be far from reassuring to the object of his worship. "Amours décomposés" refers both to the mouldering body and to the destruction of love. And, though declaring that he will preserve the divine essence, the poet creates with "A Carrion" itself a tenacious embodiment of grisly mortality for the divine essence in order to remind his beloved that his memory holds the key to her triumph over death.

In 'The Phantom," as well as in "If by Some Freak of Fortune" and "The Spiritual Dawn" but most clearly in "Evening Harmony" and "The Flask," the living woman—the body, the perfume, the hair—who furnished the poet the materials for creation, disappears, becomes a ghost or statue, and the poet creates out of remembrance the essence of his love, whether divine or not. "The Flask" in particular shows the opposition of nature and the imagination starting with the unusual, conversational opening: "Il est de forts parfums pour qui toute matière / Est poreuse. On dirait qu'ils pénètrent le verre" (ll. 1–2; "There are some powerful odours that can pass / Out of the stoppered flagon; even glass / To them is porous"). The impotence of matter to contain certain perfumes, especially the ones in "un vieux flacon qui se souvient" (l. 7; an old vial who remembers), is followed by the impotence of time to destroy them. The relationship between memory and resurrection from the dead, mentioned in the *Salon de 1859* (*OC*, 2:699), appears forcefully in the poem. The poet, metamorphosed into the vial by his art, becomes the power that resurrects and saves against time and matter, although the man in him falls victim to the disease of love.

Because of the increased separation of the physical and the spiritual, the journey through love proves no easy access to eternity and yields no lasting triumph of the imagination. The poet bemoans in "Moesta et errabunda" that in the "verts paradis des amours enfantines" ("the grass-greenest heaven of childish loves") all that one loves "est digne d'être aimé" ("is worthy to be loved"), whereas sexuality bars the possibility of worth. His limited perception, first due to innocence and then to immersion in reality, separates the "verts paradis," as it does the "parfums frais," from the richer, but corrupt, aspects of matter he wishes to experience. The knowledge he gains fragments his faculties. The titles *Black Venus* and *White Venus*, designated by critics to distinguish not only between the actual women who inspired the poems, but between their orientations—eroticism and platonic worship— indicate an ambivalent attitude toward the beloved; on the one hand, the fascination of the dark woman, on the other, the solace of the angel of light, merging unevenly in "the beauty with golden hair" and in the others. Conscious at times of the temptation to separate, analyze, and destroy, the poet attributes this fatal tendency to a demon's suggestion in "All in One," where he successfully parries the evil spirit's question, "Parmi les objets noirs ou roses / Qui composent son corps charmant, / Quel est le plus doux" (ll. 7–9; "Among the beauties, black and rose, / That make her body's charm and grace, / Which is most fair"), with praise of the whole being, of that harmony and synesthesia Baudelaire associates with Nature. But the remaining poems of the subcycle of the *White Venus*, more serious in tone, show that the poet desires only the angel of light, that any sign of the living woman rather than his idealization, such as her awareness of mortality in "Confession," makes him recoil in horror.

Consequently, in the last poem containing the process of symbolization by which the poet replaces the real being with the one created by his art, "To a Madonna," he revels in the destruction of his own creation. He has succumbed to the fate predicted by the odious wife in "The Blessing." As we see in "Conversation," his heart has been eaten by beasts, and he becomes the instrument of mortality instead of the agent of life. In "To a Madonna," the imagination does not preserve against decay, does not resurrect, but rather succumbs to the impulse to destroy the erected idol and thus the passion for the living being. The poet's mind becomes the subterranean shrine, on the one hand hidden from everyday life, from any "désir mondain" ("all worldly lusts"), on the other serving as a scene for a destruction just like that effected by daily circumstances and mortality. The parallel use of the metaphor of the target in "To a Madonna" and in "The Clock" underscores the theme of temporal destruction, and the poet, who is the executioner in "To a Madonna," becomes the victim in "The Clock," a fitting reversal for a mind that furthers fragmentation instead of opposing it.

The Symbolic Method

The poems from "The Sadness of the Moon" to "Music" form a transition from the subcycle of love to the last movement of "Bile and the Ideal." They represent the poet's last attempts to forge a unified vision and to create the symbol out of ordinary life. The metamorphosis of the cats in "Cats" from ordinary domestic animals to symbols of infinity owes its success to the fusion of the dynamic opposites, "science" and "volupté"—knowledge and sexuality—which merge instead of destroying each other. The synthesizing power cannot be sustained, however, and the remaining subcycle of "Bile and the Ideal" deals only with dissolution and death, ending in the clock's implacable refrain, "Meurs, vieux lâche! il est trop tard."[35] The antithesis of remembrance and forgetting, as well as the omnipresence of matter, becomes the haunting refrain in these last poems: the immobile agony of "The Cracked Bell," the transformation of the poet to living matter in "Spleen" (LXXVI), of his blood into the waters of the Lethe (LXXVII). "Obsession" contains amplified and distorted echoes of images of nature which in earlier poems were filled with the hope of discovery. The sea of "Man and the Sea" becomes the ocean reflecting not the depths of the human spirit recognizing itself in the sea's "plainte indomptable et sauvage" (l. 8; savage and untamed moan) but "ce rire amer / De l'homme vaincu" (ll. 6–7; the bitter laughter / Of defeated man). The forests of symbols of "Correspondances" change to vast woods, which pursue the hearts of the damned with their reminders of God. The penultimate image, the night empty of stars, is a nothingness suggesting the chaos before creation, toward which the poet yearns without being able to attain it. Against his will, he populates the darkness with projections of his mind. These are not imaginative creations, but obsessive mirrorings of remorse and failure. The hope of recognition between man and nature, expressed in "Correspondances" by the "regards familiers" ("familiar eyes") that meet him in the encounter with nature, become "des êtres disparus aux regards familiers" ("familiar . . . shapes no longer there"), the ghosts of hope.

    The problem of temporality and mortality of "Bile and the Ideal" begins to find solution in "Revolt" and in the last movement of *Les Fleurs du Mal* toward restructured innocence. In "Revolt," the poet will again make a choice, but this time his consciousness of good and evil will be neither naive nor limited by the entrapment of experience. The demons and idols who control the poet and try to destroy him will be recognized as parts of the hero's own psyche, and the fragmented vision will move toward integration, toward healing.

Even if the lessons of experience in "Bile and the Ideal" bring about the negation of youthful hopes and the crisis of despair about the human condition, in the beginning of "Parisian Scenes" the creative imagination renews itself by confronting reality and offers an alternative to the entrapment in time. This fragile alternative, always in danger of being overwhelmed by despair, belongs to the second movement of *Les Fleurs du Mal*, which begins the conflict between reality and the dream, the interior world. The first poem, "A Landscape," announces the principle governing the composition of the cycle: the attempt to make poetic creation triumph over daily circumstances. The affirmation in "A Landscape" marks the progress from "The Blessing," where the poet places himself above life. Here, as the title of the cycle points out, he is entrenched in urban existence, in his "mansarde" (garret), isolated from the bustle of mankind yet receptive to the sounds of the great city. Nevertheless, "A Landscape," like "The Blessing," bears the seed of the defeat the poet will suffer in his encounter with reality. As he proclaims his independence from the passage of seasons, he withdraws into a state of selective innocence bordering on ignorance, into the schoolboy's dream of poetic creation. In the course of the cycle, the dream will have to yield to the underestimated destructive pressure of reality.

The oppositions between "The Clock" and "A Landscape" indicate the imaginative renewal through which the poet hopes to extricate himself from the crisis of "Bile and the Ideal." Most of the verbs in the two poems are in the future tense, but whereas in "The Clock" the infallible polyglot "gosier de métal" ("brazen windpipe") of Time prophesies the future, and the poet cannot help but submit to his fate, in "A Landscape" a reversal occurs with the first two words, "Je veux" (I wish).[36] The poet's creative will determines the future: "Je verrai l'atelier" (l. 6; I will see the workshop), "Je verrai les printemps" (l. 13; I will see the springtime), "je rêverai" (l. 17; I will dream). The "gosier de métal" itself changes to the voice of "clochers" (bells), which, instead of reminding the poet of his imminent death, inspire him to dream and create: "Je veux, pour composer chastement mes églogues, / . . . / . . . voisin des clochers, écouter en rêvant / Leurs hymnes solennels emportés par le vent" (ll. 1–4; I wish, so that I may chastely compose my eclogues / . . . / . . . next to the bells, dreamily listen to / Their solemn hymns blowing on the wind). The concluding words of the first stanza, "rêver d'éternité" (dream of eternity), show that the poet's escape from his obsession with mortality has been effected through his mind's own power rather than, as in "The Blessing," through God's intervention.[37]

Other parallels emphasize the theme of renewal which contradicts the conclusion of "Bile and the Ideal" and opens "Parisian Scenes." In "The Clock" the metonymy "season" describes mortal life. As man grows old, the season loses its charms: "Chaque instant te dévore un morceau du délice / A chaque homme accordé pour toute sa saison" (ll. 7–8; "Each instant gnaws a crumb of the delight / That for his season every mortal brings"). In "A Landscape" the poet perceives seasons imaginatively, composes his eclogues, and, when the seasons lose their charms and turn to winter, he relies on his inner resources and creates a dream embodying the charms absent from nature. Whereas in the concluding poem of "Bile and the Ideal" Time sings a strange *carpe diem* heard only when it is too late ("Les minutes . . . sont des gangues / Qu'il ne faut pas lâcher sans en extraire l'or"; "Each moment . . . is like ore / From which the precious metal must be wrung"), in "A Landscape" the poet finds his riches in his creative power—"évoquer le Printemps avec ma volonté / . . . tirer un soleil de mon coeur" (ll. 24–25; to summon Spring solely with my will / . . . to draw out of my heart a sun)—the power to oppose the season of the imagination to the mortal one. The lost gold changes to the sun.

However, the triumph of "A Landscape" is still based on an escape from reality and therefore lasts only during intense moments of the dream. The poet opts this time for the "verts paradis," the "parfums frais," suggested by words like "chastement" (chastely), "enfantin" (innocent), "pupitre" (school desk). The pastoral idyll built behind shutters closed to the world contradicts the urban orientation of the title of the cycle as well

Hunger for the True Paradise

as the poet's location, his lookout on the city. It will fall victim to the sounds and the visions of the great city that will constantly assault the poet's mind, sometimes to fertilize his imagination, but finally to defeat it.

The last poem of the cycle, "Morning Twilight," reveals the extent to which reality has managed to penetrate the poet's seclusion. Brutish sexuality, the grinding routines of a humanity trapped in time, and finally death itself impress themselves upon the poet's consciousness as a result of his journey into the lives of Parisians. The dream of eternity sung by the hymn of the church bells and the calm nocturnal sky succumbs to the stridence of an external reality that will not be ignored. The sound of the bells turns to the "diane" ("reveille") of the "casernes" ("barracks"); the lamp in the window, subtly related to the star in "A Landscape," becomes "un oeil sanglant qui palpite et qui bouge" (l. 5; "quaking . . . blood-shot eye"). The dawn, in contrast to the pale enchantment of the moon in the beginning poem, heralds increased agonies. The chaste dream of spring of the schoolboy poet, a dream created by the will, gives way to the "rêves malfaisants" ("guilty dreams") of adolescents, helpless victims of nature's laws of generation. That creative will, "je veux," encumbered at last like "l'âme, sous le poids du corps revêche et lourd" (l. 7; "under the body's reluctant, stubborn weight . . . the soul") by the weight of reality, dissipates itself into a state in which "l'homme est las d'écrire" (l. 11; the writer is weary of his work).

Yet more than "Bile and the Ideal," "Parisian Scenes" contains that epic dimension of the city felt by Baudelaire himself. He writes, around the time when he composed the greater part of "Parisian Scenes," "For me, merely going through Paris becomes an Odyssey" (*Corr.*, 1:638). Unlike the defeat of "The Clock," which, though universally applicable, addresses itself to each man separately, rendering him conscious of *his* fate, the conclusion of "Parisian Scenes" includes representative types of humanity and finally personifies the city itself. The poet's consciousness exhibits the growth undergone through the repeated instances of sympathetic imagination in the cycle. His progress is not due to his social concern for unfortunates, but to his identifying with the dispossessed[38]—the pariahs of life—so that his ultimate vision of the universe will have to account for human misery in a world created by the beneficent God of the first movement of *Les Fleurs du Mal.*

As in "Bile and the Ideal," the enormous distance traveled by the poet between the beginning and final poem of the cycle occurs in gradual stages. In this cycle the inner world, sheltered by reverie and by the physical withdrawal of the poet behind closed shutters, crumbles little by little, not without being replaced in great moments of imaginative vision by transformations of the spectacle of the streets into symbols of life seen in its totality. At first, the dream, the power of the inner world, holds its own. "The Sun," whose repositioning in the 1861 edition points to Baudelaire's acute sense of the work's continuity, expands upon the phrase "tirer un soleil de mon coeur" of "A Landscape." Poet and sun alike change "le sort des choses les plus viles" (l. 18; "the value of things the most abject") and reverse the effects of time by rejuvenating nature and man. With "The Red-Haired Beggar Girl," the rejuvenation appears in the form reminiscent of folk songs and of the vocabulary of Renaissance poetry and hence of the youth of poetry, as well as in the subject matter—the young girl whose beauty shines through her poverty.

With "The Swan" and the following poems, the poet leaves youth for the maturity of an imaginative vision forged out of the mind's encounter with mutable, inexplicable, and terrifying aspects of reality. "The Swan," the poem paralleling most closely the Greater Romantic Lyric in its interplay of inner contemplation and outer observation, embodies the tension between memory—again, that imaginative, resurrecting memory—and absence, rather than forgetting. Associated with water, with "cocotiers" ("coconuts") whose fruit contains nourishing liquid, memory in the poem represents fertility, whereas absence is expressed in terms of sterility, drought, and emaciation, liquid being replaced by tears. Although all the beings of the past superimposed by the poet on the present cityscape remember and their remembrances surpass the limits of their entrapment, their memory, unlike that of the poet who identifies with them, remains sterile. They seek in vain the equivalent of their obsessive image from the past in present reality. The poet, however, knows the mutability of the world—"la forme d'une ville / Change plus vite, hélas! que le coeur d'un mortel" (ll. 7–8; the shape of a city / Changes faster, alas, than a mortal's heart)—and, lost in the "forest" of sense experience, he relies upon his memory to sound the horn, to restructure the flux of reality into intelligible "allegory."[39]

The verbs "pense" (think) and "vois" (see) play key roles in the process of transforming experience into symbol. "Je vois" appears each time the poet sees with the eye of memory rather than the bodily eye: "je ne vois qu'en esprit" (l. 9; I see only in spirit), "là je vis" (l. 14; there I saw), "je vois ce malheureux" (l. 25; I see this ill-starred one). In the last instance, the superimposition of the image of the old upon the new lends symbolic meaning to the event that in the past was no more than *spectacle:* "ce malheureux" becomes the "mythe étrange et fatal" (strange and fatal myth) of those who, "rongé[s] d'un désir sans trêve" (l. 36; gnawed by a desire without respite) and unable to find it in the world of experience, turn to cursing God for a world ill-made.

The phrase "je pense," in the sense of "I remember," builds toward the coherence of the poetic vision from the first line of the poem. The image resuscitated by that phrase fertilizes the memory, and the memory in turn begins to contrast its city with the actual one. The cumulative images of the second part of the poem come to life in the poet's consciousness with the magic phrase "je pense" that here acquires the sense of "I create," "I bring to life," as the poet battles with mutable reality against forgetfulness of things and people absent from the new scheme, the new arrangement of cities and minds. His "chers souvenirs" (dear memories), "plus lourds que des rocs" (l. 32; heavier than stones), which give coherence to the disparate components of new and old Paris, stay solid amid the flux. Unlike Andromaque, or the swan, or all the "captifs . . . vaincus" (l. 52; captives . . . vanquished), the poet does not need a fake reconstruction in nature, the "simoïs menteur" (false Simoïs), does not seek splendid Africa through the fog of Paris. But he does create, out of the superimposition of memory over external reality, the unsatisfied desire that makes these exiles sublime in their captivity.

The theme of unfulfilled and unending desire and the incipience of a revolt against the conditions of life announce the last

The Symbolic Method

movement of *Les Fleurs du Mal*, away from the limitations of experience toward an innocence built on knowledge. Yet those limitations, temporarily defeated in "The Swan," haunt the poet in his odyssey through the city. "The Seven Old Men" echoes key images and words of "A Landscape" and transforms the calm dream created by the poet in his high hiding place into the pursuing nightmare beginning in the streets and ending inside the poet's house, despite his barring the door. In this poem, as in "The Blind" and "Comes the Charming Evening," the poet engages his soul in a dialogue indicative of an inner division that leaves him particularly vulnerable to the assault of the city's obsessive sights and sounds. The specter itself comes as an image of fragmentation in time as well as space: "je comptai sept fois, de minute en minute, / Ce sinistre vieillard qui se multipliait" (ll. 35–36; "For seven times (I counted) was begot / This sinister, self-multiplying fear"). Eternity, sought for through "Bile and the Ideal" and dreamed of in "A Landscape," comes to mock the poet's hopes. The apparition not only multiplies but seems to last: "Ces sept monstres hideux avaient l'air éternel" (l. 40; "Those seven loathsome monsters had the air, / . . . of what can never die"). The poet, whose reason gives way before these images of multiplied evil, sees himself as a victim of evil chance, of the absurdity that dominates daily living. The masts of the city, his points of reference in his dreams of eternity from his garret, have disappeared as the soul dances to a music not of its own making, to the tempest that the poet naively thought he could keep out by closing physical and mental doors against the external world.[40]

Reality, associated more and more with God's design through "Parisian Scenes," seems inescapable; "la griffe effroyable de Dieu" ("the claw of God") weighs down "les petites vieilles" ("the little old women"); the blind seek in vain some answer from the heavens; the sufferers in crepuscular Paris die without having lived; and the poet, attempting to create a dream in "Parisian Dream" not only opposed to the present but to all of vegetable nature, is awakened by the clock "aux accents funèbres" which reminds him, as in "The Clock," of his entrapment in mortality.

After the inimical appearance of the seven old men, even thoughts of eternity begin to raise doubts in the poet's mind through his increased contact with reality and his skepticism about the justice of universal laws. "Bile and the Ideal" explores the decay of the physical being in death; "Skeletons Digging," "The Dance of Death," and "The Servant" raise the question of whether the whole being will find respite from the routines, the preoccupations, the sufferings of the everyday even after death. With these poems Baudelaire creates his equivalent of life-in-death. The old engraving of the skeleton digging pushes the curse of Adam beyond the grave into an eternity of labor and suffering, and the poet shudders at the punishment: "d'un destin trop dur / Epouvantable et clair emblème" (ll. 21–22; "the terrible sign . . . / Of our destiny's greater death"). The skeleton of "The Dance of Death" suffers from another fate, no less horrible, namely, the continuation in death of the insatiable desire for the Sabbath of Pleasures. Baudelaire creates the powerful image of desire as the rider spurring the dead being on in the tracks of habit, the mindless habit that deadens the living and gives no rest to the dead.

In "The Servant" the poet mixes remorse for a life ill-spent with love for the maternal figure who, like the other dead, has no rest from her concerns and pains, and suffers in addition from cold and solitude, against which the living still find some remedy. The simplicity of the conversational diction underlines poignantly the comfortable, familiar intercourse with loved ones that the dead lack without ceasing to love.

Through his encounter with the life of the great city in its realistic and hallucinatory aspects, the poet again suffers defeat. The affirmation of poetic powers in "A Landscape" is dispersed by the pressure of the external world against those shutters which cannot hold. The dream of spring and the sun created out of the poet's heart which can embellish the ugly aspects of reality change into the shroud of "Mists and Rains," to the funereal preoccupations to which the poet's mind succumbs. His own youth and the beauty of youth found in the streets of Paris disappear in the personification of the city as the old worker returning to his routine with the coming of dawn in "Morning Twilight." Yet the poet's plight gains mythical stature throughout "Parisian Scenes" as he identifies with the victims of life and raises them to symbols of the conflict between mind and external world. His consciousness grows to include outrage and revolt against the human condition and skepticism about the possibility of escape through the intervention of a merciful God. This progress, which leads to the cycle of "Revolt," propels the poet forward to the last movement of *Les Fleurs du Mal.*

Before integration can begin, the poet must traverse two archetypal stages of the quest, the false paradise and the dark night of the soul to which the delusion leads. Situated between "Parisian Scenes" and "Revolt," "Wine" and "Flowers of Evil" represent respectively these stages.[41] The initial poem of "Wine" negates the despair and lassitude of "Morning Twilight." The cruel dawn calling Paris to work changes to a setting of repose, either evening or Sunday. Wine, which throughout the cycle is associated with images of light and warmth, dissipates the cold and its effects on the poor who cannot find relief. In "Morning Twilight" the defeated soul contends with the weight of the body, the weary poet and woman of pleasure with their exhaustion, the dying with their last agony; the sterility of existence dominates man. By contrast, the stimulant in "The Soul of Wine" restores, as did the imagination in earlier cycles, life, love, even poetic inspiration. More powerful than the imagination, it manages to remedy those conditions of life against which the mind is powerless, such as the suffering of the poor: the laborer's child gains his strength and color under the wine's power.

The wine's role as supreme remedy for the "maudits"— poets and rogues alike—appears in all the poems of the cycle. Yet the homage to God of "The Soul of Wine"—"la poésie / Qui jaillera vers Dieu comme une rare fleur" (ll. 23–24; "the poetry . . . / Shall spring toward God like a great, strange flower")—which seems to attribute to God the bounty of wine, changes, through Baudelaire's revision of "The Ragpickers' Wine," to a reproach; God, stricken with remorse for the old wretches, gives them the solace of sleep, and man himself adds the consolation of wine. In earlier versions, God, praised for his goodness, gives man both.[42] The reproach emphasizes the poet's continuing awareness of human suffering and of his failure to regain paradise by means of his imagination. In "The Ragpickers' Wine" man himself seizes the external stimulant as a way to escape the dilemma of an unjust world.

The structure of the cycle reveals the delusory nature of the false paradise. The poem situated at the center of the cycle, "The Murderer's Wine," deals with the necessity of escape. The assassin justifies his deed as one of mercy: "Je l'aimais trop! voilà pourquoi / Je lui dis: Sors de cette vie" (ll. 27–28; "I loved her past bearing; and so / I said: 'You've got to die' "). Full of self-hatred and contempt for others, driven by a thirst that can hardly be assuaged, even by wine, the assassin announces the dangers of the artificial paradise and foreshadows the self-destruction of "Flowers of Evil." Apart from the dark side, namely, the discordance of the central poem, the beginning and end show no progression. In both "The Soul of Wine" and "Lovers' Wine," wine represents a successful escape into the fruitful states of mind: poetry, dreams. The overwhelmed psyche of the poet at the end of "Parisian Scenes" pauses too long, relies too heavily upon the temporary external remedy, and the beginning of "Flowers of Evil" shows the resultant devastation. As Baudelaire writes in the concluding section of *Artificial Paradises*, "The very infallibility of the method constitutes its immorality" (*OC*, 1:439–40). Poets gain the true paradise ("artificiels" functions very much as "false," in addition to "artificial") by regenerating their souls through mental efforts, not external stimulants (*OC*, 1:441).

Prolonged dependence on these stimulants plunges the poet into that modern equivalent of the fall from grace, the desolation of Boredom, which poses an even greater threat to the imagination. In the last stanza of "Lovers' Wine," the poet envisions a journey toward bliss: "Ma soeur, côte à côte nageant, / Nous fuirons sans repos ni trèves / Vers le paradis de mes rêves" (ll. 12–14; "My sister, side by side will [sic] flee, / Without repose, or truce, where gleams / The golden paradise of my dreams"). The lines that begin the cycle of "Flowers of Evil" continue the images of swimming and drinking of the preceding poem but violently oppose the hope of paradise. The sister-beloved figure metamorphoses into a demon swimming around the poet and taking the shape of "la plus séduisante des femmes" (l. 6; "woman's most seductive forms") in order to lure him into a realm of desolation. Drinking, the supreme remedy in "Wine," takes on the connotation of damnation: "Je l'avale et le sens qui brûle mon poumon / Et l'emplit d'un désir éternel et

The Symbolic Method

coupable" (ll. 3-4; "As I breathe, he [the demon] burns my lungs like fever / And fills me with an eternal guilty desire"), "[il] Accoutume ma lèvre à des philtres infâmes" (l. 8; "Lips grow accustomed to his lewd love-charms"). The demon, who first seduces the poet through his vulnerability to beauty, his "grand amour de l'Art" ("love of Art"), leads him into Boredom by making habitual to him states of consciousness exacerbated by stimulants.

Worn out by excesses, the poet's perception is at the mercy of the tempter. The demon forces the poet's sight toward a narrowly limited range of experience which must henceforth furnish the materials for his art: "Des vêtements souillés, des blessures ouvertes, / Et l'appareil sanglant de la Destruction" (ll. 13–14; "festering wounds and filthy clothes, / And all Destruction's bloody retinue"). Because of this distorted perception, the poet creates a vision of the world whose images of violence and death reflect his own imprisoned psyche.[43] The poet finally becomes the brother of the "hypocrite Reader," succumbing to Boredom and to the nightmares of cruelty dreamed up by its victims in a vain attempt to break away.

The cycle of "Flowers of Evil" explores the demonic perversion of the desire without respite sung in "Parisian Scenes," which continues to seek satisfaction, not in the sights of external reality this time, but in acts of misguided love and aberrant sexuality. In "The Martyr" the poet asks the decapitated corpse whether her killer satisfied "l'immensité de son désir" ("His monstrous, last desire"); the lesbians seek infinity, and are, as such, sisters to the poet, who sees himself now as the antithesis of his youthful self in "The Blessing," as "sinistre, ennemi des familles, / Favori de l'enfer" ("The Two Good Sisters," ll. 5-6; "curst poet, foe to married rest, / The friend of hell").

The obsessive desire for infinity and the vain struggle to appease it result in a psychic division that manifests itself in images of bodily dismemberment and mental impotence. The "martyr" is decapitated, the poet loses his blood to "ces cruelles filles" ("The Fountain of Blood," l. 14; "these cruel whores") in his attempt to escape the terror that dominates him and, worse yet, recognizes his disemboweled and castrated corpse on the island of Love. Mocked by the perversion of his ill-placed worship and hopes of love, his mind is impotent before the demons of "My

Hunger for the True Paradise

Beatrice" and divided against itself at the end of "A Voyage to Cythera," where the observing consciousness contemplates from a distance the deceived heart and polluted body to which it belongs. The poet has been enthralled by the distorted perception of Boredom. He sees only what the demon allows him: "pour moi tout était noir et sanglant désormais" (l. 54; "all was blood and blackness then to me"). The word "allegory," which in "The Swan" indicated the transformation of external reality into symbol, shows in the conclusion of "A Voyage to Cythera" the poet's horrified recognition of his psychic state, buried in a vision that mirrors its fragmentation in all he sees.

The flash of awareness in "A Voyage to Cythera" finds a direct response in the cycle's first suggestion of hope for psychic recovery. "Love and the Skull," used by Baudelaire as the final poem for the original eighteen *Fleurs du Mal*, continues to represent in the larger context a reaffirmation—even if severely limited—of creative power in a vertical movement out of Boredom, even at the price of existence. Seduced by the demon of perverted desire in the initial poem of the cycle, the poet is still dominated by a cruel power. But though in the first poem his eyes were "pleins de confusion" ("bewildered") and he was lost in the desert of Boredom, here the narrative voice, as well as the victim, is lucid. Hence, the skull seems dominated in a physical rather than a spiritual sense. As for poetic creation, in the beginning the demon furnishes the poet with the raw materials for his art, namely, images of horror. In the final poem, the poet uses the same type of matter, "cervelle, / . . . sang et . . . chair" (ll. 19–20; "my blood . . . my brain"), but it becomes living matter instead of dead, dismembered forms since it originates in the skull, in the inner suffering of mankind. It thus suggests a new dignity of the mind conscious of its condition, not seeking solace in "philtres infâmes" ("lewd love-charms") nor lost in Boredom. Instead of becoming images of murder and blood, this matter changes through the suffering inflicted by the perverse Love into "des bulles rondes / Qui montent dans l'air" (ll. 5–6; "bubbles . . . / That rise and fly"), defying physical laws. Neither the ascension nor the existence of these bubbles lasts, and it is clear that, if continued, the ferocious game of love will dissipate the living matter. Yet, though in the other poems of "Flowers of

Evil" the poet's psyche is destroyed at each turn by the horror of its enslavement, in the last poem it finds a brief affirmation in the issue of Love and the brain:

> Le globe lumineux et frêle
> Prend un grand essor,
> Crève et crache son âme grêle
> Comme un songe d'or. [Ll. 9-12][14]

Even the defeat of this élan toward "les mondes / Au fond de l'éther" (ll. 7-8; "worlds / Deep in the sky") results in an image of beauty, "un songe d'or" (a golden dream). The precious metal in "Love and the Skull" recalls "le riche métal de notre volonté / . . . vaporisé" ("the precious metal of our will / . . . vaporized") by Satan Trismegistus of "To the Reader" and the unextracted gold of Time in "The Clock." Here the vaporized gold does not dissipate itself in meaningless particles. It forms a luminous sphere, a product of the mind—the dream. The love of the beautiful which damns the poet in the beginning of the cycle saves him from total destruction by transforming his very being into images of fragile beauty, rising above the matter that goes into their making.

"Revolt" represents the poet's first sustained attempt to forge a vision of reality free from the domination of conventional concepts of good and evil, of temptation and fall attributed to external forces such as the various demons who pursue the poet. Hints of revolt make themselves heard throughout the preceding cycles, not in outright blasphemies of God, but in the poet's growing dissatisfaction with the incapacity of the world to answer to man's aspirations. The poet allies himself increasingly with those shut out of the contentment of everyday life, those who experience the greatest depths of suffering. In a draft of a letter to Jules Janin, Baudelaire exposes the contentment with the status quo and the refusal to look at the reality of human misery as characteristics of limited and self-deceiving minds: "I pity you, sir, for being so easily made happy. A man must sink quite low to consider himself happy" (*OC*, 2:233). The poet, who has experienced phases of despair culminating in the destruction of creative power in "Flowers of Evil," refuses to look away and, particularly in the militant "Abel and Cain," sees the need to restructure the world so as to save it from the tyranny of limited perceptions.

The redefinition of Satan, his complete transformation from the demon of "To the Reader" to the savior of "Litany to Satan," obviates the theological question of Baudelaire's satanism and the problem of his sincerity in the preface to "Revolt." For Baudelaire, the description of all of *Les Fleurs du Mal*, not just "Revolt," as a diabolical work (*Corr.*, 2:198; *OC*, 1: "Epigraphe pour un livre condamné") reveals the connection between *Les Fleurs du Mal* and Romanticism, which Baudelaire discusses in the same terms, as an exploration of the depths of the soul requiring a satanic perspective (*OC*, 2:168).

The move toward the rehabilitation of Satan begins with the view of God presented in "The Denial of Saint Peter." Like the profane tyrant of "Love and the Skull," God, perched over humanity, gorges himself on its suffering, on the sobs and blood of those tortured and killed. Since God presides over these atrocities and Christ takes the place of the cranium of Humanity—"Dans ton crâne où vivait l'immense Humanité" (l. 16; "your temples . . . / Which hold, of all Humanity, the sum"), his martyrdom, instead of saving mankind, serves to feed the insatiable appetite of God. The poet reproaches Christ for having failed to fulfill the eternal promise through his lack of knowledge of life. Christ, like the youthful poet of "The Blessing," commits two errors: he addresses prayers to the cruel God, and he seeks to remain faithful to his dream of innocence by escaping the conflict with a reality that contradicts the dream at every step. The remorse that pierces Christ on the cross is that he left the world unchanged. The poet envies the alternative of leaving a condition in which "l'action n'est pas la soeur du rêve" (l. 30; "dream and action disunite"), but knows that he, like Saint Peter, must live in the world and find a way to defeat human misery, since the false paradises have proven disastrous.

The third and last poem of "Revolt" opposes Satan to Christ rather than to God by pointing to the success of Satan's healing vision. Satan, the vanquished, the exile, knows the world and the uselessness of appeals to superior powers. His experience on the cosmic plane parallels the condition of the pariah on earth and renders him "le plus savant . . . des Anges" (l. 1; "of the

The Symbolic Method

Angels . . . most wise"). Unlike Christ, he stays to share his knowledge and healing throughout eternity: "Toi, qui sais tout . . . / Guérisseur familier des angoisses humaines" (ll. 7–8; "King, omniscient / Healer of man's immortal discontent"). Not only does he lighten mankind's burden of suffering, but he fulfills the eternal promise, the return to Paradise, by teaching man the way to regain it. Satan the vanquished is also the eternal challenger; his battle with God perpetually renews itself. He offers man the choice of a continual revolt against mortality. Love redeems man's isolation as pariah, as leper (l. 10), by giving him the taste of Paradise (l. 11). Hope, another of Satan's gifts, allows man to surpass his limitations by making him act as if he were immortal.

In the last part of the poem, entitled "Prayer," the poet sees Satan succeeding where Christ has failed, reuniting beneficent action—the knowledge of the external world described in the course of the litany—with the inner world of the dream. The poet, who throughout his journey has attempted a similar fusion, prays that he be admitted to the highest paradise where innocence can exist together with knowledge, where his soul, in the shade of the Tree of Knowledge, will not reach stasis but will witness its ever-growing branches and be in contact with the unknown.

The continuity between the final poem of "Revolt" and the beginning poem of "Death" indicates the thematic relationship of the two cycles. Harmony instead of opposition between cycles occurs for the first time in the transition from "Revolt" to "Death" and signifies that the poet, having experienced the power of imagination, no longer needs yet another chance to recover his psychic strength. "The Death of Lovers" answers the prayer of "Litany of Satan" ("O Satan, prends pitié de ma longue misère"; "Satan, at last take pity on our pain"). The poet envisions the paradise obtained through love for which Satan has prepared him. Like the following two poems, "The Death of Lovers" contains an image of doors beginning to open upon the unknown. Its atmosphere of "luxe, calme et volupté" ("richness, quietness, and pleasure") recalls "Invitation to the Voyage," but instead of a geographical goal, the lovers are headed for an "anywhere out of the world" of the soul's desire. The cycle of "Death," particularly as it existed in the 1857 edition, contains parallels with "Wine" which show the progression from false to true paradise. Like the earlier cycle, it presents types of humanity—lovers, artists, the poor—without the darker hint of a poem like "The Murderer's Wine." Yet within the cycle of "Death" there is a sense of growth, of a true movement toward integration rather than toward another attempt at escape, and the movement, which recapitulates the whole journey of *Les Fleurs du Mal*, defines itself through the poems added to the 1861 edition. Hence, the addition of these poems modifies the structure of the entire work.

"Dream of a Curious Person" serves as appropriate prelude to "The Voyage," the final poem. In it the poet explores for the last time the limitations of a fragmented vision, but here he is detached from the narrative voice, which unmasks its ignorant innocence despite its attempt to appear knowledgeable and experienced. The narrator cultivates his pain with the scope of having others admire his originality. His desire for death is a thirst for stimulus, for an excitement that life no longer provides. Like "l'enfant avide du spectacle" ("a child, so keen to see the show"), he waits passively to be entertained without exercising his faculties. Death disappoints him.

"The Voyage" incorporates this childish and cruel thirst for external stimuli to which the reader is made an accomplice in "To the Reader." This curiosity attempts to acquire the knowledge of the quester without undergoing the risk of the journey. In *The Poem of Hashish* Baudelaire comments on the desire for knowledge by proxy in terms similar to those of both "The Voyage" and "Dream of a Curious Person": "You could call it a childish impatience to find out, like that which people who never left their hearth display when they find themselves before a man who has returned from far away, unknown countries. Such people fancy hashish intoxication to be a prodigious country, an enormous theatre of juggling and prestidigitation . . . . We have here . . . a total misconception" (*OC*, 1: 408). The first stanza of "The Voyage," with its shift of perspectives, rectifies the misconception of passive curiosity. The universe is no bigger than a child's appetite, which, though vast, is nevertheless limited. It, of course, fails to satisfy the desire of that creative memory, the *souvenir*.

Having established the insufficiency of the universe, the

The Symbolic Method

poet, who, as in "To the Reader," speaks to us through the collective voice of humanity, recapitulates the voyage. Echoes of earlier images indicate the correspondence between each episode and the psychic stages traversed before the poet reaches the final point, itself only a point of departure. Among the motives for the quest are his circumstances in "Bile and the Ideal": "l'horreur de leurs berceaux" (l. 10; the horror of their cradles),[45] "la Circé tyrannique aux dangereux parfums" (l. 12; tyrannical Circe and her dangerous perfume). Yet the genuine travelers, as the poet realizes in "Parisian Scenes," are driven by desires without shape, dreams without name (ll. 21–24), toward something that cannot be found in the external world. The questers, "tel le vieux vagabond" (like the old bum), though similar to the victims of "The Swan," treading the mud and dreaming their images, prove their superiority because they create the "brillants paradis" (l. 46; glowing paradises) and transform the "taudis" (l. 48; wretched holes) of oppressive reality, even if temporarily, by means of their imagination.

The dialogue between the "curious" and the voyagers, between the perception limited by innocence and the one limited by experience, which takes place in parts 3–6 of the poem contrasts the innocents' eagerness with the weariness of experience felt by the poet at critical points of the journey and now summarized by the travelers. The false paradises of exoticism, unable to satisfy an ever-increasing desire, give way to the images of horror, cruelty, and Boredom which have haunted the poet throughout the quest.

In part 7, the travelers reap the fruit of experience, bitter knowledge, but this time in full consciousness of the flaws of their own perception. The smallness of the universe, its fragmentation, prove to be reflections of their own divided psyches. They realize that, paradoxically, death frees them from temporality, but they still seek in it the bliss of another false paradise, the perfumed Lotus that destroys memory and imagination.

The last section of "The Voyage" contains the resolution of the poem and the entire work. The questers finally understand the futility of a paradise of stasis and embark upon the last adventure that, like the tree of knowledge growing from Satan's brow, will expand their consciousness for eternity. Their cry,

Hunger for the True Paradise

"Plonger au fond du gouffre, Enfer ou Ciel, qu'importe" (l. 143; Plunge into the depths, Hell or Heaven, what matter), represents here, in contrast to "Hymn to Beauty," a genuine overthrow of conventional separations between good and evil, a movement toward infinity. In the cycle of "Death" Satan and other demons disappear, and in "The Voyage" the poet does away even with the intermediary angels who open the doors on the unknown. Unlike the bravado of "Hymn," where the poet plays with the fire of what he knows to be infernal beauty, the tone of the last section goes beyond that innocence and imparts the urgency of the final quest. Purged of their inner divisions, the questers plunge into the abyss, knowing that their own vision will determine whether "l'Inconnu" (the Unknown) becomes hell or heaven.

IV

Les Fleurs du Mal represents the poetic culmination of Baudelaire's aesthetics. Although the poetry is free from the polemics and contentiousness of the criticism, it parallels attitudes and ideas in the prose which gain substance from the unity and coherence of the poetic work. The concentration on the growth of the psyche in *Les Fleurs du Mal* and in the prose indicates Baudelaire's lifelong commitment to fighting the fragmentation of sensibility in the modern age. He sees such extremes as the pursuit of ideal beauty and industrial progress as part of the same intoxication with matter which makes one worship forms and the other worship copies of nature. Coleridge finds in the French Revolution the historical exemplum of the dissociation of faculties that stems from inner repression and results in bloodshed. Baudelaire chooses the material progress of his time as the mark of a diminishing respect for the mind manifested in the pursuit of contentment and the repression of anything exceeding mediocrity. Modern art, Baudelaire contends in his criticism, refuses to look at life except in its surface aspects, in disparate facets behind which there is no unifying vision.

In Baudelaire's view, the Romantic movement alone

133

The Symbolic Method

meets the challenge posed by modern life. It finds the heroism, the epic dimension of daily living because it perpetually attempts to see the world in its totality, to create an intelligible vision of its coherence in art. But such a quest requires constant imaginative effort against the mutability of experience, and, for all the dangers posed by external reality, the mind, as the movements of *Les Fleurs du Mal* demonstrate, cannot create a viable alternative without this tension. "Bile and the Ideal," a title that intrigues critics who see in it a duality and contradiction in that the "bile" poems actually follow the "ideal," suggests the synthesis originating in the initial contradiction; the ideal cannot survive without *spleen,* and *spleen* would be mere immersion, perhaps even contentment, in the everyday without the pull of the ideal.

For Baudelaire, the perception of nature in its totality, the transformation of nature into Nature—the universal analogy—depends upon the imagination. He expands Coleridge's theory of the imagination to include functions of the mind which do not always coexist with the conscious will, but which nevertheless lead to poetic creation. The dream and remembrance in *Les Fleurs du Mal* signalize the moments in which the imagination succeeds in metamorphosing the *spectacle* of the streets, of mundane reality, and even of temporal dissolution into symbol. Like Coleridge, Baudelaire focuses on the process of creating the symbol rather than on the static image. Post-Baudelarian literary developments like Symbolism and Aestheticism, which claim kinship with Baudelaire, often neglect or obscure this fundamental aspect of his contribution. They also forget, as do some contemporary critics, that Baudelaire's goal is a profoundly humane one. His search for integration, as the quest of the poet in *Les Fleurs du Mal* shows, exposes false idols and demands a constant renewal of the imagination, always the unknown, the *new,* opposing false paradises and their delusion of ecstatic stasis, even in death. In *Les Fleurs du Mal* the poet's identification with the dispossessed, the exiles from life's bounty, provides the key impetus for a reconstruction of the human condition on an imaginative level, away from and against the determinism of earthly circumstances.

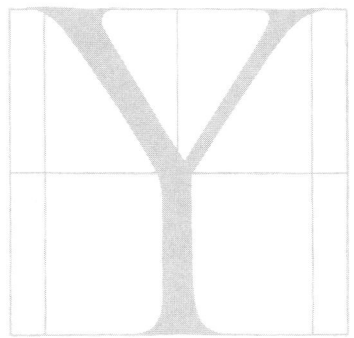

FOUR YEATS
THE QUEST FOR UNITY OF BEING

"Life is an endeavour, made vain by the four sails of its mill, to come to double contemplation, that of the chosen Image, that of the fated Image," writes Yeats in a succinct description of his lifelong quest.[1] Although terms like "four sails," "chosen," and "fated" require further elucidation from the context of *A Vision,* the dominant idea of life as an unsatisfied enterprise to reconcile or at least to make coincide circumstances (the fated Image) and desire (the chosen Image) places Yeats directly in the mainstream of Romantic tradition. Yeats's search for unity in his work and his creation of a system of symbols to give it coherence represent an advancement over Coleridge's thwarted poetic career and Baudelaire's unfinished plans for *Les Fleurs du Mal* because of the magnitude of Yeats's output. Helped by longevity and relative freedom from the painful situations of Coleridge and Baudelaire, Yeats was able to dedicate himself to shaping his life's work into unity. However, in terms of the enterprise comprised in the aesthetic of the symbol—psychic reintegration through imaginative creation—Yeats's achievement is at times flawed by the pursuit of the "double contemplation"; his contraries, yoked together by violence, are in danger of fragmenting instead of integrating.

Armed against nature by his study of Blake and his immersion in the mystical orders, Yeats separates more sharply than Coleridge and Baudelaire the realm of the senses from that of the spirit by dispensing with correspondences. He feels less strongly nature's lure, and hence his quarrel with nature is less bitter. In later years he fights repeatedly against the loss of the fated Image in the pursuit of the chosen one. Two major strands in Yeats's poetic heritage account for his much-noted vacillation between the dream in nature's spite and an almost Tennysonian fear, especially in the early work, of abandoning the consolations and sweetness of nature and of man's common lot. While the pursuit of the dream is clearly a Romantic inheritance, the latter preoccupation grows out of his Rhymers' Club experience in the Nineties. The fire of straw, burning itself in one great blaze in Johnson, Dowson, Wilde, Symons, and Beardsley, all of whom destroyed their creative capacities and sometimes themselves at an early age, warned the young poet against their version of the Romantic Quest. In his autobiographical writing, Yeats separates himself from them by mocking his own youthful penchant for theorizing and his provincialism in the midst of sophisticated, learned men, contemptuous of generalizations.[2] Yet the distance he creates between himself and the rest stands as a criticism of their attitudes. In the interests expressed with consistency over a decade in letters to Katharine Tynan and John O'Leary (*Letters*, pp. 33, 286), in the early prose,[3] as well as in the early Irish ballads, Yeats shows the need for a break with the Rhymers in his conscious orientation toward folk tradition rather than the continent, particularly France, and toward a commitment to national life that resolutely opposes the Rhymers' aspirations to cosmopolitanism.

Symons, Yeats's Rhymer friend, influenced him to see a connection between Coleridge, Rossetti, and Baudelaire. Ironically, Yeats later closely identified the triad with the Rhymers by attributing to them all the exhausting and ultimately fatal quest for "this new pure beauty" (" 'perfection of thought and feeling,' " its unity in turn with "perfection of form") (*A*, p. 188). Because Dowson and Johnson, like their precursors, "make all

The Quest for Unity of Being

out of the privacy of their thought" (*A*. p. 188), Yeats throughout the early poetry attempts to fight the privacy of thought which threatens to become incommunicable. He warns against absorption in the dream, while he himself feels irresistibly drawn to it. Fear and desire exist side by side, unabated, despite Yeats's attempt to use symbol as a focus for national life and to root his mythology in the existing folk tradition of Ireland. Major symbols like the rose awaken the poet's ambivalence. In revision, Yeats tries to sharpen the function of symbols and generally succeeds, but only at the cost of confusing the tone and attitude within the individual poems and cycles by bringing in a later consciousness too advanced for his earlier quester.

Yeats's survival beyond the Tragic Generation, his mastery of diction, and his public disclosure of the private system of *A Vision* alleviate his fear, as the later poetry and prose show. He looks upon the Tragic Generation with as much pity as terror and attributes his aesthetic of passion to his contact with it. However, the desire to leap into the supernatural is still kept in check in the later poetry by recurring symbols and the dialectical structure of the cycles, which act as correctives and recall the quester back to life. Yet Yeats's swerves from the Romantic influence, with its devastating effect upon his friends,[4] continue to haunt his career. Some, such as his development of a new diction (though that in itself is a typical Romantic endeavor), have positive results; many of them are decidedly unpleasant, particularly when Yeats undertakes to achieve Unity of Culture and, when that fails, calls down war and the world's end in order to prove that his idea of civilization is right.

The greatness of Yeats's quest consists of his desire for Unity of Being in the face of the mind's divided faculties, the four sails of the mill. This phase of Yeats's work shows influences and echoes of Coleridge and important affinities with Baudelaire. Yet there is little evidence of direct influence except via Baudelaire's French heirs—Verlaine, Mallarmé, Villiers de l'Isle d'Adam—whom Yeats admired and whose influence he himself admits was hard to measure.[5] Yeats's emphasis on the mind's primacy borrows from Coleridge's aesthetic, and a number of key poems contain clear Coleridgean echoes. The great poems of symbolization, whether traditional Greater Romantic

137

The Symbolic Method

Lyrics or not, revolve around the illumination of Coleridge's best-known Conversation Poems when natural event or object becomes symbol. Yeats's inclusion of reverie and recollection in the imaginative process enlarges Coleridge's theory of the imagination and parallels Baudelaire's. The dialectical progress of the psyche through each cycle and the recurrence of key symbols or symbolic moments within cycles and throughout the work appear as major structural methods in both *Les Fleurs du Mal* and Yeats's *Collected Poems*. Although internalized quests throughout the work characterize Romantic poetry and several Romantic poets use the cycle structure, the cycle and its function in the work as employed by Baudelaire and Yeats represent a startling parallelism, especially if Yeats had only second-hand, fragmentary knowledge of *Les Fleurs du Mal*. Both poets use the cycle to present a state of mind first contradicted, then transcended by the growing consciousness of the speaker through turning points and summings-up of the journey.

Shelley and Blake provide the most visible, central influence on Yeats's career,[6] yet the less readily perceived affinities of Coleridge and Baudelaire are essential for understanding Yeats's aesthetic of the symbol and reintegration of faculties effected by the imagination. Traditionally, Romantic scholars, like their subjects, emphasize this humanist view of the arts. The humanist aim of Coleridge's enterprise, even in his most orthodox phase, is so plain that there is little controversy about this aspect of his work. Baudelaire's humanism comes under attack primarily from critics who concentrate on isolated poems and on the prose rather than on the totality of *Les Fleurs du Mal*. Discussions of Yeats's humanism appeared frequently enough even before Bloom's uncompromising assessment in his *Yeats* to warrant that Yeats's is at best not as consistently obvious as Coleridge's and exists at worst only in portions of his work. Ultimately, the debate about Yeats's humanism centers on the critics' view of what constitutes a viable literary tradition. Denis Donoghue and Northrop Frye trace the source of Yeats's occasional movements away from reality and justice to reactionary aspects of nineteenth-century aesthetics. Frank Kermode in "The Modern Apocalypse" and Bloom in *Yeats* measure Yeats's achievement against that of the Romantics and argue that Modernist aesthetics is a departure or at least an *éloignement* from humanist values. Other critics, some of whom place Yeats within the Romantic tradition, oppose attempts to devalue Yeats's humanism.[7] Finally, the formalist and Modernist critics, who consider Romanticism a distortion of the mainstream of British literature, identify Yeats's weaknesses in the early poetry with the Romantics' debilitating influence and his unification of the sensibility with his break with Romantic tradition in his later poetry. This last interpretation receives a great deal of support from some of Yeats's own statements, though he does know better than to call the Romantics nature poets or sentimentalists.[8] While aspects of Yeats's aesthetics, like the cult of beauty and the idealization of the Renaissance, derive from nineteenth-century tradition, Symbolist and Aesthete developments taint his inheritance. External solutions for the decline of civilization and the exclusion of modern life from art had their attraction for artists in the latter half of the century, but these theories and practices distinctly broke with the Romantics' insistence on the need to reintegrate the psyche and their hope that achieved humanity could transform the world.[9]

The Romantic influence in Yeats is discussed in the context of Shelley, Blake, and even Wordsworth, but rarely Coleridge,[10] and almost never Baudelaire, who, if classified at all, generally falls in with the Symbolists and their British counterparts, the Aesthetes, in studies of influence. The same neglect, coupled at times with desultory assessments of Baudelaire, characterizes many discussions of Yeats's relationship to the Symbolists. Astonishingly, excepting Frank Kermode's illuminating *Romantic Image* and Graham Hough's *The Last Romantics*, the most just appraisal of Baudelaire remains that of Symons. If, as several scholars contend, Yeats's knowledge of Baudelaire in particular and of the Symbolists in general came through Symons's critiques and translations,[11] Yeats was well served by Symons's intermediation. In calling Baudelaire "not only a wholly original poet, but a new personal force in literature," and by perceiving that Baudelaire's art would be more influential than Hugo's, Symons anticipates the immense importance of Baudelaire to modern literature. Baudelaire, Symons writes, spent his life writing one book of poetry,[12] an endeavor of some significance to Yeats's own search for "sacred books" among other poets' writings and

The Symbolic Method

for a unified structure for his own lifetime work. As Kermode perceptively notes, connections perfectly familiar to Yeats and Symons between Romantic poets—especially Blake—and the Symbolists are now rediscovered by exegetes. The parallel drawn by Symons between Catullus and Baudelaire, which Yeats takes up, becomes the basis of his association of Baudelaire with the Tragic Generation. Kermode points out that Yeats's grouping of Catullus, Baudelaire, Verlaine, Johnson, and Dowson indicates his awareness of their common traits—the cult of the Image and its high cost, retreat into abnormality and estrangement. In a more radical departure from the critical consensus, Hough finds that Baudelaire's exploration of the human condition and the universal relevance of his work are unparalleled by any poet in England in the last part of the century and that only Yeats undertakes Baudelaire's metaphysical enterprise and his revolutionary experiments with language.[13]

Despite Kermode's and Hough's reappraisals of Baudelaire, the great majority of critics are intent upon proving Yeats's independence from the Nineties and from the Symbolist influence that dominates them. Since most critics consider Yeats's later poetry superior to the early work, they see his forsaking the Nineties poetics as a positive move, and hence his distance from figures such as Baudelaire a measure of his progress. In order to distinguish—to Yeats's advantage—between Baudelaire and Yeats, some critics pair Baudelaire with another poet (Rimbaud and Eliot respectively) and discuss the poetics of the two as if they were identical.[14] Other critics distinguish even less among poets when they group Mallarmé, Verlaine, Rimbaud, and Villiers de l'Isle d'Adam under the common name of Symbolism; whether Baudelaire is included under the same label is generally not clear. Discussing the Symbolist poem or the Symbolists' use of symbols without establishing whether the use of symbols is consistent in the several poets so labeled or whether there is such a commonly agreed-upon genre as the Symbolist poem (such as the Greater Romantic Lyric and the internalized quest in British Romanticism) leads to distortions.[15] And since few critics use the terminology associated with the word "symbol" with precision,[16] conclusions about Yeats's symbol and the collective poetics of the French[17] often leave out the particulars of Yeats's interest in Baudelaire.

The Quest for Unity of Being

II

For Yeats, Coleridge and Baudelaire appear on the literary horizon as forerunners of the Tragic Generation and partakers of the same fate, the engulfment in the pursuit of ideal beauty. Their personal absorption, admirable in its intensity and integrity, represents a danger to be avoided through the external validation of private vision. Yeats will take alternate roads in a search to verify vision which will last his whole career. Those alternatives constitute departures from a heritage whose cost Yeats strove to avoid, because to him, on the immediate level, it meant an early poetic death. When Yeats begins to accept the burden of his tradition, Coleridge and Baudelaire occupy high places in his hierarchy of predecessors. In the poetry, a similar process of distancing and return occurs in regard to Coleridge, although both movements contain distortions. It is more difficult to measure Baudelaire's presence in Yeats's poetic creation beyond the startling parallelism of method in the dialectical structure of the cycles and in their relationship to one another.[18] Apart from Yeats's stated and inferred use of Coleridge and Baudelaire, his own *oeuvre* occupies a major position in the continuity of an aesthetic of the symbol which develops and changes as each post-Romantic poet systematically makes use of it.

When Yeats associates Coleridge and Baudelaire with the Rhymers, he obscures the integration sought by both poets in favor of the doomed pursuit of the larger-than-life dream at the cost of exile from reality. The doomed quest preoccupies Yeats, particularly in the isolation it brings to the quester and in its disastrous effects on the poet's own life. "The Trembling of the Veil" and "The Phases of the Moon," both written in 1922, a watershed year in respect to Yeats's defining his relation to predecessors, group Coleridge and Baudelaire with the most promising and the most isolated members of the Tragic Generation, namely, Johnson, Dowson, and Beardsley. He writes: "All poets . . . until our age came . . . have had some propaganda or traditional doctrine to give companionship with their fellows. . . . But Coleridge of the *Ancient Mariner* and *Kubla Khan*, and Rossetti in all his writings . . . sought this new, pure beauty, and suffered in their lives because of it." For these, as for the triad of

The Symbolic Method

the Tragic Generation, "the whole life is art and poetry" (*A*, p. 188). In an earlier essay, Yeats places Coleridge among solitaries associated with Synge, a different type from the Rhymers. The key element binding this group is the same absorption in art at the expense of living insisted upon in the earlier passage: "Such men [Wordsworth, Coleridge, Goldsmith, Keats, and Synge] have the advantage that all they write is a part of knowledge, but they are powerless before events and have often but one visible strength, the strength to reject from life and thought all that would mar their work, or deafen them in the doing of it" (*E&I*, p. 329). That Yeats grants these artists only a "part of knowledge" underlines his reservations about the exclusiveness of their quest. Coleridge's appearance with Synge in 1910 and with Rossetti in 1922 indicates Yeats's awareness of various facets of Coleridge (i.e., "Coleridge of the *Ancient Mariner*") and his emphasis of the aspect necessary to him at this particular point in his evaluation of tradition. In the thirties, when Yeats attempts to forge a philosophical tradition for Ireland, Coleridge as sage joins Swift and Berkeley in Yeats's reconstructions, and his visionary poetry, the only kind to which Yeats ever makes reference, shows the beneficent influence of Asia upon Europe (*E&I*, pp. 410, 432–33). The need to show the one-sidedness of the quest and thus to exorcise his own attraction to the dream becomes so imperative in the first two decades of the twentieth century that Yeats suppresses one of his important insights—albeit incomplete and characteristically distorted—present in an 1886 article on the Irish poet R. D. Joyce. He proceeds to his customary bipartite classification of tradition into two opposing movements: one, represented by Wordsworth, Coleridge, and Shelley, looks inward: "[these poets] investigate what is obscure in emotion, and appeal to what is abnormal in man, or become healers of some particular disease of the spirit" (*Uncoll.*, 1:105). The healing of the disease, as Yeats himself will articulate it, consists of a search for unity of thought and feeling (*A*, p. 188). But Yeats's somewhat forced preference for the opposing tradition of bards who "speak to the manhood in us" serves as guard against the isolation of these poets from the larger part of mankind ("they write for a clique, and leave after them a school") and against the feminine, reflective souls produced by the late nineteenth-century Romantic schools.[19]

The Quest for Unity of Being

If Yeats occasionally acknowledges that his estimates of Coleridge apply to only one aspect of the man, he makes no such distinction in Baudelaire's case, though his opinion of Baudelaire also undergoes changes. Yeats's view of Baudelaire derives in large part from Symons and in lesser part from Swinburne, who devotes a few warm paragraphs to Baudelaire in his essay on Blake, with which Yeats was acquainted. A letter dated September 1899 contains the earliest reference to Baudelaire and provides evidence that Yeats held Baudelaire in esteem since, in a moment of humility, he doubts his own dismissal of Poe in light of Poe's impact on Baudelaire and Villiers de l'Isle d'Adam (*Letters*, p. 325). Although Baudelaire figures little in Yeats's writings, he, rather than Mallarmé or Verlaine, finds a place among the representative types of artist Yeats chooses as illustrations of phases of the moon in *A Vision*. Again, "The Trembling of the Veil" and *A Vision* illuminate each other; in both Yeats draws a rapprochement of temperament and artistic purpose between Baudelaire and Beardsley and groups them in phase 13 with the luckless Dowson as types of "the sensuous man." The characterization is much more complex than the phrase suggests, for, contradicting the commonplace view of Baudelaire as a decadent trading in grotesque perversions, Yeats assigns him the antithetical phase where "complete intellectual unity, Unity of Being," becomes for the first time possible (*Vision*, p. 129). Although in "The Trembling of the Veil" Yeats makes specific references to Beardsley's life and work and transposes them to the description of the phase-13 type, the passage echoes Symons and Swinburne on Baudelaire. Both emphasize unity of sensibility in Baudelaire; Symons even describes Baudelaire's work as "made out of his whole intellect," recalling not only "Unity of Being" but also the recurrence of the word "intellect" in "Phase 13."[20] Symons comments that Baudelaire's work "is without abundance, but it is without waste." Yeats in turn states, "As the *primary tincture* has weakened, the sense of quantity has weakened, for the *antithetical tincture* is preoccupied with quality." More importantly, Symons discussed Baudelaire's asceticism of passion ("a hermit of the brothel"), his "deliberate science of sensual and sexual perversity," and his deliberate choice of a tragic life, all of these causing his isolation from society and his vilification.[21] Yeats develops a corresponding theory of "victimage" by which the artist becomes a scapegoat, taking upon himself "the knowledge of sin" and the hatred of society in order to enable others to recover innocence (*A*, p. 199). The artist's relation to sin incorporates another saintly trait, "a virginal purity of emotion" (*Vision*, p. 129), "a kind of frozen passion" (*A*, p. 200). Yeats ends "Phase 13" with a prophecy for the men in it and typically changes Symons's deliberate choice to the paradox of the System, the inevitable choice of tragedy as "all life grows more tragic" (*Vision*, p. 130).

Yeats's insistence upon self-expression as the *True Mask* of phase 13, of the perfect achievement of the phase as "expression for expression's sake," bears similarities with Swinburne's references to Baudelaire in *William Blake*. Swinburne arduously defends art for art's sake and uses as authority Baudelaire and his "hérésie de l'enseignement." He warns against compromises with "Philistia" and glorifies sincerity,[22] thus perhaps prompting Yeats's comment that "certain writers . . . exalt intellectual sincerity to the place in literature which is held by sanctity in theology" (*Vision*, p. 130). In a note to the passage on art for art's sake, Swinburne delivers a short eulogy for Baudelaire in which he assesses the uniqueness of Baudelaire's genius: "He could give beauty to the form, expression to the feeling, most horrible and most obscure to the senses and souls of lesser men." Yeats recasts the passage in the language of *A Vision*: "The self discovers, within itself, while struggling with the Body of Fate, forms of emotional morbidity which others recognize as their own. . . . There is almost always a preoccupation with those metaphors and symbols and mythological images through which we define whatever seems most strange and most morbid" (*Vision*, p. 130). Swinburne's descriptions of Baudelaire—beauty of form and expression of hidden feelings—become for Yeats a preoccupation with artistic embodiments of whatever may be obscure and unrecognized—metaphors, symbols, images—so that "others recognize [them] as their own" and art triumphs even over the souls of "lesser men" (*Vision*, p. 130).

Although Yeats articulates more sharply the suggestions given by his two sources, he nevertheless overrides Symons's opinion in one important respect. Symons, like many critics after him, distinguishes between the terms "romantic" and "classic" on the basis of a writer's excess or moderation. He concludes that Baudelaire, improperly called "romantic," "had something classic in his moderation, a moderation which becomes at times as terrifying as Poe's logic."[23] Yeats counters in "Phase 13": "there are moments of triumph and moments of defeat, each in its extreme form, for the subjective intellect knows nothing of moderation" (*Vision*, p. 130). When Yeats follows Symons's lead and writes about frozen purity and virginity of passion, he may be offering an insight into Beardsley's emotional make-up, but he underestimates the descent into the abyss of the self by means of sensuality in *Les Fleurs du Mal*; there is, of course, a strong intellectual element in Baudelaire's portrayal of sensuality, and Yeats will hint at its metaphysical significance only later. However, when Yeats strikes out on his own and contradicts or enlarges upon his sources, he comes much nearer the mark. The extremes of triumph and defeat, the anything-but-moderate anguish or exaltation of descent and ascent describe the very fabric of *Les Fleurs du Mal*.

In this evaluation of phase 13, two poles of Yeats's own desire struggle against each other:[24] one is Yeats's lifelong attraction to passion, excess, and his distrust of logic; the other is the warning image of the False Mask, self-absorption, which haunts his account of Romantic precursors and Nineties friends.[25] The subjective intellect's danger appears even more clearly in the *Autobiography*, where he writes that Beardsley's inspiration could not have come from anywhere "outside his own head," just as the other Rhymers had to "make all out of the privacy of their thought" (*A*, pp. 200, 188). Out of his own needs, Yeats fashioned Baudelaire's portrait. He underlined Baudelaire's solitude, his excessive devotion to the quest, and the inevitable tragedy, while at the same time emphasizing the artist's occasional triumphs, his discovery and embodiment of universal aspects of the self.

Why does Yeats need to present images of the artist as an isolated, tragic figure, particularly when the artist is a Romantic or a member of the Tragic Generation? Yeats, like Wordsworth, seems obsessed with the fate of poets who end in despondency and madness. These immediate precursors show all too

The Symbolic Method

clearly the devastation produced by the age upon its imaginative men, and Yeats struggles toward his brand of resolution and independence, bracing himself against internal and external pressures that destroyed the others. By dwelling on incommunicability, victimage, loss of contact with reality, he envisions forms of artistic death which will permit *him* to survive. The distortion of the significant influences of his youth allows him to progress beyond them, beyond the dead end of *The Wind among the Reeds*, but also demonstrates Yeats's desire for the dream quest with its intensity and its exclusion of nature and the mundane. In three important essays around the turn of the century (1897, 1898, 1900), Yeats not only sides with the dream questers but prophesies that the literature of the dream, of inwardness, of immortality will produce the new sacred book that will transform the arts into religion. This art, as the title of one of the essays—"The Autumn of the Body"—suggests, is melancholy, weary of the world; Yeats's statements manifest a strong yearning for apocalypse. The new "embodiment of the imagination" "has done with time" (*E&I*, p. 163): "Man has wooed and won the world, and has fallen weary, and not, I think, for a time, but with a weariness that will not end until the last autumn, when the stars shall be blown away like withered leaves" (*E&I*, p. 193). The widespread influence of Baudelaire and Rimbaud on the Nineties and Yeats's close association with the climate of the times make themselves felt in the frequent appearance of the artist as the supreme *savant*, the alchemist dethroning the matter-oriented chemist with his spiritual transmutations (*E&I*, p. 193). The onesidedness of the quest, its divorce from the natural world, becomes allied to the desire for apocalypse and to alchemical transformations of all matter into spirit. *Rosa Alchemica* exemplifies through its extreme articulation the seductive aspect of the dream quest and through its plot the retreat from it. Yeats sums up in one memorable phrase the yearning that haunted the Nineties as "a cry of measureless desire for a world made wholly of essences" (*Myth*, p. 267).

Yeats's groups of lyrics up to the turn of the century center on the pursuit of the dream which finds no analogue in the natural world. The movement toward the supernatural is initiated either by the speaker or by supernatural beings who answer his

The Quest for Unity of Being

desires or lure him away from common life. The breach brings a sense of loss, of isolation from mankind, which is a characteristic feature of the Romantic Quest. Yeats attempts to use Irish folklore as an antidote to the dream and the escape from life, but the antidote is poetically less convincing than the ill it tries to cure, particularly since Yeats's Irish questers—Fergus, Aengus, King Goll—and his tempters and temptresses resemble their Romantic counterparts more than figures of folklore. In *Crossways, The Rose,* and *The Wind among the Reeds,* progressively, the supernatural speaks through the natural not to reveal itself in symbolic moments of perception but to blast nature and give no hope of reconciliation between the two. The 1889 version of "Ephemera" in *Crossways,* together with a passage of a review of *Axel,* looks forward to *The Wind among the Reeds* and demonstrates the progression toward the separation of nature and the supernatural that appears so unmistakably in the last group. In the review of *Axel,* Yeats speaks of the hierarchy "of those recollections which are our standards and our beacons" (*Uncoll.,* 1:324) in terms of which other works of art ought to be judged. His highest one is that of "the wind blowing in a bed of reeds by the border of a little lake," and it is significant that the recollection should occur in a section dealing with the lovers' renunciation of life in *Axel* and with the striving for the infinite, which "is the possession of the dead." In the 1889 "Ephemera," the concluding stanza contains the lady's reproof to the lover's assertion that eternity lies before them. The wind-swept reeds "cry, 'Eternity!' " (1. 24f),[26] but they represent generation and mortality, and the cry, though uttered through them, does not impart immortality. Rather, it gives sharper contrast to their lifespan of a year. The title of the last nineteenth-century cycle of lyrics, *The Wind among the Reeds,* announces Yeats's commitment to the pursuit of the infinite by forsaking mortality.

But before plunging into the resolute supernatural orientation of *The Wind among the Reeds,* Yeats presents the loss incurred by the quester who chooses the dream. In "The Stolen Child" the fairies lure a mortal away from "a world more full of weeping than he can understand," but they also take him away from the consolations and the "peace within his breast" brought by rural domestic sounds and sights. The child suffers the fate of

The Symbolic Method

the dream quester, as does "The Man Who Dreamed of Faeryland" in *The Rose;* once embarked for the supernatural, he loses his ties to life and, with them, his peace. The theme of loss pervades *The Rose* even more than *Crossways* since the narrator from the beginning invokes the supernatural in the guise of the rose, but not without trying to keep the visitation at a sufficient distance so that he may not lose contact with mortality. Although the invocation appears at first as a desire for a Coleridgean imaginative revelation of the universal through and in the natural—"In all poor foolish things that live a day, / Eternal beauty wandering on her way"—the second stanza presents the unmistakable conflict between the rose and "common things that crave," "mortal hopes," despite Yeats's protest that his Intellectual Beauty suffers with man (*VP*, p. 842). If the rose comes too close, the speaker will find himself isolated from humanity and from life itself. The two heroes of *The Rose,* Fergus and Cuchulain, are less successful than the poet at keeping the visitation at bay and holding on to "a little space" between themselves and it. The first grows to "nothing" after having changed a life of action for the Druid's "little bag of dreams"; the other perishes in a fight with the sea, victim of a web of magical delusions.

Yeats's awareness of the toll taken by the quest is nowhere more apparent than in *The Wind among the Reeds.* There, devotion to the supernatural inevitably brings destruction of the self and the world. Yet the orientation toward death in *The Wind among the Reeds* derives from a psychic state at opposite poles from the one that cries in "The Voyage," "O Mort, vieux capitaine! Il est temps! levons l'ancre" (O Death, old captain! It is time! Raise the anchor). In *Les Fleurs du Mal* the speaker has resolved the pull of contraries in his quest, and the integrated psyche has gone beyond the choices of "Enfer ou Ciel" (Heaven or Hell). But *The Wind among the Reeds* presents the reader with "principles of the mind" instead of the whole psyche,[27] and these principles do not even stand for the various faculties of the mind, but for a divided imagination (*VP*, p. 803). The speakers of the greater number of poems tremble with apocalyptic yearnings and prophecies.[28] But why this unrelieved desire for the end of the world? On the one hand, there is the correlation of the poetry to the essays on twilight and autumn and stories about a new revela-

The Quest for Unity of Being

tion like "The Adoration of the Magi"; these, too, foresee the end of the materialistic, inimical world and a revelation of the sacred through art this time, not religion. On the other hand, the end would bring release from the only solution to life offered in *The Wind among the Reeds*, which consists of division and ultimate destruction of the self. Yeats sees the danger of the False Mask of his own phase, 17, as "Dispersal," and it is tempting to see that formulation as a diagnosis of the psychic state represented in his own early lyrics.

The central poem of *The Wind among the Reeds* in which desire finds fulfillment provides a key to the apocalyptic orientation of the cycle and to Yeats's acute awareness of the cost of dreams separated from reality. The poem, an accomplished variation on the theme of *la belle dame sans merci* and the Salome figure which haunted the Nineties, is "The Cap and Bells." I would add to Bloom's most satisfying reading, with its emphasis on the sinister aspects of the jester's success as lover, only that dispersal forms the heart of the lover's perception of the beloved and consequently of his fate. If his offers to the beloved are the conventional stock of love poetry, heart and soul, so are his soul's worship of her footfall and his heart's worship of her hair. The lover divides himself into different faculties that seize upon parts of the beloved for devotion without declaring, as does the speaker of *Les Fleurs du Mal*, his love for her "tout entière." The ending of the poem, though it reunites all the dismembered parts of lover and beloved, contains a disquieting sense of continued dispersal. The faculties are not fused, and their song seems inconsequential: "a noise like crickets, / A chattering wise and sweet." The lady, touched by love at last, appears fulfilled in the last lines of the poem.[29] In view of the dismemberment of her lover, her satisfaction hints at Salome's dance with the head of John the Baptist, at a vampiric satiety in this poem where owls call and bats cry (ll. 6 and 14 of the 1894 version). Supreme beauty exacts the supreme cost—the life of its worshipper, his Unity of Being.

Although it is undeniable that the developments of Yeats's life affected his work, the poetry itself shows signs of strain which necessitate departures in subject matter as well as style. *The Wind among the Reeds* represents a superb articulation of Yeats's attraction to the dream and wariness of it. Whatever the changes in his relationship with Maud Gonne, it is hard to imagine him continuing the themes of *The Wind among the Reeds* in the same style. In the twentieth century, Yeats opts for a new poetic vocabulary and new themes. The very word "dream" appears much more rarely after the close of the nineteenth century.[30] Yet the roots of Yeats's deliberate break with a heritage that grew too burdensome and showed evidence of exhaustion exist in statements of the early Yeats so that the transformation is neither complete nor abrupt. Yeats sees several antidotes to the lassitude, the weariness of the *fin de siècle* which touched his work and the life and work of the Tragic Generation. One of these is his reinterpretation of the theory of the imagination through emphasis of passion to a much greater degree than anything encountered in Coleridge or Baudelaire. By combatting weariness, passion becomes one of the attributes or gifts of the imagination.

The primacy Yeats places on passion spans the length of his artistic life. In *Reveries over Childhood and Youth*, the time when, Yeats acknowledges, his father's influence on him was at its greatest, J. B. Yeats "read passages from the poets, and always from the play or poem at its most passionate moment." In seeking the unifying principles behind his father's seemingly fragmented judgment of the arts, Yeats discovers one that contains central aspects of his own aesthetics: "All must be an idealization of speech, and at some moment of passionate action or somnambulistic reverie" (*A*, pp. 39-40). The impact of J. B. Yeats's insistence on the passions in art extends from Yeats's youth to old age. When age, rather than the twilight of the Nineties, makes the poet feel weary, the elemental passions of rage and lust are called upon to "spur [him] into song" (*VP*, "The Spur," p. 591).

For Yeats, passion constitutes the major component of imaginative vision and of the symbol, sometimes to the detriment of reason. Yeats's emphasis represents a departure from the theory of imagination elaborated by Coleridge and adopted with modifications by Baudelaire. Coleridge and Baudelaire show little patience with cold-bloodedness in the creative process; Coleridge condemns wit because its conceits result from a mind unaffected by emotion; Baudelaire berates artists who behold the world and are content, unmoved by desires for more. Like Bau-

The Quest for Unity of Being

delaire, Yeats attributes a large part of the creative process to the unconscious, but he links unconscious operations of the mind to passion as well as reverie. Yeats's view of the imagination as passion departs, however, from Coleridge's insistence on the imagination as the mediating faculty that fuses head and heart and from Baudelaire's assertion that the imagination permeates all of man's faculties and calls upon each in turn during creation. Clearly, Yeats uses passion to oppose threatening forces, whether internal, like his attraction to the dream quest, or external, like logic and reason put to the use of a materialistic society intent upon progress. This double parrying leads to inconsistencies. When Yeats approves of a movement or work, the object of his admiration displays passion. When he criticizes it, it is often lacking in passion. As the object under consideration rises or falls with Yeats's changing values, so does its measure of passion. Moreover, Yeats throughout his life seeks external validation for the vision arising out of passion to the point where imagination and symbol become tools to shape class or race rather than integrate the psyche.

Yeats in his early career hopes that passion can save the arts by infusing the exhausted, over-subtle literature of Britain with the vitality of Ireland's folk tradition. The articles "Hopes and Fears for Irish Literature" and "Nationality and Literature" contrast the Tragic Generation and the Romantic movement respectively with the art that stays firmly attached to "the general tide of life" (*Uncoll.*, 1:271), namely, the dawning art of the Irish, who "have behind [them] in the past the most moving legends and a history full of lofty passions" (*Uncoll.*, 1:250). Those "lofty passions" help tie Yeats's nationalism to his other intense preoccupation, occultism. They provide the antidote to the gravest danger facing the Tragic Generation—the isolation of the artist—by means of an external validation of imaginative experience. Individual experience becomes absorbed into the Great Memory so that all men partake of it: "Whatever the passions of man have gathered about, becomes a symbol in the Great Memory, and in the hands of him who has the secret it is a worker of wonders, a caller-up of angels or of devils. The symbols are of all kinds, for everything in heaven or earth has its association, momentous or trivial, in the Great Memory, and one never knows

The Symbolic Method

what forgotten events may have plunged it, like the toadstool and the ragweed, into the great passions" (*E&I*, p. 50). The focus of the energy generated by great passions is the symbol.[31] Yeats therefore calls it "the greatest of all powers" and, significantly, distinguishes between its conscious use "by the masters of magic" and its half-unconscious use by "their successors, the poet, the musician and the artist" (*E&I*, p. 49). The imaginative users seem to have lost some of the control over the operations of the creative imagination, which, according to Coleridge, coexists with the conscious will. As Yeats's 1924 note to the text informs us, the wisdom of the subconscious—a collective one—compensates for loss of control by giving instead access to sources beyond the individual.

Passion becomes a much used term in Yeats's critical vocabulary. On the one hand, it saves from artistic isolation and even death brought on by too great a degree of self-absorption. On the other hand, it can be used to combat realist and nature schools of poetry with "a return to the subjective." In "Miss Fiona Macleod as a Poet," the French, rather than the Irish, raise the banner of the new art based on "a franker trust in passion and beauty than was possible to the poets who put their trust in the external world and its laws." Yeats's image of the mirror reflecting not outer reality but the mind expresses the inward orientation of this art: "We . . . wish . . . to make our work a mirror, where the passions and desires and ideals of our own minds can cast terrible or beautiful images" (*Uncoll.*, 1:422). When, in 1909 and 1910, Yeats's concern with the impingement of the external world upon his imaginative freedom comes to the fore, the Tragic Generation regains its status. Yeats writes that he and the other Rhymers belonged to the "second wave" of the Pre-Raphaelite movement "and had more passion because more confidence than the first."[32] Similarly, his criticism of modern acting turns upon its lack of passion, and the attributes of passion resemble the ones given to the imagination by Coleridge and Baudelaire: "It realizes, substantiates, attains, scorns, governs, and is most mighty when it passes from our sight" (*Memoirs*, p. 246).

The relationship of passion to imagination and the subconscious and its visitation in privileged moments are articulated most clearly in *Per Amica Silentia Lunae,* where Yeats begins his extraordinary effort to marry individuality and universality by means of a system of patterns. He effectively subverts the findings of psychoanalysis in favor of a higher doctrine, that of imaginative vision. The repressed desire of dream analysis changes to "starved and banished passion," and that, in turn, when accompanied by awareness, takes us back to the dream quest: "The passions, when we know that they cannot find fulfillment, become vision; and a vision, whether we wake or sleep, prolongs its power by rhythm and pattern, the wheel where the world is butterfly. . . . Whether it is we or the vision that create the pattern, who set the wheel turning, it is hard to say" (*Myth,* p. 341). The same uncertainty regarding conscious control encountered in Yeats's description of artists' use of the symbol is evident in this passage, which ends with a moving eulogy to the privileged moment of vision. Yet the distinction between repressed desire and passion consists of the tragic recognition, "when we know that they cannot find fulfillment," and in this Yeats parallels the heroism of Coleridge's and Baudelaire's admissions of the inherent failure of their quests.

Despite his acknowledgement of the impossibility of fulfillment in *Per Amica* and much of the poetry, Yeats searches throughout his life for some measure of external confirmation of vision, for kinship of experience beyond just the realm of aesthetics. This need of Yeats's leads him to distance himself from Romanticism, embroils him in unsavory politics, and commits him to a determinist interpretation of history and individual life, though it does produce changes in style which plant his verse firmly in the twentieth century. At first, Yeats's involvement with nationalist literary societies and the Irish movement for independence gave him hope that, by establishing institutions such as the Abbey Theatre, artists could create a unified national consciousness. Yet, like Maud Gonne, who bore a large share of responsibility for Yeats's patriotic fervor,[33] Ireland proved intractable and turned a deaf ear to the poet's ideals for a Unity of Culture through the arts. As early as three years before his break with the Abbey Theatre, Yeats begins to voice his discontent not with the ideal, which becomes more stringent, but with the world he tried to reform. In "Discoveries" and "Poetry and Tradition" Yeats

The Symbolic Method

traces the sources of his discontent to the external reality that betrayed his hopes, much as the first-generation Romantics expressed their disappointment at the outcome of the French Revolution. However, unlike them, Yeats seeks new external alliances, and one wonders if the Second World War would have finally satisfied Yeats that history, like individual life, breaks the coherent imaginative pattern desired by the artist. In "Poetry and Tradition" Yeats recalls his early hopes and the reason for their failure. Folklore, the revitalizing source, would have provided needed passion and the weight of evidence which "could change the country spiritism into a reasoned belief that would put its might into all the rest" (*E&I*, pp. 248–49). Ireland would give the artist a system of belief combined with a traditional mythology. Out of these "we were to forge in Ireland a new sword on our old traditional anvil for that great battle that must in the end re-establish the old, confident, joyous world" (*E&I*, p. 249). Yet a "type of mind"—the antithesis of tradition and aristocracy—began to have influence in the modern world and to oppose the old Ireland with "a new nation" (*E&I*, p. 250). This mind represents for Yeats the urban culture expressed in newspaper rhetoric, the rising working class displacing the peasant and the nobleman who, together with the artist, deserve to share Ireland:

> Three types of men have made all beautiful things. Aristocracies have made beautiful manners, because their place in the world puts them above the fear of life, and the countrymen have made beautiful stories and beliefs, because they have nothing to lose and so do not fear, and the artists have made all the rest, because Providence has filled them with recklessness. All these look backward to a long tradition, for, being without fear, they have held to whatever pleased them. [*E&I*, p. 251]

The backward glance, the worship of a past that contained an integrated culture, was a trademark of Yeats's poetry even before his change in the great wind of 1903. Now, however, his tradition finds unity in the *sprezzatura* mask he considered typical of the Renaissance: gaiety replaces the dream as the means of dealing with loss.[34]

The Quest for Unity of Being

"The Fascination of What's Difficult," a representative poem of Yeats's middle period, with its exaltation of Renaissance manners and virtues, embodies most clearly Yeats's deliberate departure from such Romantic poems of loss as "Dejection," "Les Sept Vieillards," and "La Destruction," in which the outer world takes on supernatural power and defeats the mind. "The Fascination" begins with an account of intellectual pursuit that has fragmented the being because it has exhausted the speaker's emotional resources. Yeats takes up the vegetation imagery of stanza 6 in "Dejection" both in the opening lines of "The Fascination" and in the second poem following it, "The Coming of Wisdom with Time." Instead of using the imagery, however, as Coleridge does, to show the mind's fruitfulness when whole and its blasting by fragmentation, he turns the loss into qualified gain, particularly in the second poem. In the first, he veers from the expectations set up by the distinctly Coleridgean echoes of the first three-and-a-half lines. The loss of natural content recalls Coleridge's lines about the loss of "all the natural man," and the division of the self from "spontaneous joy" echoes the emotional center of "Dejection" in which joy and spontaneity of feeling stand for the integrated psychic state whose loss the poet laments in his despondency. The nonchalance of language, the wit of the Pegasus device, the defiance of the conclusion, all combine to give a sense of irritation with the mundane and of bravura in dealing with it, but they present no tension of the pressure of reality upon the imagination. Yeats began a poem of loss in the high Romantic manner and then opted for his new-found mask not so much to show recovery as to move the plane of the poem from a psychic one of inner division to a historical one of the artist against the multitude and thus to avert the crisis.

Although the stance of artist isolated from the masses is associated with Romanticism and reveals itself emphatically in nineteenth-century French literature—for example, Baudelaire's criticism of art—its implications in Yeats are those of a break with his Romantic predecessors. In his middle period, he begins his lifelong search for an ideal model of culture to be found in a historical past. Baudelaire and Coleridge, like other Romantic artists, dreamed of a return to paradise, but this was to be effected on a psychic level. As Baudelaire's cry "anywhere out of

The Symbolic Method

the world" makes explicit, these poets would not place their faith in the outer world, particularly in history. Even Coleridge, who pinpoints the dissociation of sensibility in the seventeenth century, does not glorify the Renaissance as a historical period. Yeats's Byzantium, Urbino, and Versailles are imaginative projections of a utopian desire, but he consistently and systematically proposes external solutions to the problem of psychic integration. His disappointment with the modern world incites him to theories of tradition, which in turn lead to pronouncements on eugenics and to sympathy for an oligarchical tyranny. He expects deliverance from historical circumstances by an equally external turn of the tide, a return to antithetical dominance, which makes him detached to the point of occasional callousness from the events of his time and makes his anticipation of apocalypse, in poems like "The Second Coming," not entirely disinterested.

Despite Yeats's idealization of the peasant, which seems in need of the corrective Coleridge applies to Wordsworth's idealization of the rustic, Yeats associates himself as artist with the aristocracy since it provides the suitable audience for his art, the select brotherhood that validates his vision. In "Discoveries," in "Certain Noble Plays of Japan," Yeats insists upon the relationship between genius and good breeding that provides "antiquity of thought" and "memory of old emotions" necessary for the archetypal resonances he seeks for his symbols. Like Baudelaire, he defends traditional forms, but whereas Baudelaire claims them to be laws of the inner being, Yeats's argument rests on the authority conferred by nobility and blood: "He [the cultivated man] is above all things well-bred, and whether he write or paint will not desire a technique that denies or obtrudes his long and noble descent" (*E&I*, p. 284). In a revealing passage of his journal, Yeats creates out of his personal grievances and his dreams a spiritual rapprochement between artists and aristocrats: "Every day I notice some new analogy between [the] long-established life of the well-born and the artist's life. We come from permanent things and create them, and instead of old blood we have old emotions and we carry in our head that form of society which aristocracies create now and again for some brief moment at Urbino and Versailles. We too despise the mob and suffer at its hands" (*Memoirs*, p. 156). That he relegates historical achievement to aristocracy and psychic creation to artists shows a sense of balance in Yeats's judgment; yet the irritation with circumstances, a feeling that he himself tries to combat (*Memoirs*, p. 157), makes him utter the absurdity of the last line. Although artists may suffer at the hands of the mob, the mob itself, as well as independent-minded artists, had far more to fear at the hands of the aristocrats of Urbino and Versailles.

Yeats's allegiance to subjectivity through emphasis on passions and to the past through his identification with the ruling class leads him to some of the fragmenting formulations of the System presented in *A Vision* and in *Essays and Introductions* of the thirties. Although Yeats is careful to point out that no human life can exist at the extremes of the antithetical or primary tincture, the System nevertheless rests upon a division of mental faculties: "the *antithetical tincture* is emotional and aesthetic whereas the *primary tincture* is reasonable and moral" (*Vision*, p. 73). Whereas in human life the two tinctures interpenetrate to a certain extent, the interplay of the contraries is practically nonexistent in Yeats's account of the "two thousand and odd"-year periods of history, except insofar as the annunciatory being retains physical characteristics associated with the preceding phase. Robartes, the persona through which Yeats chooses to speak, summarizes the essence of each age: "After an age of necessity, truth, goodness, mechanism, science, democracy, abstraction, peace, comes an age of freedom, diction, evil, kindred, art, aristocracy, particularity, war" (*Vision*, p. 52). Yeats's much noted preference for the antithetical might startle in this context, where each period offers such distinct disadvantages. But Yeats is ready to embrace the vision of evil he faults Shelley for lacking, and, since the new age will clearly give ascendancy to the powers he approves and to which he allies himself, he anticipates it in numerous prophecies. There is something decidedly inhumane about Yeats's impatience to see the new age dawn and something inhuman about the determinism of a system that predicts historical cycles as if these were set in motion by a universal mechanism turning mindlessly despite the will and choice of the humans who, after all, make history.

The *Later Essays and Introductions* shed some light on Yeats's commitment, though they do not help humanize it. In his

The Symbolic Method

continual search for external validation of poetic vision, Yeats no longer considers traditional mythology alone sufficient to sustain the symbolic structure of a work; he is looking for a system of belief outside the internalized Christianity of the Romantics, a system that would bring a unity of pattern to his political, occult, and poetic enterprises. When in "*Prometheus Unbound*" he faults Shelley for not attending to the "whole drama of life," for repressing evil and therefore finding himself forced to project it onto nightmarish and unconvincing creations, he discloses his own attraction to nightmare in the form or intention of divinity: "I understood that we must not demand even the welfare of the human race, nor traffic with divinity in our prayers. It moves outside our antinomies, it may be our lot to worship in terror" (*E&I*, p. 425). In a later essay, the certitude about our lot deepens: "I think profound philosophy must come from terror" (*E&I*, p. 502). The terror that Yeats found inevitable surely relates to the division within his own mind, to his resolute turning away from modern life into anachronistic stances that cut him off from the reality and justice sought in *A Vision* but found in poems that rise above its determinism. Yeats acknowledges his "own dark," but the recognition, instead of leading to reintegration, calls up a vision of cosmic fragmentation:

> When I stand upon O'Connell Bridge in the half-light and notice that discordant architecture, all those electric signs, where modern heterogeneity has taken physical form, a vague hatred comes up out of my own dark and I am certain that wherever in Europe there are minds strong enough to lead others the same vague hatred rises; in four or five or in less generations this hatred will have issued in violence and imposed some kind of rule of kindred. I cannot know the nature of that rule, for its opposite fills the light; all I can do to bring it nearer is to intensify my hatred. [*E&I*, p. 526]

"The Second Coming" is a poem of intensified hatred. To the many and brilliant analyses of this well-known and often-quoted poem I want to add my sense of context. Written at a time when Yeats envisioned ruin for civilization,[35] "The Second

The Quest for Unity of Being

Coming," when divorced from its position in *Michael Robartes and the Dancer* and from Yeats's illuminating notes, embodies a powerful articulation of modern anxiety about the ever-increasing violence and irrationality of our world. But Yeats's historical thought severely limits the poem; it relegates humanity to a position governed by the higher order of history revealed to a speaker content to understand and worship in terror. If the apocalypse yearned for in the early poems rose against a divided mind and announced an age of the arts, the vision called up in "The Second Coming" appears in response to cultural disintegration and prophesies the coming of the antithetical age. Although "every nerve trembles with horror" (*Letters*, p. 851) before it, the speaker worships this new divinity whom he endows with the attributes of godhead.

In the notes to the poem, Yeats emphasizes the inevitability of the new age, the uselessness of resisting it, and makes very clear that the future is of an antithetical nature. More importantly, he suggests in a brief sentence why the new god takes his shape from a rough beast instead of becoming flesh in the form of a beautiful infant: "The revelation which approaches will however take its character from the contrary movement of the interior gyre" (*VP*, p. 825). Its ugliness, like Christ's beauty, belongs to the dominant age which nears its end. Yet its nature, its "character," mirrors the antithetical annunciation. Yeats's simile "as the sun" (l. 15) has presented the largest obstacle to interpreting the vision as antithetical. Yeats, however, is not quite as rigid in his use of sun and moon in the poetry as his theories might indicate. Other moments of illumination, in "The Cold Heaven" and "Stream and Sun at Glendalough," for example, occur through the agency of sunlight. Moreover, the modifiers of "gaze"—"blank and pitiless"—are characteristics prized in *A Vision*, the first because it typifies antithetical art, the second because it is a prime antithetical virtue, one that separates the outward-turning, fragmenting concern with the world from the concentration upon inner vision, the sight before the mind's eye. Both Pound and Maud Gonne incur Yeats's disapproval since both exhibit a pity for the world that Yeats associates with the decaying primary civilization (*Vision*, p. 6) and that will be excluded from the ruthless, aristocratic age to come. As for the

The Symbolic Method

blank gaze of the Sphinxlike creature, it finds antecedents in another antithetical age, the civilization of Greece. Both in the Introduction to *A Vision* where he muses upon the similarity of his thought to Spengler's and in "Dove or Swan," Yeats writes about the difference between Greek culture and the Roman primary dispersal of it and uses as the chief example the sculpture of the two civilizations, particularly their method of portraying the eyes. Greek statues have blank eyes, Roman ones pierced eyes (*Vision*, p. 18). To oppose Rome's "world-considering eyes" (*Vision*, p. 277), Yeats contemplates "vague Grecian eyes gazing at nothing." Finally, the ambiguous adjective "rough" has secondary connotations of harsh, violent, overbearing, angry, passionate, all of which are traits Yeats approves when they relate to antithetical ascendance. After all, Zeus's shape in "Leda and the Swan" is that of a "rough beast," and his visitation engenders the classical age of Greece.

The certainty of the last lines, "but now I know / That twenty centuries of stony sleep / Were vexed to nightmare by a rocking cradle" (ll. 18–20), prepares for the question of the last two lines to be asked with anticipation as well as terror. The seemingly purposeless irrational disintegration of the modern world presented in the first half of the poem suddenly becomes understandable in the revelatory dawn of a new age. What rough beast can bring a worse nightmare than that described by the speaker as the last rule of two thousand years of Christian civilization? "Leda and the Swan" evokes in a few lines the tragedies of antithetical culture, but there Yeats gives majesty to burning Troy and a hero's death, whereas "The Second Coming" gives a horrifying sense of loss of control, of unleashed violence. In the context of Yeats's historical thought, the first part of the poem can be read as representing Yeats's revulsion not so much at violence but at the loss of power of those who ought to have kept control. The image of the aristocratic endeavor gone wrong which begins the poem sets the tone for the speaker's indignation at the reversal of power in the modern world. The victims of the "blood-dimmed tide" are the aristocrats,[36] those bred and trained in the custom and ceremony Yeats associates throughout his poetry with the life in and surrounding the great houses of Ireland, the tradition he hopes to save for his daughter against the howling storm of change. Passion and intensity, traits of culture of the Renaissance and of those who created it, now lodge in "the worst." Against this background, the "vast image" satisfies Yeats's call for the revelation. History falls into order once more as the speaker moves from dismay and horror to knowledge. In his "Introduction to *The Resurrection*" Yeats himself accounts for his need to create a myth more powerful than the myth of progress prevalent in his youth and thus to oppose it. As a child, he looked for external evidence to substantiate his "aversion to that myth": "I took satisfaction in certain public disasters, felt a sort of ecstasy at the contemplation of ruin."[37] Later, coming to a judgment of history, Yeats decided that "our civilization was about to reverse itself," and sought an image that would frighten the believers in progress and that at the same time would accord with his hopes of history: "I began to imagine, as always at my left side just out of the range of the sight, a brazen winged beast that I associated with laughing, ecstatic destruction" (*Ex.*, p. 393). Lest any doubt remain about the image in his reader's mind, Yeats identifies the beast in a footnote as the one "afterwards described in my poem 'The Second Coming.' "

The poem's success when divorced from context measures the distance Yeats has traveled from his Romantic predecessors and from his own ideal of a unified structure of the work; it indicates the damage suffered by the work when Yeats insists on authenticating his vision outside the confines of human life. In this sense, there is an irony to humanist evaluations of Baudelaire and Yeats. Baudelaire's poems save themselves from even formidable attacks through their context; though generally Yeats's poetry gains magnitude from the work and commentaries related to it, context occasionally harms a famous poem like "The Second Coming."

III

Yeats's vacillation, his attraction to antinomial thought, appears in his commitment to the Romantic enterprise, which continues parallel to his deterministic patterns for history and pro-

The Symbolic Method

vides a counterpoint for them. Along with Unity of Culture achieved by violent external means, Yeats seeks Unity of Being. Conflict, the war of opposites, plays the largest part in the mind's progress toward unity. In this quest intellectual wars replace corporeal wars and lead to recognition of our common humanity rather than the tyranny of class victory. Coleridge's thought and poetry gain new importance on this plane, though not without misinterpretations, and Baudelaire, too, reappears briefly in a new light. Yeats focuses upon concepts central to Coleridge's thought, such as the primacy of the mind, mental faculties and their interrelationships, the moment of imaginative illumination, the necessity to fuse thought and passion, and attributes their sources to Coleridge. Others—the *ouroboros*, the symbol as embodiment, and the union in poetry of a more than usual state of emotion with more than usual order—echo Coleridge closely enough to warrant influence, although Yeats's extensive knowledge of the Romantics makes likely the tracing of these passages to more than one source. As to Coleridge as artist, Yeats mentions with admiration his so-called visionary poetry, which has little effect upon his own, in essays, but echoes the Greater Romantic Lyrics in several poems. Apart from the direct references to Baudelaire, which show approval of the French poet's thinking and, more importantly, evidence that Yeats understood the orientation of *Les Fleurs du Mal*, Yeats's inclusion of reverie and memory in the imaginative process and the dialectical structure of his cycles suggest strong kinship with Baudelaire.

Yeats's quest for Unity of Being injects a new-found bitterness into the early poetry by means of revisions. *The Rose* offers the most consistent evidence of Yeats's shift in thought. Discontent, rage, bitterness supplant the moments of satisfaction or desire to belong, the sweetness of nature and the common lot; antithetical defiance takes the place of resignation to circumstance. Yeats averts the dangers of the dream anticipated in "To the Rose Upon the Rood of Time" by proving he has learned a language men will understand and by circumventing world weariness and melancholy through an emphasis on man, not the world, on vigor, not languor. Perhaps *The Rose*, with its ambivalence to the ideal, seemed to Yeats most in need of an opposing conviction. Yet *The Rose* still lacks the dialectical opposition of Yeats's later cycles,

The Quest for Unity of Being

and neither its last poems nor *The Wind among the Reeds* presents a synthesis of its contraries. Despite Yeats's protest that "Whatever changes I have made are but an attempt to express better what I thought and felt when I was a very young man" (*VP*, p. 842), the very process of expressing "better" changes the nature of the early poetry to a mixture, held loosely in solution, as Coleridge would say, of the consciousness of the "very young man" and the more developed, experienced view of the older man.

In terms of the overall quest pattern of the work, themes of the early poetry and perceptions that need the correction of experience are obscured and overpowered by the masterful intrusions. I shall not add here to the debate about the success of the early versus the revised versions since to me the shift in substance from world to man and in tone from melancholy to bitterness and defiance makes the versions of "The Dedication to a Book of Stories Selected from the Irish Novelists," "The Sorrow of Love," and "The Lamentation of the Old Pensioner" different poems. It is sufficient to note that in "The Sorrow" "earth's old and weary cry"—the weariness of "The Autumn of the Body" and "The Celtic Twilight" coupled with the expectation of apocalypse—becomes "man's image and his cry." The primacy of man and his sorrow in the revised version ties in nicely with the Helen image of the second stanza and its association for Yeats with the tragedy of antithetical civilization; it does not, however, tie in with the other poems of the cycle or with the narrator's announced desire to "Sing of old Eire and the ancient ways." In "The Dedication," the speaker plucks the bell-branch of forgetfulness from "the green boughs of old Eri, / The willow of the many-sorrowed world" (ll. 15-16 of versions before 1924), which, like earth's cry in "The Sorrow," are "weary, weary, weary." In the revised version, the sap of summer has grown weary of sustaining the wind-tossed branches now barren, an image recalling the withering into truth undergone by the poet himself in "The Coming of Wisdom with Time." Instead of being placed in the larger perspective of the sorrowing world, Ireland itself becomes the setting that inflicts grief on man. While "we and our bitterness" may have left no traces on "Munster grass and Connemara skies," the poem is profoundly changed by the accent on personal grief. The shift from the veiled patriotic re-

The Symbolic Method

proach to the exiles to the open attack against Ireland as the ideal opposes too violently the commitment of the beginning and last poems of the cycle, although the revisions of "To Ireland in the Coming Times" attempt to create some consonance between the consciousness of "The Dedication" and the concluding poem. Unlike the other two poems, "The Lamentation of the Old Pensioner" offers no substitution of world for man, but it does change lamentation to defiance, focusing on the strength of the old man's rage instead of his helplessness. The battle against circumstance despite the recognition of defeat—"I spit into the face of Time / That has transfigured me" (ll. 17–18)—is a characteristic of the quest pattern, but, as in the other two poems, its appearance is premature in this cycle, which maps the lure of the dream and the fear of losing contact with the world.

The early poetry does provide Yeats with lasting images for the later work, despite his dissatisfaction with the achievement of the very young man and his correction of it. What Yeats echoes from the early work, however, serves to enforce his theory of inner conflict as the basis for Unity of Being. The obvious example is "The Two Trees," but there is another, more neglected, connection between the early and later Yeats, namely, the image of the parrot in "The Indian to His Love." The parrot, "raging at his own image in the enamelled sea," supplies Yeats with a means to express the conflict between ideal image and actual image in the self when the self desires love or has great beauty. The "dim enamelled sea" (variant of l. 4) appears in "The Two Trees" as the dim bitter glass "of outer weariness," the unsatisfying, distorted external reflection of love and beauty. In *The Tower*, where the central theme consists of the dichotomy between desire and the confines of grotesque and aged physicality, the memory of love set against itself sharpens the bitterness of the volume. The presence of the green parrots in "On a Picture of a Black Centaur" maddened the poet's youth with unattainable, unfulfilled love and haunts his self-questioning in "The Tower." "The Hero, the Girl, and the Fool" returns to the feeling of rage of lover and beloved when self-perception fails to match the image in the other's eye. Yeats's doctrine of the mask is more optimistic in 1909; the lover bridges the contrast of the two images if he is wise: "the lover or the beloved sees an image

The Quest for Unity of Being

to copy in daily life" (*Memoirs*, p. 145). The commentary of the fool and the conclusion of the speaker in "On a Picture" indicate, however, that in the later Yeats the self-division, the rage, the bitterness of love are overcome only in death or only by reaching an equanimity of mind which keeps the danger of insanity and remorse at a distance. The emotion of bitterness arising out of inner conflict allows Yeats to progress beyond the unresolved tug-of-war between desire and fear of loss in much of nineteenth-century poetry, but brings with it its own dangers.

Although Yeats remains faithful to his emphasis on passion, his quest for Unity of Being impels him to develop a more inclusive theory of the mind and its functions, and he often turns to Coleridge for support. In "The Completed Symbol" of *A Vision*, Yeats hints at the relationship between his classification of the mind's Principles—and implicitly its Faculties—and Coleridge's. He refuses to accept Coleridge's terminology which exalts "reason" as the faculty for perceiving the divine and substitutes "mind" (*Vision*, pp. 187–88). Yeats's description of each Faculty's realm makes the kinship between the two terminologies even more explicit than the passage on the Principles. The Will is a combination of Coleridge's senses and the unconscious, our most basic perception and response to the external world; the Body of Fate, the historicobiographical baggage, is in Coleridge's terms the Understanding. Mask and Creative Mind, the "memory of the moments of exaltation in his [man's] past lives" and the "memory of ideas—or universals" (*Vision*, p. 83), have a similar relationship to each other as Imagination and Reason or, "in the most *antithetical* phases" (*Vision*, p. 142) such as Yeats's own, as symbol—embodiment of the ideal—and the secondary Imagination. Divergences between Coleridge's theory and method and Yeats's certainly abound. Apart from the prominent role of the subconscious in it, Yeats's System depends on occult lore, on a division of *tinctures* and thus of the nature of historical ages and individual lives. Nevertheless, in Yeats's account of the individual mind, four faculties explain man's relationship to his immediate environment, to his history, to his own self, and to the divine, and this classification, granted the differences mentioned, comes very near Coleridge's. Yeats acknowledges Coleridge's role in teaching him that one may arrive at "measurements and classifications" that, though abstract, "continually bring [him] back to concrete reality" (*Ex.*, p. 303) because they unite thought and passion. As Yeats turns to the eighteenth-century Irish tradition and attempts to obscure his relation to the Romantics and particularly to Shelley, he includes Coleridge, as well as Mallarmé, in the group that "played . . . in a unique drama . . . played it . . . with the whole soul" (*Ex.*, p. 301), reproaching Shelley for excluding parts of the drama from his art.

Although Yeats uses Coleridge frequently in the thirties to buttress his arguments, he is not above distorting him even in the context of the antirealist aesthetic. In a discussion of Berkeley's thought, he turns to Coleridge "for a clue": "I think of Coleridge's contrast between Juliet's nurse and Hamlet, remember that Shakespeare drew the nurse from observation, from passive sense-impression, but Hamlet, the Court, the whole work of art, out of himself in a pure indivisible act" (*E&I*, p. 410). Yeats emphasizes Unity of Being in the creative act, but he completely misrepresents Coleridge's clue. In fact, Coleridge argues that the nurse could not have been drawn from observation, that her characterization is the product of Shakespeare's protean imagination.[38] Coleridge would never have allowed that Shakespeare descended to representations of "passive sense-impression." But for Yeats, who worships the aristocratic and passionate world of *Hamlet*, the nurse as a member of the servant class insufficiently in love with service to be rendered mute or loftyspoken by it needs to be demoted to a lower level of artistic creation. Coleridge differs so completely from the Shakespearean criticism ascribed to him by Yeats that in the *Essay on Method* he declares both Hamlet and Mistress Quickly incapable of method, one from excess of reflection and generalization, the other from lack of it (*Friend*, 1:453).

In "The Holy Mountain," where the "single timeless act" appears not in relation to the work of art but to stages of mystical meditation, Yeats ends the passage with a truncated quotation of Coleridge's "What Is Life" and reverses its meaning. For Coleridge, Life becomes boundless light through man's consciousness, and our apprehension of shades and colors, as of joys and pains, is due to death's "encroach of darkness." In Yeats's description of the fourth state of meditation, absolute self can exist only in

The Quest for Unity of Being

death since life limits its completeness. Yeats's readiness to pursue Unity of Being beyond the confines of life may bear striking similarity to Baudelaire, but certainly not to Coleridge.[39]

Despite his distortions of Coleridge, when Yeats accepts his heritage and renews the quest, he recognizes his own humanity. In some of his statements on the symbol, in moments of symbolic illumination, and, most humanly, in acknowledgments of defeat, Yeats demonstrates his kinship with the Romantics and, at times, specifically with Coleridge. In *A Vision* Yeats explains his sometimes dismaying preference for the antithetical phases by relegating them to moments of the mind rather than to ruling signs of individual lives: "the *antithetical* phases are but, at the best, phases of a momentary illumination like that of a lightning flash" (*Vision*, pp. 283–84). Coleridge's light in crystal, the eternal I AM in the finite mind represent imaginative illumination, and Yeats associates the visionary insight with Coleridge: "Why does Coleridge delight me more as man than poet? . . . I think the reason is that from 1807 or so he seems to have some kind of illumination which was, as always, only in part communicable. . . . The end attained in such a life is not a truth or even a symbol of truth, but a oneness with some spiritual being or beings" (*Ex.*, p. 299). Yeats's qualifications about illumination—its brevity, its incommunicability—indicate his awareness that the intensity of vision cannot be sustained.

In the poetry these largely atypical, Coleridgean moments of the mind creating nature's wedding garment, overflowing with light and sweetness, occur in the context of remorse, uneasiness, and a keen sense of temporality. The first of such illuminations holds little sweetness, though the instance is a close echo of the final lines of the preceding poem, "Friends," in which remembrance of the beloved brings overflowing sweetness to the mind and makes the body tremble. "The Cold Heaven" contains a like moment of exaltation when the speaker finds himself "riddled with light" after "imagination and heart" compose a coherent picture of his youth and unrequited love. The way he went about winning the beloved accords ill with the icy passion of the sky, and regret becomes the only fruit of the illumination. Seven years later, in "Demon and Beast," fragmenting hatred and one-sided desire make way for a reconciliation with outer things that

The Symbolic Method

"laugh in the sun" because the poet's "whole nature," the healed psyche of the older man, has won him freedom from bitterness toward the past and from responsibility for it. However, that freedom is short-lived, the contraries must war again, and the poet can but wish "to make it linger half a day." The complete illumination, though the shortest when measured in clock time, appears in "Vacillation," where the fourth section provides the fullest answer to the question "What is joy?" which sets in motion the mental process. Yeats again times the vision to "twenty minutes more or less," but the clock minutes sharpen the contours of the timeless moment of "so great [a] happiness" and separate it from everyday life. As in "Demon and Beast," the poet returns from illumination to acknowledgment of the fragmenting powers of the mind with section 5, where remorse breaks the psychic wholeness capable of embracing nature. "Stream and Sun at Glendalough" echoes closely the first stanza of section 5 and amplifies the theme of repentance destroying happiness. The conclusion, however, gives perhaps the greatest ascendance to nature encountered in all of Yeats's poetry, except for the chestnut tree of "Among School Children." The sun or stream or eyelid (an intervention of the supernatural or a fusion of natural and human as in "Among School Children"?) "shot the gleam" that transfigured the poet so that he became like "these that seem / Self-born, born anew." Yeats's only qualification, "that seem," distinguishes these from the Presences of "Among School Children," which mock human enterprise, but bring them closer to the "self-sown, self-begotten shape that gives / Athenian intellect its mastery" (ll. 10–11 of "Colonus' Praise"), and especially to the olive tree, a natural, yet miraculous, creation. Yeats's antithetical flashes illuminate in poetry moments of imaginative transformation that parallel as closely as Yeats could Coleridge's process of symbolization: the mind/nature opposition, the mind overcoming nature and so incorporating it, and most significantly, the mind's inability to effect union when the psyche is wounded and divided against itself. When the mind's wholeness becomes of prime importance, Yeats sheds the *sprezzatura* mask of poems like "The Fascination of What's Difficult" in favor of the Romantic mode of expressing imaginative vision and its loss.

The Quest for Unity of Being

In their use of light as an emanation of the mind's fullness, both Coleridge and Yeats follow Platonic tradition; they follow an equally ancient tradition in adopting the *ouroboros* to symbolize eternity and in using it to clarify the relationship of immortal to temporal and of the "timeless" artistic creation to natural object or event. Coleridge confers upon the poet the power, analogous to that of the Creator, to "convert a *series* into a *Whole,*" to see and create "the great Cycle," the circular motion of the world, which, to "our short sight," appears as a straight line (*CL,* 4:545). Yeats in his prose is less generous. "Changeless eternity" (*Vision,* p. 68), symbolized by the sphere, cannot be perceived by men except as the thirteenth cone because "their serpent has not its tail in its mouth" (*Vision,* p. 69), because "all things fall into a series of antinomies in human experience" (*Vision,* p. 193). Instead of the bleak renunciation of *A Vision* where the instructors do not even bother to reveal the sphere to one living in the phenomenal world, there is the more optimistic rhetorical question of Yeats's middle years to the effect that "the poet has made his home in the serpent's mouth" (*E&I,* p. 288). Like Coleridge's poet, who transforms events that "move on in a *strait* line" into circular structures following the pattern of the cycle, Yeats's poet, in love with "whatever is most fleeting," keeps to the circumference of the eternal circle, seeks that which "comes round again." For both poets, the Greater Romantic Lyric and Quest, with their circular form, become the chief modes of presenting the symbolizing process. But Yeats, like Baudelaire, expands the structural device of these poetic genres to a number of returns throughout the cycles which create an overall circular pattern, culminating in the next to last poem of *Last Poems,* "The Circus Animals' Desertion," where the lyric serves as a return for the whole body of Yeats's work. The sphere as an image of eternity is a dominant theme of *Supernatural Songs,* and its relation to sexual union in these and in *A Vision* will be discussed in a later context. But the sphere also appears in two poems celebrating love written before *Supernatural Songs.* In "Among School Children," the poet recalls a moment of Platonic union with the beloved effected through sympathetic imagination. That image of youth and love remains unchanged and proclaims its superiority over a present marked by temporal loss—

The Symbolic Method

bodily decay and disappointment of hopes. The disparity between sphere and mortal life is so acute that earlier versions of the poem cannot move beyond defeat.[40] The sphere also concludes section 6 ("Chosen") of *A Woman Young and Old*, and though it represents sexual union—"utmost pleasure with a man"—it alludes to "Plato's parable" as the lovers' identities merge ("his heart my heart did seem") and they escape the "blind network of stars" of the zodiac by moving into the divine, the sphere.

Sympathetic imagination, which breaks through bitterness and hatred, exists in Yeats's poetry at times when the Coleridgean mode manifests itself in him, but, just as Yeats uses Coleridge in the thirties to endorse opinions that Coleridge could not have shared, he pays him the compliment of echoing a significant passage of *Biographia Literaria* in one of his last poems, "The Long-Legged Fly." The poem, like several of Yeats's last ("Under Ben Bulben" and "The Statues" are chief examples), attempts to embrace both Unity of Being and Unity of Culture. The arts achieve Unity of Being, and the artist's legacy to his country, his race, is the images according to which the nation will shape itself. In *Explorations*, Yeats writes:

> If . . . the family is the unit of social life, and the origin of civilisation which but exists to preserve it, and almost the sole cause of progress, it seems more natural than it did before that its ecstatic moment, the sexual choice of man and woman, should be the greater part of all poetry. A single wrong choice may destroy a family, dissipating its tradition or its biological force, and the great sculptors, painters, and poets are there that instinct may find its lamp. [*Ex.*, p. 274]

In this notion of the use of the arts Yeats differs from Coleridge and Baudelaire, who see the arts as a means of reproducing in the mind of the beholder the healing, unifying imaginative process that creates. Perhaps both hopes prove equally unfeasible, but one centers on the mind's growth, the other on the improvement of the race. Notwithstanding this major difference, "The Long-Legged Fly" celebrates Unity of Being, the act in which the mind shapes the world through its own powers, either to pre-

The Quest for Unity of Being

serve, destroy, or further civilization.[41] In its subjective absorption of the self not in its own division but in a unifying image, the quester in the poem finds at last a most Coleridgean "unity of being, the subordination of all parts to the whole" (*Ex.*, p. 250).

Yeats goes beyond even the reevaluation of Coleridge and Coleridgean echoes in his poetry when he expands upon Coleridge's principles regarding the symbol and creates a unified work of the type Coleridge had hoped Wordsworth would write. Yeats's deliberate use of symbols and his critically prophetic study of "symbolism" in art and poetry reveal his kinship with Coleridge. Yet in his elevation of memory and reverie to the status of imaginative processes and in his addition of "phantasmagoria" as a theoretical term for a system of symbols in art and as a stage of completion after death he resembles Baudelaire more than Coleridge. The symbol for Yeats, as for Coleridge, is a medium that permits the expression of an invisible essence otherwise unperceived by the bodily eye, a "transparent lamp about a spiritual flame" (*E&I*, p. 116). What distinguishes Yeats's symbol from allegory is not that it embodies the "spiritual flame" but that it is "the only possible expression," whereas allegory "is one of the many possible." This distinction approaches Baudelaire's mathematically exact correspondences, which also are the only possible expression of the eternal because they belong to the vaster system of the universal analogy of earthly things and their spiritual counterparts. As for Baudelaire, for the early Yeats the symbol embodies beauty rather than ideas, and "impossible beauty" is as inaccessible to the senses as Coleridge's amorphous light: "the beauty . . . cannot be seen . . . or pictured other than by symbols" (*Memoirs*, p. 284). Despite the symbol's absolutely necessary role as medium through which the spiritual—equated in early Yeats with beauty, later with the supernatural—can manifest itself, Yeats experiences a sense of dissatisfaction with the symbol expressed even in such constructions as "the only possible expression," "other than symbols," and the frequent "but symbols," as if he, as Coleridge at times, felt the need for embodiment of the ideal, yet regretted its limitations. A more radical departure from the customary prestige associated with "symbol" is Yeats's use of the word in his occult experiments to identify an object that induced trances totally unrelated to itself (*Memoirs*, p. 61).

The Symbolic Method

Yeats takes up the aesthetic built around the symbol through the nineteenth century much more purposely and powerfully when he turns from the contemplation of the single symbol or its distinction from allegory to asserting the significance of systems of symbols in works of art. As early as 1900 Yeats writes essays like "The Philosophy of Shelley's Poetry" and "The Symbolism of Poetry" in which he demonstrates profound understanding of the function of symbols in poetry in general and in Romantic poetry in particular. Of Shelley, he writes: "One finds in his poetry, besides innumerable images that have not the definiteness of symbols, many images that are certainly symbols, and as the years went by he began to use these with a more and more deliberately symbolic purpose" (*E&I*, p. 78). What distinguishes symbols from images is their definiteness and the deliberate use a poet makes of them throughout the years; as Yeats's analysis of Shelley shows, images become symbols when they recur throughout the work and acquire cumulative meaning from their new contexts, where they recall earlier poems and thus project the present text upon the background of the whole *oeuvre*. In later years, Yeats gives the name of "phantasmagoria" to the systematic building of symbols in art. Like the symbol, phantasmagoria becomes the only means of expressing not the spiritual this time, but personality—"through which I [Yeats] can alone express my convictions about the world" (*VP*, p. 852). In his 1937 introduction to his work, Yeats elaborates upon the relationship of phantasmagoria and personality; the poet, not as man but as poet, is inseparable from his phantasmagoria, the creation of his imagination, "and we adore him because nature has grown intelligible, and by so doing a part of our creative power" (*E&I*, p. 509). Yeats affirms Coleridge and Baudelaire's hope for art, the partaking in the creative power of those who are not themselves artists, but he brushes aside any use of the phantasmagoria to illuminate external reality in order to render it intelligible. "Nature" means human nature, and we adore because we understand ourselves. Ultimately, Coleridge's symbol and Yeats's phantasmagoria both activate portions of the mind hitherto mechanical and unselfconscious, thereby creating "something intended, complete"—a reintegrated psyche that in turn translates vision into art.

The Quest for Unity of Being

For Yeats, however, as for Baudelaire, ultimate wholeness of self occurs only in death. Yeats describes a state of being after death in the section titled *Phantasmagoria*, whose function goes beyond that of giving knowledge of the past to the soul; *Phantasmagoria* completes "the objects of hope," namely, that which could not have been realized in life, and hence "completes not only life, but imagination" (*Vision*, p. 230). Although the goal of this phase is completion, not knowledge, its tutelary guides are the "Teaching Spirits" of the "Thirteenth Cone," who, as Yeats warns, may not be "pure benevolence," but who nevertheless help the soul amend events of the past. *Phantasmagoria*, which completes the imagination through a reliving of "moral and emotional suffering" (*Vision*, p. 231), resembles Baudelaire's "Revolt" cycle, with its strong emphasis on moral and emotional suffering and its hope for completion under the guidance of a tutelary spirit of equal ambivalence, Satan. The purification of good and evil, which in *A Vision* occurs in the next state, *Shiftings*, has a parallel in the last cycle of *Les Fleurs du Mal*, "Death," which follows "Revolt" and in which the quester finally moves beyond the antinomies of good and evil toward completion of desire. The parallel, of course, works only in rough outlines yet indicates an affinity between Baudelaire and Yeats in regard to the quest's goal, namely, the resolution of antinomial divisions only in death; in this Baudelaire and Yeats's orientation is much closer to the second-generation Romantics than to Coleridge. The embrace of reality and of the totality of experience seems to need the perspective of after-death for both poets since both use an *outre-tombe* distance to impart vision in their last poems.

Yeats's creation of a System accounting for imaginative completion after death, however, did not prevent him from seeking that sort of wholeness in his life's work. Like Baudelaire, Yeats understood the enormous importance of creating a unified *oeuvre* and employed the favorite Romantic and Baudelairian metaphor of the work as architectural structure, opposing it to images of mechanical arrangements of lyrics similar to Baudelaire's beads on a string. In "Art and Ideas," Yeats surveys the fragmentation of nineteenth-century and modern art and asks, "What long modern poem equals the old poems in architectural unity, in symbolic importance?" (*E&I*, p. 354). Almost twenty years later, still haunted by the need to find the cause for the failure of the Romantic enterprise, Yeats, unable to deny the Romantics' coherent use of symbols, declares that the Romantic poet—the prototype of the poet *engagé*—becomes obsessed with the symbol, unlike the mystic, who is able to suspend all desire. The deliberate purpose in symbolic creation praised in the early essay gives way here to an emphasis on the importance of reverie, of a suspension of the will in "a form of meditation which permits an image or symbol to generate itself, and [in which] the images and symbols so generated build themselves up into coherent structures" (*E&I*, p. 422). This passage recalls Baudelaire's account of the creation of a painting; the dream is the generating idea that produces the world of the painting through successive layers completing each other and thus creating the complexity and coherence of a world. But Yeats's self-generated symbols seem to belong to the *Phantasmagoria* of afterlife since they are "a symbolical revelation received after the suspension of all desire," and Yeats perhaps admits the unfairness of his criticism of Shelley's determinately unsuspended desire when he concludes, "That life, and all lives, would be unintelligible to me did I not think of them as an exfoliation prolonged from life to life; he sang of something beginning" (*E&I*, p. 424). More relevant to the idea of unity in the work as opposed to the life is Yeats's reliance on the familiar metaphors of organicism. Of William Morris, he writes, "with him every book was a new planting, and not a new bud on a old bough" (*A*, p. 78). In "Art and Ideas," however, he criticizes Arnold's mistaken notion of reintegration: "his *Sorhab and Rustum* proves that the unity he imagined was a classical imitation and not an organic thing, not the flow of flesh under the impulse of passionate thought" (*E&I*, p. 354). As in "*Prometheus Unbound*," in "Art and Ideas" Yeats affirms that reverie is the imaginative mode; the system of symbols, the means; and the unified work, the product of artistic creation.

Whereas other poets await critical discovery of the coherence of their work, Yeats and Baudelaire both actively propagandized the unity of theirs. Baudelaire's audacious use of echoes and recurrences of key symbols and his tenacity in keeping to the original quest pattern of *Les Fleurs du Mal* were so novel that they brought him charges of repetitiveness and lack of imaginative abundance. Yeats, who remade himself through major stylistic changes throughout a long, productive life, escapes such attacks. Nevertheless, in his work, as in *Les Fleurs du Mal,* a network of recurring images develops into symbols through the same process Yeats observed in Shelley's poetry; Yeats's use of these images in individual poems alters the poems' ontological self-sufficiency by placing them within the larger architectural structure. To continue Wordsworth's informing metaphor, some poems are only stones of the great cathedral, while others serve as antechapels, recesses, foundations. The dialectical movement within cycles and from cycle to cycle naturally gives importance to beginning and final poems. Although a thesis-antithesis-synthesis pattern does not occur in mechanical, predictable order from cycle to cycle, certain poems acquire importance partly through their positions in the cycle and partly because they represent false starts, turning points, summings-up of experience, recoveries of vision. Their greatness consists of the indivisibility of their own merits as single poems from their function as stages of the quest in the work as a whole.

Despite the similarities between Yeats's method of constructing his *oeuvre* and Baudelaire's, Yeats mentions the French poet infrequently. It is safe to assume that, even if Yeats is sometimes silent about works that impressed him enough to reverberate in his own poetry ("Frost at Midnight," "Dejection: An Ode," *Biographia Literaria,* to mention only the Coleridgean echoes), Yeats does not count Baudelaire among the great influences upon his art. Yet his references to Baudelaire indicate an awareness of *Les Fleurs du Mal,* combined with his usual uncanny ability to reveal the essence of another poet's creation. In *A Vision* Yeats opposes Christ "who went into the abstract sky" to Oedipus, who "sank . . . into the earth," and he places *Gulliver's Travels* and *Les Fleurs du Mal* in the same non-Christian, antithetical category as Oedipus; their point in common is "horror," the emotion attendant upon the revelation of the hitherto hidden self (p. 28). Approximately at the same time, two years before the publication of the *The Tower,* Yeats mentions in a letter to Olivia Shakespear (*Letters,* pp. 714–15) that he brought only two books for his stay at Thoor Ballylee: Baudelaire and MacKenna's *Plotinus.* Since Yeats does specify "MacKenna's

The Symbolic Method

Plotinus," the "Baudelaire" must have been a book authored by Baudelaire rather than a biography. Although Yeats continues, "Plotinus is a most ardent and wonderful person" and makes no more mention of Baudelaire, the context is illuminating. Just before the reference to Baudelaire and Plotinus, he muses that all his poetry, no matter how begun, "becomes love poetry before I am finished with it." A few lines following it he writes, "One feels at moments as if one could with a touch convey a vision—that the mystic way and sexual love use the same means—opposed yet parallel existences." Several paragraphs later he adds, "The other day I found at Coole a reproduction of a drawing of two charming persons in the full stream of their Sapphoistic enthusiasm, and it got into my dreams at night and made a great racket there, and yet I feel spiritual things are very near me." The conjunction of Plotinus and Baudelaire seems to result in the recurring ruminations about the opposing means of sexuality and mysticism and their common end. Yeats could hardly have read Baudelaire without being struck by the resolute search for the absolute through sexuality that pervades *Les Fleurs du Mal* and specifically by Baudelaire's insistence that the lesbians are, like the quester himself, seekers of infinitude. The insight derived from his thinking in the spring and summer of 1926 informs much of his subsequent work, such as the Crazy Jane poems and, more significantly, the *Supernatural Songs,* where the image of the sphere becomes related to the wholeness achieved in copulation, where copulating spirits and godhead produce momentary illuminations for the mystic ("Ribh at the Tomb of Baile and Aillinn," "Ribh in Ecstasy") and lead him to intimations of apocalypse ("There," "The Four Ages of Man").

The renewal of the quest from *Responsibilities* to *Last Poems* attempts to embrace the kind of wholeness possible only in afterlife within the System of *A Vision.* Yeats recognizes, however, that triumph is momentary and the endeavor vain except in the quester's commitment to begin again. Throughout the quest, many images achieve symbolic status. The images of birdsong and heart become significant in relation to Yeats's search for Unity of Being; their presence occurs in moments when the psyche needs the synthesizing illumination of birdsong or the insistently human pull of the heart to overcome division and reach creative wholeness. Like the swimming sensation and the diffuse light of Coleridge's poetry, the recollections, perfumes, ascents, and descents in *Les Fleurs du Mal*, birdsong and heart signal the moment of symbolization, in which the mind gains freedom from its fragmented vision of reality, from its obsessions, and creates. In 1906 Yeats faces the choices open to a post-Romantic: "upward into ever-growing subtlety," "or downward taking the soul with us" (*E&I*, p. 267). He identifies the soul with the bird and develops the archetypal association so that it illuminates the inevitability of his choice:

> That is the choice of choices—the way of the bird until common eyes have lost us, or to the market carts; but we must see to it that the soul goes with us, for the bird's song is beautiful, and the traditions of the modern imagination, growing always more musical, more lyrical, more melancholy . . . are . . . the frenzy of those that are about to see what the magic hymn printed by the Abbé de Villars has called the Crown of Living and Melodious Diamonds. [*E&I*, p. 267]

Yeats rejects the isolation of "ever-growing subtlety" without, however, renouncing the bird, its song—the imaginative vision. In later years bird and song become even more strongly identified with his art[42] and with the psychic healing that occurred when Yeats turned from the search for knowledge to an affirmation of life. In a moving passage of *A Vision* Yeats comes to recognize the abstraction and antihumanism of his Systematized account of life. The bird here represents not the soul but "a reality which is concrete, sensuous, bodily," and which can be attained when the imagination reaches unity: "My imagination was for a time haunted by figures that, muttering 'The great systems,' held out to me the sun-dried skeletons of birds, and it seemed to me that this image was meant to turn my thoughts to the living bird. That bird signifies truth when it eats, evacuates, builds its nest, engenders, feeds its young; do not all intelligible truths lie in its passage from egg to dust?" (*Vision*, p. 214). The living bird, like the birdsong in the poetry, provides the needed corrective to the frequent temptation in Yeats to exclude much of life in exchange for "truth."

The Symbolic Method

In *Responsibilities* birdsong breaks through the poet's quarrel with the past or doubts about past commitments that have endangered his imaginative powers. The bitterness that breaks through the *sprezzatura* mask of poems like "To a Wealthy Man," "September 1913," and "To a Friend Whose Work Has Come to Nothing" finds remedy in the brief illuminations of "Paudeen." The poet in his indignation internalizes the world until he resembles the thing he despises, substituting for the "fumbling wits" of the aged shopkeeper his stumbling blindness. The bird's cry "in the luminous wind" brings the necessary fusion of sensibility to the poet, who in a visionary moment transcends the sound and fury of everyday events for a God's view of things, for the perspective of eternity in which each soul, regardless of its station in life, finds its own "sweet crystalline cry." Yeats rarely gives himself to the magnanimity of vision in "Paudeen," and yet this is a poem of wisdom greater than the *sprezzatura* of the middle period or the gaiety of the last. It looks forward to the inclusiveness and humanity of "Cuchulain Comforted." "The Three Hermits" reinforces the sense of the eternal revealed in the bird's cry. The two hermits who are still plagued by fleas and by the fear of afterlife fail to see the transformation of the third, who, having reached the embodied wisdom imperceptible through theological speculation, "sang unnoticed like a bird."

Much of the remorse over the past which haunts the poet in *Responsibilities* results from the "barren passion" of his youth. In the subcycle of irresponsibility—the beggar poems—Yeats envisions the alternative to the rootlessness of his existence by having the beggar imagine the acquisition of "a comfortable wife and house" where "I'll grow respected at my ease" ("Beggar to Beggar Cried"). The beggar would gain this comfort were he to forsake the unfulfilled sexual passion for a beautiful woman. Yet once at ease, his peace would be broken by "the wind-blown clamour of the barnacle-geese," the same kind of daring bird into which the poet metamorphoses while ascending to heaven in "High Talk." The clamor troubles his wishful dreams as it reminds him of the tenacious devils "in . . . shoes" and "between . . . thighs" who need much more powerful exorcism than the fantasy of well-being, the delusion of the lower paradise, if

The Quest for Unity of Being

the quester is to find fulfillment. As if to belie the barrenness of the passion, Yeats returns to the persona of the poet in the subcycle commemorating his star-crossed love for Maud. "A Memory of Youth," which builds toward loss of passion and youth in the service of unrequited love and thus resembles the awakening to reality portrayed in "Adam's Curse," ends in a reversal where "the cry / Of a most ridiculous little bird" suddenly illuminates the poet's imagination with "the marvellous moon" of love. The silence "of stone" of the estranged lovers having been broken, the poet recovers youthful passion, with all it contains of praise, blame, and remorse, and transforms the barrenness into poetic creation as he promised his ancestors in the opening poem of the cycle.

The image of the bird and its cry all but disappears from *The Wild Swans at Coole*, where the poet again counters loss of vision by recovering passion through the agency of memory, and from *Michael Robartes and the Dancer*, where, with two exceptions, the many birds keep silent. Yet the birdsong imagery continues, even if submerged; *The Wild Swans* begins with the disparity between the poet's aging heart and the "unwearied" birds and ends with the poet having supplanted the bird by internalizing the agent of imaginative fusion and thus taking over its function. The dialogue of *Hic* and *Ille* in "Ego Dominus Tuus" centers on a debate about song, and *Ille* insists that song is the exclusive domain of the imaginative man seeking his Daimon, who will "disclose / All that I seek," and whose whispers replace the birds' "momentary cries before it is dawn" (ll. 75–76, 78). Fittingly, in "The Double Vision of Michael Robartes," the poet celebrates the long-awaited vision by arranging it "in a song" (l. 65). *Michael Robartes and the Dancer*, perhaps the most thematically divided of Yeats's cycles, initiates the dichotomy of real and supernatural bird. The cockerel in "Solomon and the Witch" and the "terrified, invisible . . . bird" in "An Image from Past Life" both scream or crow out of the supernatural either to bless or blight mortal union. To these images "of poignant recollection" of unattainable paradise Yeats opposes a series of natural birds which contradicts the pursuit of the absolute when that ideal turns to abstraction. The sweetness from the living thing drives out the skeleton. In "Easter 1916" and "On a Political Prisoner"

The Symbolic Method

Yeats ascribes the abstraction resulting from the political commitment to the men and the woman whom he commemorates with such great reservations. The "one purpose alone" to which they have given themselves stands like a stone amid the "living stream" of things that "minute by minute live." The indictment of the political prisoner grows even sharper, no doubt mixed with Yeats's detestation of causes that rob women from their lovers. The "bitter abstract thing"—the skeleton of the mind—contrasts with the seaborne bird taking flight for the first time, an image of wholeness of body and mind engaged in maintaining equilibrium. The descent from the magnificent, lonely gull braving the storm to the linnet having "no business but" and hanging on to the leaf in "A Prayer for My Daughter" may be a touching instance of the father's protectiveness but shows a disquieting parsimony of hopes for the child which, for me, flaws the poem. The poet wishes his child to move from innocence to "radical innocence," sheltered from the storm of experience instead of facing and defeating it. Although the poem abounds in wishes for an antithetical culture to sustain the poet's daughter, she herself appears as a primary figure shielded from antithetical intensity. She becomes the "kind gladness," the hidden flowering tree, not the brave, heedless beauty whose scattering "in the thoroughfares" Yeats decries as the unmaking of "Plenty's horn." The serenity and detachment from life projected by the poet for his daughter uncomfortably recall the situation of the naive speaker of "The Blessing." At this point in the quest Yeats knows better than to hope that innocence untried by experience can withstand and rise above external circumstances or the more awesome divisions within. In "Demon and Beast" the poet, finally recognizing that his own inner forces of negation as much as an exclusive devotion to external causes can change the heart to stone, frees himself long enough to taste the sweetness of imaginative wholeness as he watches the movements of the "absurd / Portly green-pated bird."

Yeats makes full symbolic use of bird and birdsong in *The Tower,* where he opens the cycle with "Sailing to Byzantium," in which the birds caught in the music of generation force the poet to a different singing school. Yet the soul's clapping and singing are not so much a study of "its own magnificence" as an

The Quest for Unity of Being

attempt to cover up the "tatter in the mortal dress," the process of aging which has isolated the poet from the country of the young. Aware of what ails him, the speaker calls upon the sages to divide him from his heart and his desire and to remake him into an unnatural, but also inhuman form; "Sailing to Byzantium" is an instance of Yeats's readiness to exchange the sensuous embodied truth of the living—and dying—bird for knowledge and hence to give up Unity of Being (*Vision*, p. 214). The knowledgeable bird appears again in "Byzantium" (*The Winding Stair and Other Poems*), this time distinct from the poet's own person or at least from aspects of his mind; here it behaves much like other crazed birds and lovers of Yeats's poetry who rage at their imperfect reflection, as it does at its "common," living counterparts. The mere "glory of changeless metal" seems to yearn for a completion that only generation—the "complexities of mire and blood"—can provide, and both "The Tower" and "Vacillation" return to the true theme of the singer and his subject, namely, the eternal desire for ephemeral things: "Man is in love and loves what vanishes" ("Nineteen Hundred and Nineteen," l. 42). In *The Tower*, despite the bitterness that Yeats saw in it, the quester manages to overcome the dissolution of historical order and the divisions of his own mind to the point where in "All Souls' Night" he accepts the inevitable isolation of his creed and is content for once to take the way of the bird into subtlety at the risk of being outside the range of human understanding. (I shall discuss further the resolution in *The Tower*.)

"Cuchulain Comforted," which completes the cycle of the hero's journey all the way into stages of the soul on its way to Beatitude, presents birdsong for the last time in Yeats's poetry and, as such, is an apt culmination of this symbol of unity.[43] The state following *Phantasmagoria* in Yeats's account of afterlife is *Shiftings*, and Yeats's description in *A Vision* provides a clue for the hero's arrival amid spirits who were all "convicted cowards." In it, "the *Spirit* is purified of good and evil. In so far as the man did good without knowing evil, or evil without knowing good, his nature is reversed until that knowledge is obtained" (*Vision*, p. 231). Yeats envisions a different kind of leveling from the historical, which he resisted all his life, taking place at this stage of the soul's journey. Ideas of good and evil "according to the code

The Symbolic Method

accepted during life" (*Vision*, p. 231) must be transcended in order for the soul to complete itself, and a culminating transformation occurs in this symbol-concluding poem, as in "Le Voyage"; hence the reversal of the hero into coward. Cuchulain has yet to become his opposite, while the Shrouds, former heroes, have already accomplished the great change. They are cowards precisely because they have attained complete knowledge of their antithetical opposite. Their identification has become so unconditional that it necessitates a confession of cowardice to the newly arrived soul of the hero. The Shrouds pass into Beatitude, leaving Cuchulain to shed his individuality and sew his new habit of mind until communal fears become his and he too can change his tune to birdsong. In "Cuchulain Comforted" Yeats makes a magnificent admission of the insufficiency of heroism, of any antithetical virtue, for the attainment of complete being. The Shrouds' acknowledgment of cowardice shows that they have reached knowledge beyond antinomies of good and evil, have reached birdsong, that symbol Yeats builds throughout his poetry for "complete equilibrium" (*Vision*, p. 232) and wholeness of mind.

Alternating and at times combining with the symbol of birdsong, the heart restores unity by balancing the quester's extreme absorption in a fragmenting and often inhuman pursuit. Unlike the supernatural, equalizing illumination of birdsong, which attracts the quester's eye away from inner division, the heart will not let him forget or disown parts of his humanity and continually calls him back to his own self, preparing him for Unity of Being.[44] Yeats had been made aware quite early in his career of the importance of integrating the heart into poetry in order to give credibility to vision. Whether Verlaine made his remark about the heart casually or not, Yeats seized upon it as a statement of the major difference between the exhausted literature of Britain and the tradition that he chose for himself: "Tennyson is too noble, too Anglais; when he should have been brokenhearted, he had many reminiscences" (*A*, p. 206). The distinction evidently struck Yeats, who reported it first in 1896 (*Uncoll.*, 1:399), following it with his own musings; then, as he rearranged the order of his recollections in 1922 for "The Trembling of the Veil," he moved it to a more prominent position as Ver-

The Quest for Unity of Being

laine's concluding statement. Like birdsong, the humanizing wisdom of the heart contrasts in Yeats with single-minded pursuit and its attendant abstractions, whether the pursuit is his own or that of others. In 1909 and 1910, before renewing his poetic enterprise, Yeats attempts to account for his increasing estrangement from the woman and the national cause that consumed so much of his youth. Both the *Memoirs* and *The Cutting of an Agate* contain passages on the exclusion of the living thing from a mind in thrall to "some fixed idea" (*E&I*, pp. 313–14). Anticipating the heart's metamorphosis to stone in "Easter 1916" and its growing brutality in "Meditations in Time of Civil War," Yeats writes, "A stone is always stronger, more masculine than a living thing," and, looking forward to "Among School Children," elaborates: "living thought, an intricacy of leaf and twig" (*Memoirs*, p. 196).

The quester in Yeats's later cycles begins either in imaginative exhaustion or seeks a renewal of vision which would counteract "bodily decrepitude." Yet his ultimate search centers upon finding an affirmation of vision which does not break the heart but acknowledges it as the matrix of imaginative creation. The consistency of Yeats's thought in regard to the image of the heart is evident in the associations of heart with psychic unity, with the imagination, and with the quest appearing in the early and middle poetry as well, though these associations do not acquire the cumulative force of the later usage. The stargazers of Yeats's first lyric in *Collected Poems* have suffered a dissociation of sensibility characteristic of men of science, so that the knowledge they gain has no relevance to "human truth" ("The Song of the Happy Shepherd," l. 34). Men who have kept integrity of mind are the artists, who, like the speaker in "To Ireland in the Coming Times," "cast [the] heart into . . . rhymes" and remain faithful to the quest. Despite Yeats's admiration for the mask in the middle period, he recognizes the damage suffered by the heart through hatred and bitterness, though he can banish hatred only temporarily. What he cannot part with for all the attraction of the nonchalant Renaissance manner is the devotion to the cruel muse and ultimately to his quest, his art. The heart tenaciously holds on to its wisdom as it cries in "The Folly of Being Comforted," "No, / I have not a crumb of comfort, not a grain" and spurs the quester on. The inability to deny the heart does reap its moments of supreme reward, in which the memory of love stored in the heart wells up and overwhelms the poet with its sweetness ("Friends").

The later cycles show increased emphasis and dependence on heart as the repository of images and memories that renew faltering or misled poetic vision. *The Wild Swans at Coole* begins with the poet's dejection over lost youth, cooled passion and an aged heart. The original concluding stanza (ll. 19–24) of the introductory poem opposes the swans' permanence to the ravaging mutability ("All's changed," l. 15) of the poet's life:

> Unwearied still, lover by lover,
> They paddle in the cold
> Companionable streams or climb the air;
> Their hearts have not grown old;
> Passion or conquest, wander where they will,
> Attend upon them still.

Surprisingly, Yeats refuses here the traditional contrast between art—images that "keep a marble or a bronze repose"—and the flux of experience in favor of renewed, continued passion versus growing old. The lament is heard again in "Men Improve with the Years," in the apostrophe to the heart in the "The Living Beauty," and in the refrain to "A Song." Yet bidding his heart "to draw content / From beauty that is cast out of a mould / In bronze, or that in dazzling marble appears" ("The Living Beauty," ll. 3–5) because he and it have grown old leaves the heart discontented, and *The Wild Swans* moves toward recovery of passion's spur.

The heart fuels Yeats's poems of loss and changes them from merely "many reminiscences" to passionate celebrations of dead and dying friends and lost love. In the last stanza of "In Memory of Major Robert Gregory" Yeats comments on his attempted method for honoring the men he admired; he began with memory—"to have brought to mind" (l. 10)—sought to change it to imaginative vision, but recognizes that his grief gives the last eloquent silence to the heart. Yeats's faithfulness to heartache throughout the cycle rejuvenates his imagination. "To a Young Girl" and "The People" oppose the wisdom, the instant recogni-

The Quest for Unity of Being

tion, of the heart to the extinguished passion of old age and "the definitions / Of the analytic mind" ("The People," ll. 32–33). In "Broken Dreams" and "Upon a Dying Lady" the poet creates out of "all heart's ache" a vision of what was lost, ranging "from dream to dream and rhyme to rhyme" until "vague memories" take shape and life. His progress from "The Wild Swans" to "Ego Dominus Tuus" becomes clear in *Ille's* affirmation, "Those men that in their writings are most wise / Own nothing but their blind, stupefied hearts" (ll. 68–69). This recognition of the heart's primacy allows the poet to recover his psychic unity and results in the reward of "The Double Vision of Michael Robartes," where the visionary moment becomes "time overthrown"—a glimpse of eternity.

Whereas in *The Wild Swans* the quester triumphs over mutability by recovering passion, in *The Tower* he seeks the wisdom that can satisfy the passionate heart, and in *The Winding Stair* he attempts to go beyond passion and wisdom to find joy. "Sailing to Byzantium" shows the speaker ready to exchange the heart, "sick with desire / And fastened to a dying animal," for an eternity that no longer plagues him with the incompatibility of the heart's desire and bodily decay. Yet as the quester progresses through the cycle, he recognizes the necessity to incorporate the heart into the self in order to achieve a wisdom greater than that of the prophetic, but disturbingly inconsequential, bird at the emperor's court. Far from being consumed in the holy fire, the heart is apostrophized at the beginning of "The Tower": "What shall I do with this absurdity— / O heart, O troubled heart—this caricature, / Decrepit age . . ." (ll. 1–3). The poet seeks an answer by calling upon "images and memories" that arise at the bidding of the imagination but whose source is the troubled heart. In turn, the poet creates out of images and memories "a superhuman / Mirror-resembling dream" that dismisses Stendhal's nature-reflecting mirror and thus defeats temporal decay. Yet the soul's school at the end of "The Tower" is not unlike the singing school of "Sailing to Byzantium," in that both turn away from the decaying animal and human ties, which, too, fall prey to mutability. "Meditations in Time of Civil War," particularly sections 3, 6, and 7, reverses the conclusions of "The Tower" by renewing faith in the "aching heart," the "ambitious heart" that

The Symbolic Method

spurs the poet toward creation of "a changeless work of art" and that, embittered by its insubstantial diet of "fantasies" (abstractions), prompts the poet to seek the sweetness of imaginative embodiment even amid the "loosening masonry" of psychic and cultural structures.

"Among School Children" represents the culmination and resolution of the poet's attempt to school his soul at the expense of his heart. All of man's accomplishments in building "monuments of its [the soul's] magnificence" are punctured by the heartrending irony of time's power: "Old clothes upon old sticks to scare a bird." The Presences, who, like the "sages standing in God's holy fire," symbolize "all heavenly glory," become a measure of man's defeat instead of the means of his salvation. In the last stanza, the poet turns from the heartbreaking Presences to images of indissoluble integrity which satisfy the whole self. Yeats's revision of "hawthorn tree" into "chestnut-tree"[45] indicates his care in excluding possible religious associations from his last images in order to separate them from the "heavenly glory." The hawthorn tree, traditionally the source of Christ's crown of thorns, changes to the nondenominational, aesthetically impressive, yet natural chestnut tree. "All Souls' Night," the concluding poem of the cycle, contains an equal expression of psychic integrity which finally releases the poet from the obsession with the "battered kettle at the heel":

> Such thought—such thought have I that hold it tight
> Till meditation master all its parts,
> Nothing can stay my glance
> Until that glance run in the world's despite
> To where the damned have howled away their hearts,
> And where the blessed dance. [Ll. 91–96]

The poet has moved beyond the golden bird's "what's past, or passing, or to come" into a vision of eternity that obviates the backward look over the mutable world. The extravagant, prolonged hilarity and grief, recalling the emotions of "Reconciliation," represent the effect of vision upon an audience—"all that hear"—as improbable as the emperor and his court, but indicate the incomparably greater import of the poet's thought at the end of the cycle. As in "Reconciliation," the poet has accepted his heart, "sick with desire," and has found a wisdom that rejects the sundering of soul and heart.

In *The Winding Stair* Yeats proposes to remedy the bitterness he found so prevalent, to his surprise, in *The Tower*. Major poems of the cycle, such as "A Dialogue of Self and Soul," "Vacillation," and "Stream and Sun at Glendalough" proclaim the centrality of the heart to imaginative creation, and the cycle moves toward a casting out of remorse in order to purify the heart and discover joy. The ecstatic Self declares in "A Dialogue of Self and Soul": "I am content to follow to its source / Every event in action or in thought; / Measure the lot; forgive myself the lot" (ll. 65–67). It becomes evident in "Vacillation" that the source of "every event" is "man's blood-sodden heart" (l. 67). The recognition brings the quester the honeycomb he had desired in "Meditations in Time of Civil War," since for once the poet's lot—"a predestined part" (l. 86)—is one with his choice—"Homer is my example and his unchristened heart" (l. 87)—and life's endeavor finds temporary fulfillment in a state of blessedness, in the ecstasy of the Self of "A Dialogue" and in the illuminations of "Vacillation" and "Stream and Sun."

Joy and the coincidence of Chance and Choice are of necessity short-lived in the Romantic Quest, and Yeats's poetry does not deviate in this respect. The fulfillment of *The Winding Stair* sinks again under the bitterness of *From "A Full Moon in March"* and the gay mask of some of the *New Poems* and *Last Poems*.[46] Despite Yeats's resurgent desire to extend Unity of Being into Unity of Culture, the last poems are haunted by the discrepancy between desire and achievement, by Plato's "ghostly paradigm" mocking life in the world ("What Then"). Refrains puncture the claims made by the speaker in the stanzas, the echo treacherously throws back reminders of mortality to the man who has his eye on the afterlife, and the quester himself declares, in judgment over himself, "I am not content." His discontent in the face of approaching night urges the quester on. He arrives at two choices, both using the imagery of the circus, that most self-conscious make-believe, for the poet's life and art; one, "High Talk," ends in ascent to the sky; the other, "The Circus Animals' Desertion," necessitates a descent into the source of "every event," the heart. Yeats's revision of an early draft reveals the

The Symbolic Method

extent of his ultimate acceptance of the Romantic enterprise.[47] Gaiety, the *sprezzatura* mask, will not do in this last instance of reckoning. The only action that suffices is a descent back from the top of the ladder—the pure mind almost dissociated from the rest of the self—to the storehouse of images and memories, the stuff of imaginative creation. Like Baudelaire with the last poem of *Les Fleurs du Mal*, "Le Voyage," Yeats transcends antinomial divisions in the circus poems; the props, scenery, and characters are stripped away with the same severity as the travelers' replies to childish believers in illusion, throwing the mind back upon itself; ascent or descent matters only in that each offers a road toward renewal.

IV

Unlike Coleridge and Baudelaire, Yeats had time and will to remake himself more thoroughly as a poet than did his predecessors. He understood early in his career the necessity of hammering one's thoughts into unity, and his extensive reading of the Romantics, as well as his kinship with the generation growing under the shade of Baudelaire and his French heirs, provided him with models for the creation of unity through use of sustained, coherent symbols. Yeats to a large extent invented the failure of the Romantic enterprise by distorting its causes, but he showed extraordinary insight and independence of mind in distancing himself from the self-destructive path taken by the Tragic Generation. Yet his attempt to save his vision from incommunicability and early death by seeking external validation for it continually endangered his quest. Nature, *la belle dame sans merci*, which so often seduces and defeats the Romantic imagination, plays little part in Yeats's poetry. But the external world enters it nonetheless in the form of equally dangerous seductions, such as the hope of fraternity with the aristocracy, the inevitable movement of history which will revenge the poet upon his detractors, and, finally, the mill of the System, spiraling back and forth complexities that for all their subtleties determine human life. Despite his consistent return to Romantic models, Yeats ends his

The Quest for Unity of Being

life's work with "Politics," not the much more significant "Circus Animals' Desertion," or, if one wishes to pursue the table of contents to its end, with *Purgatory,* as heartless a last vision as the extreme statements of *On the Boiler.*

Yet the attraction of external solutions, which seduces the quester away from Unity of Being only to be repulsed by the structure of each major cycle in turn, represents only part of Yeats's departure from the Coleridgean and Baudelairian pattern for the enterprise. Despite his deliberate and astonishingly successful shift in diction and his inclusion of traditionally unaesthetic subjects in his verse, Yeats resolutely banished the modern age from his poetry. To him, there was no heroism of modern life, no modern beauty, no modern act worth all his admiration. When Yeats praises men and women, he likens them to paragons of the past, not merely to give them the mythical dimensions of cultural associations but to show them inevitably unsuited for a context too pathetic, too small for them, or to place them in a context whose allegiance to the past makes it the antithesis of modern life. Had Yeats begun his visions more frequently in the low-key, realistically recognizable outer locus of "Among School Children," his poetry might have imparted a greater sense of modernity. His choice, simplification through intensity, did not allow such inclusiveness and perhaps preserved his poetry from dispersal. It did create the unified structure of the work and the quest for Unity of Being. However, it certainly left his younger contemporary, James Joyce, room to take up the continuing enterprise toward psychic reintegration and bring it back to the city, in the lives of Paudeens to whom Yeats would concede imaginative illumination, the "sweet crystalline cry" of completion, only in death.

That Coleridge continues to be regarded as the cornerstone of Romantic theories of the symbol and of the language of poetry and as a major influence on his contemporaries and on subsequent writers is evident.[48] Critics who take a formalist approach to the vocabulary of Romanticism still dismiss him as an abridgment of German Romanticism and see Mallarmé's work as the synthesis of Romantic intransitiveness of language.[49] Such polarities of opinion are not new in the history of criticism. What is novel, perhaps, is a certain failure of nerve on the part of some

The Symbolic Method

of those presently engaged in the study of the humanities. Methodologies that borrow the aura of scientific investigation lend authority to what seems to be regarded as the otherwise indefensible activity of thinking about works of art. Given the impotence of the humanities to affect modern life, the desire to move literary criticism to the domain of science is not surprising. Such an alliance, however, tends to reduce the status of art and the meaning of "human." It is as if we focused on the failure of regenerative efforts in previous periods because images of ruin mirror the fragmentation visible in our own age; we have an uneasy feeling that man's scope has drastically diminished, and we can read the great Romantic enterprises only from the confines of our beleaguered position.[50]

The present study has been guided by Coleridge's statement on Method, which gives the book its epigraph. Despite all the vicissitudes of his life, Coleridge was a systematic thinker. His poetic achievements in genre and imagery represent the early and at times the most successful articulations of his theory of the symbol and the imagination. His Greater Romantic Lyrics and *The Rime of the Ancient Mariner,* that formidable example of the Romantic Quest, become two principal poetic modes for expressing the process of the mind encountering external reality. The success of imaginative vision, which occurs when the mind transforms reality into a sublime moment of revelation, appears in Coleridge through imagery in which light suffuses the contemplated or remembered object or landscape. The human presence—friend, child, beloved—is an essential element of the imaginative transformation. In formulating a theory of imagination and symbol, Coleridge relies upon identical imagery to distinguish the genuine fusion of intellect and feeling from the mundane operations of the mind. However inapplicable the words "symbol" and "imagination" seem to certain critics, Coleridge uses them as criteria that raise the work of art and the process of beholding that work to the level of heightened consciousness; imaginative constructs free man from the thralldom of ever-changing sensations

Coleridge looked to an epic poem that, like his symbol, was to reflect the experience of his time and to make reality intelligible. By consciously shaping their lyrics into *oeuvres* of

The Quest for Unity of Being

epic scope, Baudelaire and Yeats in turn rediscover and expand upon Coleridge's symbolic method. Apart from affinities between Coleridge and Baudelaire apparent in Baudelaire's pronouncements about beauty, the role of art, and the nature of imagination and language, the connection between the two poets appears in Baudelaire's use of a structure similar to that of the Greater Romantic Lyric for each of the cycles of *Les Fleurs du Mal*, and in his construction of the *oeuvre* as a quest. These patterns provide the poetic forms through which consciousness shapes and reshapes itself in response to life. Acts of symbolization differ in imagery and setting from those of Coleridge, but their regenerative function remains the same, that of reintegrating a psyche assaulted by the fragmentariness of mere existence.

Yeats, like Baudelaire, uses the structure—often flawed—of the Greater Romantic Lyric for the cycles of his *Collected Poems* and the Quest as the unifying movement of the work. Two recurring images, birdsong and heart, signalize the act of symbolization which in Yeats saves consciousness from the dangers of solipsism on the one hand and disintegration on the other.

Resonances of Baudelaire's and Yeats's *oeuvres* and, implicitly, of Coleridge's work can be heard not only in twentieth-century poetry but in fiction and drama. Thus, the best defense of the present approach is that the achievements of these three men, in both their finished and projected states, inform so much that is central to modern literature. The most courageous writing of our century continues to explore the problems raised by the Romantics about the human capacity to find meaning other than a strictly religious one in the *spectacle* of life. Consequently, symbolization as structural method, progressing in cycles and moving toward an overall unity, could be applied successfully to such works as Joyce's *Ulysses*, Proust's *A la recherche du temps perdu*, and even Beckett's trilogy. Ultimately, I believe that the Romantic enterprise will survive in these poets' works, as it does in their literary heirs, not because it amuses us or gives occasion for learned playfulness, but because it offers the extratemporal order to our lives which, outside of art, only a prospect from the undiscovered country can give—and such a prospect is all too problematic for most of us.

NOTES

CHAPTER ONE

1. Samuel Taylor Coleridge, *Biographia Literaria and Aesthetical Essays*, 1:167. Henceforth, this edition will be cited as *BL*.
2. See M. H. Abrams, "Structure and Style in the Greater Romantic Lyric"; Harold Bloom, "The Internalization of Quest Romance"; and M. H. Abrams, *Natural Supernaturalism: Tradition and Revolution in Romantic Literature*, chaps. 3 and 4.
3. Walter Benjamin, *A Lyric Poet in the Era of High Capitalism*, p. 152.
4. See Harold Bloom, *The Anxiety of Influence: A Theory of Poetry*.
5. Leon Edel, in chap. 2 of *The Modern Psychological Novel*, mentions in passing just such a continuity.
6. *Lay Sermons*, in *The Collected Works of Samuel Taylor Coleridge*, 6:30. Henceforth *Collected Works* will be cited as *CW*.
7. See "On the Principles of Genial Criticism Concerning the Fine Arts," *BL*, 2:238.
8. See Frank Kermode's definition of the Image in *Romantic Image*.
9. See Harry Levin, *The Gates of Horn: A Study of Five French Realists*, pp. 64–83, 215–19.
10. See Baudelaire's *Salon de 1859*, under the subheadings "The Queen of Faculties" and "The Rule of Imagination," in *Oeuvres Complètes*, vol. 2. Henceforth, this edition will be cited as *OC*. The translations of prose passages in the text are the author's. The translations of poetry in both the text and the notes are from *The Flowers of Evil;* author's translations are in parentheses, without quotation marks, following the quotations in French.
11. See Northrop Frye, "Three Meanings of Symbolism," "The Drunken Boat: The Revolutionary Element in Romanticism," and *Anatomy of Criticism: Four Essays*, pp. 79–81.
12. *Mythologies*, p. 267. Henceforth, this edition will be cited as *Myth*.
13. See *The Letters of W. B. Yeats*, pp. 714–15. Henceforth, this edition will be cited as *Letters*.
14. "The Philosophy of Shelley's Poetry," in *Essays and Introductions*. Henceforth, this edition will be cited as *E&I*.
15. See Hugh Kenner, "The Sacred Book of the Arts."
16. See Harold Bloom, *Shelley's Mythmaking;* Northrop Frye, *Fearful Symmetry: A Study of William Blake;* Jack Stillinger, "The Order of Poems in Keats's First Volume"; Denis Donoghue, *William Butler Yeats;* and John Unterecker, *A Reader's Guide to William Butler Yeats*.
17. M. H. Abrams, *The Mirror and the Lamp: Romantic Theory and the*

Notes to Pages 26-33

Critical Tradition, pp. 320, 327-28, and "Coleridge, Baudelaire, and Modernist Poetics"; Margery Sabin, *English Romanticism and the French Tradition;* Robert Langbaum, *The Poetry of Experience*, p. 35; and Edward Engelberg, *The Vast Design: Patterns in W. B. Yeats's Aesthetic*, pp. 110-12.

18. See Lloyd James Austin, *L'Univers poétique de Baudelaire: Symbolisme et symbolique*.

19. See T. S. Eliot, "Baudelaire in Our Time," in *For Lancelot Andrews: Essays on Style and Order*, pp. 68-78. For a critique of Eliot's opinion, see Victor Brombert, "T. S. Eliot and the Heresy of Romanticism."

20. Erich Auerbach, "The Esthetic Dignity of the *Fleurs du Mal.*"

21. See Harold Bloom, *Yeats*, and George Bornstein, *Yeats and Shelley*.

22. George Bornstein, *Transformations of Romanticism in Yeats, Eliot, and Stevens;* Thomas Whitaker, *Swan and Shadow: Yeats's Dialogue with History;* Theodor Klimeck, *Symbol und Wirklichkeit bei W. B. Yeats;* Donald Pearce, "Yeats and the Romantics"; and Cleanth Brooks, "W. B. Yeats as a Literary Critic," in *A Shaping Joy: Studies in the Writer's Craft*.

23. Harold Bloom, *Poetry and Repression: Revisionism from Blake to Stevens*, p. 209.

24. Denis Donoghue, *The Sovereign Ghost: Studies in Imagination*, pp. 40-44.

25. The representative reading of Yeats in the light of the poetics of vision is Bloom's *Yeats*.

26. See Frank Kermode, "The Modern Apocalypse," in *The Sense of an Ending: Studies in the Theory of Fiction*, p. 108.

CHAPTER TWO

1. *The Notebooks of Samuel Taylor Coleridge*, 2:2274. Henceforth, this edition will be cited as *Nb*, followed by volume and entry number.

2. John Beer, *Coleridge the Visionary*, pp. 16-17, and R. H. Fogle, *The Idea of Coleridge's Criticism*, pp. 50, 58, point to contradictions they find inherent in Coleridge's idea of the symbol and its function.

3. I am using Nature as *natura naturata*, the world as it is received by the senses and generalized by the Understanding. The word will be capitalized when used in this Coleridgean sense.

4. Faculties, as defined by Coleridge, will be capitalized in order to distinguish them from common usage.

5. For Coleridge's ambivalence toward nature, see Douglas Brownlow Wilson, "Two Modes of Apprehending Nature: A Gloss on the Coleridgean Symbol."

6. George McLean Harper is the first to discuss Coleridge's Lyrics in "Coleridge's Conversation Poems"; M. H. Abrams definitively establishes the genre of these poems in "Structure and Style in the Greater Romantic Lyric."

7. For a different account of Coleridge's bad conscience in "The Eolian Harp," see John Beer, *Coleridge's Poetic Intelligence*, p. 67.

8. "The Nightingale" exhibits the same reluctance, though in it Coleridge subverts "Nature's sweet voices, always full of love / And joyance" by adding to the supposedly sufficient setting a profusion of nightingales (ll. 55-56) and moonlight, thus correcting the single voice of the nightingale, which, despite his protests, puts the speaker in mind of Milton's "melancholy man" and the "dimness of the stars" (l. 11).

9. Both J. Robert Barth, *The Symbolic Imagination: Coleridge and the Symbolic Tradition*, and Thomas McFarland, "The Origin and Significance of Coleridge's Theory of Secondary Imagination," insist on religiosity and minimize

Notes to Pages 34–37

the importance of his theory to aesthetics. For a resounding refutation of the separatist view of Coleridge's religious concerns and poetry, see Elinor S. Shaffer, *Kubla Khan and "The Fall of Jerusalem": The Mythological School in Biblical Criticism and Secular Literature, 1770–1800.*

10. See Paul Magnuson, *Coleridge's Nightmare Poetry,* and Norman Fruman, *Coleridge, the Damaged Archangel.*

11. James Volant Baker, *The Sacred River: Coleridge's Theory of the Imagination,* p. 211; Manfred Wojcik, "Coleridge: Symbolization, Expression, and Artistic Creativity," pp. 121–22; Stephen Prickett, *Coleridge and Wordsworth,* p. 70; and James D. Boulger, "Coleridge on Imagination Revisited."

12. The exception is J. Robert Barth, *Coleridge and Christian Doctrine.*

13. I. A. Richards, *Coleridge on Imagination,* p. 58.

14. Baker, *The Sacred River,* p. 119.

15. For variations on Richards's view, see M. H. Abrams, *The Mirror and the Lamp: Romantic Theory and the Critical Tradition,* p. 68; R. H. Fogle, "Coleridge's Critical Principles," pp. 62–63; Owen Barfield, *What Coleridge Thought,* p. 81; and D. G. James, *Skepticism and Poetry: An Essay on the Poetic Imagination,* pp. 24, 70–74. On the other side of the controversy, see J. A. Appleyard, "Coleridge and Criticism: I. Critical Theory," and J. R. de J. Jackson, *Method and Imagination in Coleridge's Criticism,* p. 116.

16. "Symbol as Sacrament in Coleridge's Thought," *Studies in Romanticism,* no. 11 (1972), pp. 320–31 (see p. 325).

17. D. G. James, "The Thought of Coleridge," pp. 100–112, explains Coleridge's retreat as growth.

18. Abrams, "The Greater Romantic Lyric," p. 528; Albert S. Gérard, *English Romantic Poetry: Ethos, Structure, and Symbol in Coleridge, Wordsworth, Shelley, and Keats,* pp. 63, 251, 258; and Max F. Schulz, "Oneness and Multeity in Coleridge's Poems."

19. The same view of the process appears in Abrams, "The Greater Romantic Lyric," p. 548; in R. H. Fogle, "Coleridge's Conversation Poems"; in Panthea Reid Broughton, "The Modifying Metaphor in 'Dejection: An Ode' "; in Michael E. Holstein, "Poet into Priest: A Reading of Coleridge's 'Conversation Poems' "; and in Anne K. Mellor, "Coleridge's 'This Lime-Tree Bower My Prison' and the Categories of English Landscape."

20. Morris Dickstein, "Coleridge, Wordsworth, and the 'Conversation Poems,' "; A. R. Jones, "Coleridge and Poetry: II. The Conversational and Other Poems."

21. Abrams, "The Greater Romantic Lyric," p. 553.

22. R. H. Fogle, "The Genre of the Ancient Mariner."

23. See ibid., p. 122, for a defense of verisimilitude, A. M. Buchan, "The Sad Wisdom of the Mariner," for an attack. Note also Robert Penn Warren, "A Poem of Pure Imagination"; Humphry House, "The Ancient Mariner," in his *Coleridge: The Clark Lectures, 1951–1952,* pp. 84–113; Harold Bloom's brief treatment in *The Visionary Company,* pp. 206–12; Magnuson, *Coleridge's Nightmare Poetry;* and Beer, *Coleridge's Poetic Intelligence.* For charges of irrationality, see Edward Bostetter, "The Nightmare World of *The Ancient Mariner*"; James D. Boulger, "Christian Skepticism in *The Rime of the Ancient Mariner*"; Daniel McDonald, "Too Much Reality: A Discussion of 'The Rime of the Ancient Mariner' "; L. M. Grow, "*The Rime of the Ancient Mariner:* Multiple Veils of Illusion' "; Lorne J. Forstner, "Coleridge's 'The Ancient Mariner' and the Case for Justifiable 'Mythocide': An Argument on Psychological, Epistemological, and Formal Grounds"; and Lawrence Lipking, "The Marginal Gloss."

24. See, for example, the following passage in *Biographia:* "Thus to express in one word, all that appertains to the perception, considered as passive, and merely recipient, I have adopted from our elder classics the word *sensuous*" (1:109).

25. Coleridge uses the word "living" in contexts in which he opposes organicism to mechanism. He equates mechanic philosophy with death. Note the contrasts between "all the products of the mere *reflective* faculty" which partake of "DEATH" (*BL*, 1:98) and "life and progressive power" (*BL*, 1:104 n.); between the "*discursive* understanding" acquiring "a knowledge of superficies without substance" and "the IMAGINATION, impregnated with which the understanding itself becomes intuitive, and a living power" (*Lay Sermons*, p. 69). See particularly *Theory of Life* (app. C in *Aids to Reflection*, in *CW*, 1:373–416), where Coleridge proposes a theory of life in opposition to scientism, and concludes: "Life itself is not a *thing*—a self-subsistent *hypostasis*—but an *act* and *process*" (p. 416). For a strictly religious context, see *Confessions of an Inquiring Spirit:* "The Eternal I AM, the Ever-living Word, of whom all the elect from the arch-angel . . . to the poor wrestler with the spirit . . . are but the fainter and still fainter echoes" (p. 70).

26. See J. Shawcross (ed., *BL*) on Reason and the secondary Imagination as mental faculties belonging to part or all of mankind.

27. In *BL* Coleridge writes that the "I AM" will be indiscriminately expressed "by the words spirit, self, and self-consciousness. In this, and in this alone, object and subject, being and knowing are identical, each involving, and supposing the other" (1:183). The coincidence of object and subject, the basis of all knowledge, is then effected when the primary Imagination informs perception.

28. *Nb*, 3:4066.

29. Marginal note to Schelling, *Phil. Briefe über Dogmatismus u. Kriticismus*, in *BL*, 1:lxxxv.

30. *Collected Letters of Samuel Taylor Coleridge*, 2:961. Henceforth, this edition will be cited as *CL*.

31. In *Nb*, 2:3158, Coleridge develops a metaphor of the philosopher lacking imagination, who is unable to transform essence into existence, and who instead uses forms devoid of meaning, currency without value.

32. *The Friend*, in *CW*, 1:522. Henceforth, this edition will be cited as *Friend*.

33. *OED*, "*translucent*," *a*. 2b. Although the more distinctive meaning of "translucent" came into usage in 1784 at the earliest, Coleridge does contrast the word with terms such as "opaque" and "transparent." The earliest usage listed, moreover, is in Cowper, with whose poetry Coleridge was well acquainted.

34. See *BL*, 2:238. The essay was written in 1814, four years earlier than the *Essays on Method*, and the subject is aesthetics, hence the orthodox censor is not present here as it is in the later work.

35. Ibid.

36. *Anima Poetae*, pp. 136–37.

37. *The Philosophical Lectures of Samuel Taylor Coleridge*, pp. 193–94.

38. See Walter Jackson Bate, *Coleridge*, pp. 179–81.

39. Notebook 29 (the "clasped vellum" Notebook), pp. 61–62, The Berg Collection of the New York Public Library. The Notebook covers the period from 1814 to 1825, and since Kathleen Coburn in the introduction to *Nb*, 3, writes that all entries including Notebook 29 thought to have been written between 1808 and March 1819 are contained in that volume, Coleridge's discussion on the symbol, which is absent from *Nb*, 3, must postdate March 1819.

40. *Coleridge's Miscellaneous Criticism*, p. 411. Henceforth, this edition will be cited as *MC*. Coleridge's disappointment with Wordsworth was double-edged, for, though Wordsworth did not fulfill Coleridge's prophecy by writing the philosophical poem, Coleridge endeavored to create a system of philosophy, but without success. See Thomas McFarland, *Romanticism and the Forms of Ruin: Wordsworth, Coleridge, and Modalities of Fragmentation*, for Wordsworth's and Coleridge's failed enterprises.

41. In his view of Nature, Wordsworth compares favorably with Bowles (*CL*, 2:1034), but comes short of Shakespeare and Cervantes (*MC*, p. 99).
42. *CL*, 2:714. Coleridge precedes his comment with the question, "Have you seen the second Volume of the Lyrical Ballads, & the Preface prefixed to the first?" In the rest of the passage, he indicates only the profoundest respect for Wordsworth's powers as a poet and no dissatisfaction with his poetic theory.
43. Passion, for Coleridge, distinguishes poetry from other types of composition, and he faults another idol of his youth, Bowles, for lacking it (ibid., p. 864).
44. Coleridge's extensive annotations of copies of *Friend*, reissued in three volumes in 1818, as well as letters to his friends clarifying his position when their copies did not contain the long additions, testify to his extreme anxiety that his statements not be taken to be pantheistic. His note, inserted after a passage on substantive and abstract knowledge, insists that, lacking faith and left to its own powers, the intellect is insufficient for the proper apprehension of Nature, confuses "the Creator with the Aggregate of his creatures," and, when refusing "to acknowledge a higher or deeper ground than it can itself supply," leads to pantheism, whose consequences are atheism (1:522–23, n.1).
45. See also *BL*, 2:42–43.
46. See *Coleridge on Logic and Learning, with Selections from the Unpublished Manuscripts*, pp. 126–27.
47. See also *BL*, 2:11.
48. Coleridge, *Poetical Works*, p. 178. Henceforth, this edition will be cited as *PW*.
49. See *BL*, 1:202 (where Coleridge relegates to the law of association the "fixities and definites," the "materials ready made" with which Fancy and memory play), and p. 77.
50. See Magnuson, *Coleridge's Nightmare Poetry*, pp. 16–17.
51. Note Reeve Parker's discussion of the *sententia* in *Coleridge's Meditative Art*, pp. 38–39.
52. Coleridge included ll. 26–33 as they are in the *Errata* of *Sibylline Leaves*, 1817, but did not see them in print until 1828. On the revisions, see Magnuson, *Coleridge's Nightmare Poetry*, and Abrams, "Coleridge's 'A Light in Sound.' "
53. The version of *Sibylline Leaves* does not vary substantially from the 1803 version, but does from the 1828 version. The early versions of 1796 and 1797 move directly from l. 25 of the present text to l. 34, as does the second draft of "Effusion 35" (*PW*, app. 1, p. 520).
54. For this insertion, see Abrams, "Coleridge's 'A Light in Sound,' " pp. 468–70.
55. See Jones, "Coleridge and Poetry," p. 115, and Michael Cooke, "The Manipulation of Space in Coleridge's Poetry," p. 184.
56. Mark Littmann, "The Ancient Mariner and Initiation Rites."
57. For similarities with other Romantic Quests, see my article, "*The Rime of the Ancient Mariner* as Romantic Quest."
58. For Coleridge, belief in the supernatural agency of forms of Nature is a delusion (*BL*, 2:5).
59. The original meaning of the word "bless," according to the *OED*, is "to make 'sacred' or holy with blood."
60. The "Letter to [Asra]" is published in the app. to George Whalley, *Coleridge and Sara Hutchinson and the Asra Poems*, pp. 155–64.
61. While Coleridge continues to explore the mind/Nature dialogue in such poems as "To William Wordsworth," "To Nature," and "Constancy to an Ideal Object," his most powerful poetry contains a devotional strain combined with the confessional which seems to anticipate Gerard Manley Hopkins's work

(see particularly "The Pains of Sleep," "The Visionary Hope," "Human Life," "Limbo," "Ne Plus Ultra," and "Work without Hope").
62. Sara Coleridge, in *BL*, in *The Complete Works*, 3:36 n.
63. *Lectures, 1795: On Politics and Religion*, in *CW*, 1:339.
64. *Aids to Reflection*, in *The Complete Works*, 1:252 n. Henceforth, this edition will be cited as *AR*.
65. *Letters of Samuel Taylor Coleridge*, 2:742–43.
66. Cf. the 1825 letter to Gillman with *Nb*, 3:4060, 1811, in which Coleridge proclaims the mind's independence from Nature in triumphant terms.

CHAPTER THREE

1. See Robert Vivier, *L'Originalité de Baudelaire*, pp. 117–19.
2. See Jack Stillinger, "The Order of Poems in Keats's First Volume."
3. Barbey D'Aurevilly refers to the "secret architecture" in one of the first reviews of *Les Fleurs du Mal* in "Articles justificatifs pour Charles Baudelaire, auteur des *Fleurs du Mal*," in *Les Fleurs du Mal*, pp. 410–19. "Architecture" has since become a frequently used term in relation to the unity of *Les Fleurs du Mal*.
4. William Wordsworth, *The Prelude, Selected Poems and Sonnets*, p. 198.
5. *Correspondance*, 2:615. Henceforth, this edition will be cited as *Corr*. The translations in the text are the author's. See also *Corr.*, 1:364, 2:196. In "Notes pour mon avocat" (*OC*, 1:193–96), Baudelaire refers to *Les Fleurs du Mal* as a whole work, the morality of which should be judged only in terms of its totality. The parallels between the prose poems and the lyrics are conscious. Sometimes, as in "Un Monde dans une Chevelure" and "La Chevelure," even the titles are similar.
6. Baudelaire shows some marginal knowledge of Shelley, alludes to Tennyson's "The Lotus Eaters" and "The Charge of the Light Brigade," has read Byron, and translates De Quincey's *Confessions of an Opium Eater*. For Baudelaire's acquaintance with English literature, see Francis Scarfe, "Baudelaire angliciste?"; Margaret Heinen Matheny, "Baudelaire's Knowledge of English Literature"; and Michael Shanks, "Coleridge et son influence sur la conception baudelairienne de l'imagination."
7. *Corr.*, 1:554. It appears from the evidence available to date that Baudelaire did not read either Coleridge's poetry or the prose works. He nowhere mentions Coleridge in his essays and mentions him only once, in passing, in his correspondence. Pichois tracks down the reference: Baudelaire is responding to Sainte-Beuve's request that he give Sainte-Beuve information about Poe's mentions of Coleridge. Baudelaire replies that he has had no time for "the Coleridge."
8. G. T. Clapton, "Baudelaire and Catherine Crowe"; Randolph Hughes, "Une Etape de l'esthétique de Baudelaire: Catherine Crowe"; Garnet Rees, "Baudelaire and the Imagination," pp. 203–15; Richard Beilharz, "*Fantaisie* et *Imagination* chez Baudelaire, Catherine Crowe et leurs prédécesseurs allemands."
9. See Lloyd James Austin, *L'Univers poétique de Baudelaire*, pp. 148–55; W. T. Bandy's edition of Baudelaire's *Edgar Allan Poe: Sa Vie et ses ouvrages*, pp. xi–xlvi; and Arnolds Grava, *L'Aspect métaphysique du Mal dans l'oeuvre littéraire de Charles Baudelaire et d'Edgar Allan Poe*, p. 8. For opposing views about Poe's influence on Baudelaire, see P. Mansell Jones, *The Background of Modern French Poetry: Essays and Interviews*, pp. 38–58, and M. H. Abrams, "Coleridge, Baudelaire, and Modernist Poetics."
10. Baudelaire has an ambivalent attitude toward the towering domineering figure of Victor Hugo, whom he alternately courts, flatters, and attacks, but

he acknowledges his debt to Hugo in *Réflexions sur mes contemporains*, as well as in the dedication of the great poems of the cycle "Parisian Scenes" in *Les Fleurs du Mal*. To Vigny, he writes letters of profound respect and admiration and musters for him the most eloquent defense of the unity of *Les Fleurs du Mal* (*Corr.*, 2: 196). Sainte-Beuve is a lifelong friend and advisor, and, if Baudelaire, as the younger man, differs with him, he is careful to hide those opinions in order to maintain his relationship with "oncle Beuve." Finally, when Baudelaire scandalizes the French world of established men of letters by introducing his candidacy for Lacordaire's chair at the académie Française, he justifies himself as a deserving successor because the man was a "*Romantique*" (*Corr.*, 2:198).

11. Note, for instance, F. W. Leakey, "Baudelaire: The Poet as Moralist"; Martin Turnell, *Baudelaire: A Study of His Poetry;* Léon Bopp, *Psychologie des Fleurs du Mal;* and Leo Bersani, *Baudelaire and Freud.*

12. Georges Bonneville, *Les Fleurs du Mal: Analyse Critique,* and J. M. Cocking, "The Texture of Sensibility in 'Les Fleurs du Mal.' "

13. René Galand, *Baudelaire: Poétiques et Poésie.*

14. Marcel Françon, "*L'Unité des Fleurs du Mal,*" and Marcel A. Ruff, *L'Esprit du mal et l'Esthétique baudelairienne.*

15. D. J. Mossop, in *Baudelaire's Tragic Hero: A Study of the Architecture of Les Fleurs du Mal,* opts for the 1861 edition; Albert Feuillerat, "L'Architecture des 'Fleurs du Mal,' " and Turnell, *Baudelaire,* find the 1861 edition less impressive in its unity.

16. Austin, *L'Univers poétique de Baudelaire,* and Vivier, *L'Originalité.*

17. See Austin, "Baudelaire: Poet or Prophet?"

18. Auerbach, "The Esthetic Dignity of the *Fleurs du Mal*"; Cocking, "The Texture of Sensibility"; Colin Burns, " 'Architecture Secrète': Notes on the Second Edition of 'Les Fleurs du Mal' "; Turnell, *Baudelaire;* and Bersani, *Baudelaire and Freud.*

19. Benjamin Fondane, *Baudelaire et l'expérience du gouffre,* p. 114.

20. Fondane chooses as archetypal situation of Baudelaire in his life and work vis-à-vis his audience Baudelaire's sketch titled "Le Joujou du Pauvre"; Galand analyzes the reversal of archetypes in Baudelaire's poetry. Fondane proposes the poet identification (pp. 168–80). See also Charles Mauron, "La Personnalité affective de Baudelaire," *Le Dernier Baudelaire,* and esp. "Premières Recherches sur la Structure inconsciente des *Fleurs du Mal.*"

21. See Pierre Emmanuel's *Baudelaire* and Alfred Engstrom's "Baudelaire's Title for 'Les Fleurs du Mal.' "

22. Northrop Frye notes this tendency of Romanticism in "The Drunken Boat: The Revolutionary Element in Romanticism," p. 17; see also Bernard Levine, *The Dissolving Image: The Spiritual-Esthetic Development of W. B. Yeats,* p. 144.

23. Baudelaire's development of cumulative meaning for symbols, a notable practice of English Romantics, is seen by several critics as evidence of a flagging vision and imaginative poverty: Peyre, *Qu'est-ce que le Romantisme?,* pp. 252–53; L. F. Benedetto, "L'Architecture des 'Fleurs du Mal' "; A. E. Carter, "Baudelaire"; and Marcel A. Ruff, *Baudelaire,* pp. 123–25.

24. René Wellek, *A History of Modern Criticism: 1750–1950,* and Austin, *L'Univers poétique,* hold that Baudelaire succeeds in his attempt to transform ugliness and tragedy. For an opposing view, see Luc Decaunes, "La Victoire esthétique de Baudelaire," and Turnell, *Baudelaire,* pp. 238, 290. Baudelaire's own views on the nature of poetic diction, on technique and its role in symbolization, appear most explicitly in *Salon de 1859* and *The Painter of Modern Life* (see *OC,* 2:612, 685).

25. Bersani, *Baudelaire and Freud,* p. 151.

26. The best poet is "the poet who puts himself in constant touch with the

men of his time and exchanges with them thoughts and feelings translated into a noble and satisfactorily exact language" (*OC*, 2:27). Note the vagueness of the last words.

27. "It dissolves, diffuses, dissipates, in order to re-create; or when this process is rendered impossible, yet still at all events it struggles to idealize and to unify" (*BL*, 1:202). "It is possible, and barely possible, to attain that ultimatum which I have ventured to propose as a blameless style" (*BL*, 2:115–16).

28. On sensitivity of heart and critical quality of imagination, see *OC*, 2:116–17; on adherence to form without imagination, see *OC*, 2:626–27.

29. *OC*, 2:133. See Coleridge's "Nature ne'er deserts the wise and pure," Chapter 2, p. 61.

30. Note the similarity of "*Le Confiteor de l'artiste*" with Coleridge's letter of 1825, in regard to the rarity of triumph in the mind's duel with nature (*OC*, 1:278–79).

31. See the section entitled "Jugements portés par l'Auteur sur son Livre," in *Les Fleurs du Mal*, and *Corr.*, 1:364, in which Baudelaire emphasizes his intention to participate in the ordering of his poems in their first edition (1857).

32. See Barbey D'Aurevilly, "Articles justificatifs pour Charles Baudelaire," pp. 403–6, 410–19.

33. You walk upon the dead with scornful glances,
    Among your gems Horror is not least fair;
    Murder, the dearest of your baubles, dances
    Upon your haughty breast with amorous air.

34. All forms receded, as in a dream were still,
    Where white visions vaguely start
    From the sketch of a painter's long-neglected idyll
    Into a perfect art!

35. Note the frequency of the word "temps" (time): according to Robert T. Cargo, *Concordance to Baudelaire's Fleurs du Mal*, the word appears seventeen times in the 1861 edition, thirteen of which are in poems of "Bile and the Ideal."

36. Author's translation for "A Landscape."

37. At this point of the Quest, the hero of *Les Fleurs du Mal* and the Mariner free themselves when they accept responsibility for the world of horror they see and when they rely upon the imagination to redeem it.

38. See Karlheinz Stierle, "Baudelaire and the Tradition of the *Tableau de Paris*." For an opposing view see Burns, " 'Architecture Secrète.' "

39. Author's translation for "The Swan."

40. Note the resemblance between the obsessively multiplied curse in *The Rime* with the events of "The Seven Old Men."

41. For the importance of "Wine" to *Les Fleurs du Mal*, see Mossop, *Baudelaire's Tragic Hero*, p. 195; Ruff, *L'Esprit du Mal;* Abraham Avni, "A Revaluation of Baudelaire's 'Le Vin': Its Originality and Significance for *Les Fleurs du mal*"; and Peter Hambly, "The Structure of *Les Fleurs du Mal:* Another Suggestion."

42. See *OC*, vol. 1; Notes et Variantes, 1049–51, mss. A and B of 1852 and variants of 1854; the change does not occur until the 1857 revision.

43. Note the resemblance between the creations of the fragmented psyche in the cycle of "Flowers of Evil" and in Coleridge's "Fears in Solitude" and "Dejection."

44. Each luminous and fragile whole
    Lifts like a thought,
    Then spits its little spray of soul
    Out and is not.

45. Author's translation for "The Voyage."

CHAPTER FOUR

1. William Butler Yeats, *A Vision*, p. 94. Henceforth, this edition will be cited as *Vision*.
2. W. B. Yeats, *The Autobiography of William Butler Yeats*, pp. 91, 111–12. Henceforth, this edition will be cited as *A*.
3. *Uncollected Prose by W. B. Yeats*, 1:248. Henceforth, this edition will be cited as *Uncoll.*
4. *A*, pp. 188–89; see also *E&I*, pp. 424–25, where Yeats connects the tragedy of the Rhymers with Shelley's influence on their lives.
5. See *A*, pp. 192–93; *Uncoll.*, 1: "A Symbolical Drama in Paris" and "Verlaine in 1894."
6. See especially Harold Bloom, *Yeats*, and George Bornstein, *Yeats and Shelley* and *Transformations of Romanticism in Yeats, Eliot and Stevens*. Note also Hazard Adams, *Blake and Yeats: The Contrary Vision;* W. Y. Tindall, "The Symbolism of W. B. Yeats"; B. D. Cheadle, "Yeats and Symbolism"; George Mills Harper, "Yeats's Quest for Eden"; Margaret Rudd, *Divided Image: A Study of William Blake and W. B. Yeats;* and W. H. Stevenson, "Yeats and Blake: The Use of Symbols."
7. Donoghue, *William Butler Yeats*, p. 132; "Yeats and Modern Poetry"; and "Tradition, Poetry, and W. B. Yeats." Frye, "Yeats and the Language of Symbolism," p. 220. Frank Kermode, *The Sense of an Ending*, pp. 105, 106, 108. For Bloom, see 'The Composite God," in *Yeats*, pp. 470–71. Alex Zwerdling, "W. B. Yeats: Variations on the Visionary Quest"; George Mills Harper, "Yeats's Quest for Eden"; Richard Ellmann, *The Identity of Yeats*, pp. xvii, 4, 225, and *Yeats: The Man and the Masks*, pp. 285, 291; and Thomas Parkinson, "The Modernity of Yeats."
8. Donald Davie, "Yeats, Berkeley, and Romanticism"; Cleanth Brooks, "Yeats: The Poet as Myth-Maker," and "W. B. Yeats as a Literary Critic," in *A Shaping Joy: Studies in the Writer's Craft;* and Allen Tate, "Yeats's Romanticism: Notes and Suggestions." Among anti-Romantic critics are Frank Lentricchia, *The Gaiety of Language: An Essay on the Radical Poetics of W. B. Yeats and Wallace Stevens*, pp. 55–58, and Malcolm Magaw, "Yeats and Keats: The Poetics of Romanticism."
9. It is curious that, apart from Bloom's, no voice like Auerbach's or Abrams's on Baudelaire is heard about Yeats's inhuman aspect in the poetry, where admittedly it appears least, or in the prose and plays, where it is much more in evidence. The fact is all the more curious considering the resolute attacks of Abrams and Auerbach against Baudelaire, whose poetry and essays are freer by far from horrific historical and cultural judgments than those of Yeats.
10. See chapter 1, note 21.
11. Note Ellmann, in his *Yeats* and *The Identity of Yeats;* W. Y. Tindall, in "The Symbolism of W. B. Yeats," pp. 267–68; and George Brandon Saul, in "In . . . Luminous Wind."
12. Arthur Symons, "Dante Gabriel Rossetti," in *Figures of Several Centuries*, p. 202, and *The Symbolist Movement in Literature*, pp. 114–15.
13. Frank Kermode, *Romantic Image*, pp. 63, 111; Graham Hough, *The Last Romantics*, pp. 192–95, 211–15.
14. Edward Engelberg, *The Vast Design: Patterns in W. B. Yeats's Aesthetic*, pp. 111–12; Peter Ure, *Towards a Mythology: Studies in the Poetry of W. B. Yeats*, p. 56.
15. See, for instance, Cheadle, "Yeats and Symbolism"; Donald Stauffer, *The Golden Nightingale: Essays on Some Principles of Poetry in the Lyrics of William Butler Yeats*, pp. 28–30; and Dwight Eddins, *Yeats: The Nineteenth Century Matrix*, pp. 132–33.

Notes to Pages 140–54

16. Northrop Frye, "Yeats and the Language of Symbolism," and Theodor Klimeck, *Symbol und Wirklichkeit bei W. B. Yeats*, are two who do so.
17. Note Gayatri Spivak, "A Stylistic Contrast between Yeats and Mallarmé."
18. For my reading of Yeats's cyclical structure I am indebted to Denis Donoghue, who, in *William Butler Yeats*, emphasizes Yeats's poetry of process and the dialectical relationship of the books in *Collected Poems;* to Richard Ellmann, who, in *Yeats* and *The Identity of Yeats*, traces Yeats's development of an *oeuvre;* and to John Unterecker, who gives the most detailed study of the dialectical structure of Yeats's cycles in *A Reader's Guide to William Butler Yeats*.
19. Yeats levels the charge of femininity and passivity of mind at "the ideal of culture expressed by Pater" and the followers of that ideal, *A*, pp. 289–90.
20. Symons, *The Symbolist Movement*, p. 115. Algernon Charles Swinburne, in *William Blake: A Critical Essay*, writes about Baudelaire's achievement of deep "unison of sense and spirit" (p. 100).
21. Arthur Symons, trans., *Charles Baudelaire: Prose and Poetry*, p. vi.
22. Swinburne, *William Blake*, pp. 100–103.
23. Symons, *The Symbolist Movement*, p. 115.
24. In "From Puzzle to Paradox: New Light on Yeats's Late Career," James Lovic Allen speculates that Yeats himself belonged to phase 13.
25. Yeats begins his assessment of Romantic precursors as followers of the unfulfilled dream which separates them from life early in his essays and, with few reappraisals, maintains the same thesis throughout. For Rossetti's and Shelley's pursuit of the star, "mother of impossible hope," which cuts one off from nature, see *E&I*, pp. 53–54 (1902); for Blake's incommunicability and the *dividing* power of the imagination, which separates us from mortality, see *E&I*, pp. 111–12 (1897); for the inner strife and loss of contact with reality in Coleridge, Villiers de l'Isle d'Adam, and Blake, see *E&I*, p. 128 (1897); finally, see Yeats's strongest indictment of Shelley's quest and its influence upon the tragic life of his friends, as well as a restatement of Blake's isolation because of his "arbitrary symbolism," *E&I*, pp. 424–25 (1932).
26. *The Variorum Edition of the Poems of W. B. Yeats*. All quotations from Yeats's poetry will be from this edition and will be accompanied by line numbers in parentheses when necessary. Henceforth, this edition will be cited as *VP*.
27. See Bornstein, *Transformations of Romanticism*, p. 72.
28. See particularly "He Mourns for the Change That Has Come upon Him and His Beloved, and Longs for the End of the World," "The Valley of the Black Pig," "He Hears the Cry of the Sedge," and "The Secret Rose."
29. For the hint of castration see Allen R. Grossman, *Poetic Knowledge in the Early Yeats: A Study of the Wind among the Reeds*, pp. 192–93.
30. Stephen Maxfield Parrish, ed., and James Allan Printer, programmer, *A Concordance to the Poems of W. B. Yeats*, pp. 221–23.
31. When Yeats wishes to distinguish between allegory and symbol, he either relies on Blake and uses much of the traditional Romantic terminology that presents allegory as static and symbol as dynamic, or he produces his own criterion, which consists of "wizard frenzy" in the act of symbol-making, of coldness in that of allegory-making (*E&I*, p. 382). The only instance in which allegory can be accepted as moving is when it contains "enough sheer passion" to make one forget that it is allegory.
32. W. B. Yeats, *Memoirs*, ed. Denis Donoghue, pp. 224–25.
33. Yeats writes that in his fervor there was "much patriotism and more desire for a fair woman" (*Memoirs*, p. 59).
34. Compare Yeats's poems "In the Firelight" (*Letters*, p. 110) and "Lapis Lazuli."

35. Note the context of the other poems in *Michael Robartes and the Dancer*. In "A Prayer for my Daughter" Yeats devotes much thought to ways of preserving his child from being uprooted by the coming frenzy. The last lines of the poem that concludes the cycle are "When all is ruin once again," "all" being Yeats's attempt to create a historical symbol for his art, the tower, and meaning the whole of civilization.

36. See Harold Bloom, *Poetry and Repression: Revisionism from Blake to Stevens*, p. 218.

37. W. B. Yeats, *Explorations*, p. 392. Henceforth, this edition will be cited as *Ex*.

38. *Shakespearean Criticism*, 2:99.

39. For an opposite opinion, see Robert Langbaum, *The Mysteries of Identity: A Theme in Modern Literature*, p. 172.

40. For early versions of "Among School Children," see Thomas Parkinson's *W. B. Yeats: The Later Poetry*, pp. 104–5.

41. For a detailed discussion of the Coleridgean allusion in Yeats's poem, see William Elford Rogers, "Yeats's 'Long-Legged Fly' and Coleridge's *Biographia Literaria*."

42. In letters spanning 1916–35, Yeats writes that birdsong "is perhaps subjective, and expression of feeling alone," and that likewise art has similar freedom from imitation: "In the last analysis there will always be an intensity of pattern that we have never seen with our eyes" (*Letters*, p. 607). Almost thirty years later, Yeats emphasizes the psychic wholeness of song: "I want to plunge myself into impersonal poetry, to get rid of the bitterness, irritation and hatred that my work in Ireland has brought into my soul. I want to make a last song, sweet and exultant . . . not doctrine but song" (p. 836).

43. For differing views on the setting of "Cuchulain Comforted," see Helen Hennessy Vendler, *Yeats's Vision and the Later Plays*, pp. 247–51; Bloom, *Poetry and Repression*, p. 231; and Langbaum, *The Mysteries of Identity*, pp. 234–35.

44. See Bornstein, *Transformations of Romanticism*, pp. 86–87.

45. See Parkinson, *W. B. Yeats*, p. 107.

46. I am following Yeats's own arrangement of *Last Poems* as demonstated by Curtis Bradford in "Yeats's Last Poems Again."

47. See Curtis Bradford, *Yeats at Work*, pp. 162–63.

48. For a number of recent studies see M. Jawiga Swiatecka, *The Idea of the Symbol: Some Nineteenth-Century Comparisons with Coleridge;* Emerson R. Marks, *Coleridge on the Language of Verse;* John Beer, *Wordsworth and the Human Heart*, a study of Wordsworth's emotional attachment to Dorothy and Coleridge and of his intellectual dependence on Coleridge; Thomas McFarland, *Romanticism and the Forms of Ruin: Wordsworth, Coleridge, and Modalities of Fragmentation;* and Kathleen M. Wheeler, *The Creative Mind in Coleridge's Poetry*, whose argument touches on the one I advanced in my "*Reintegration of the Mind:* Symbolization in Coleridge, Baudelaire, and Yeats," Ph.D dissertation, University of Michigan, 1977.

49. Tzvetan Todorov, *Théories du symbole*, p. 340.

50. Note McFarland's assertion in *Romanticism and the Forms of Ruin* that the Romantics' humanity is more evident in their failures than in their aspirations (p. 216); and Tilottama Rajan's argument in *Dark Interpreter: The Discourse of Romanticism* that Coleridge's poetry ultimately fails because of his vacillation between sentimentality and irony.

BIBLIOGRAPHY

Abrams, M. H. "Coleridge, Baudelaire, and Modernist Poetics." In *Immanente Aesthetik-Aesthetische Reflexion: Lyric als Paradigma der Moderne*, edited by Wolfgang Iser, pp. 113–38. Munich: Wilhelm Fink, 1966.

―――. "Coleridge's 'A Light in Sound': Science, Metascience, and Poetic Imagination." *Proceedings of the American Philosophical Society*, no. 116 (1972), pp. 458–76.

―――. *The Mirror and the Lamp: Romantic Theory and the Critical Tradition*. New York: Oxford University Press, 1953.

―――. *Natural Supernaturalism: Tradition and Revolution in Romantic Literature*. New York: W. W. Norton, 1971.

―――. "Structure and Style in the Greater Romantic Lyric." In *From Sensibility to Romanticism: Essays Presented to Frederick A. Pottle*, edited by Frederick W. Hilles and Harold Bloom, pp. 527–60. New York: Oxford University Press, 1965.

Adams, Hazard. *Blake and Yeats: The Contrary Vision*. Ithaca, N.Y.: Cornell University Press, 1955; reprint ed., New York: Russell and Russell, 1968.

Alexander, Ian W. "The Consciousness of Time in Baudelaire." In *Studies in Modern French Literature presented to P. Mansell Jones*, edited by Lloyd James Austin, Garnet Rees, and Eugène Vinaver, pp. 1–17. Manchester: Manchester University Press, 1961.

Allen, James Lovic. "From Puzzle to Paradox: New Light on Yeats's Late Career." *Sewanee Review* 82 (1974): 81–92.

Appleyard, J. A. "Coleridge and Criticism: I. Critical Theory." In *Writers and Their Backgrounds: S. T. Coleridge*, edited by R. L. Brett, pp. 123–46. London: G. Bell & Sons, 1971.

Auerbach, Erich. "The Esthetic Dignity of the *Fleurs du Mal*." *Hopkins Review* 4 (1950): 29–45.

Austin, Lloyd James. "Baudelaire: Poet or Prophet?" In *Studies in Modern French Literature Presented to P. Mansell Jones*, edited by Lloyd James Austin, Garnet Rees, and Eugène Vinaver, pp. 18–34. Manchester: Manchester University Press, 1961.

―――. *L'Univers poétique de Baudelaire: Symbolisme et symbolique*. Paris: Mercure de France, 1956.

Avni, Abraham. "A Revaluation of Baudelaire's 'Le Vin': Its Originality and Significance for *Les Fleurs du Mal*." *French Review* 44 (December 1970): 310–21.

Baker, James Volant. *The Sacred River: Coleridge's Theory of the Imagination*. Baton Rouge: Louisiana State University Press, 1957.

Bibliography

Barfield, Owen. *What Coleridge Thought.* Middletown, Conn.: Wesleyan University Press, 1971.
Barth, J. Robert. *Coleridge and Christian Doctrine.* Cambridge, Mass.: Harvard University Press, 1969.
———. "Symbol as Sacrament in Coleridge's Thought." *Studies in Romanticism* 11 (1972): 320–31.
———. *The Symbolic Imagination: Coleridge and the Symbolic Tradition.* Princeton: Princeton University Press, 1977.
Bate, Walter Jackson. *Coleridge.* New York: Macmillan, 1968.
Baudelaire, Charles. *Correspondance.* 2 vols. Edited by Claude Pichois with Jean Ziegler. Paris: Bibliothèque de la Pléïade, 1973.
———. *Edgar Allan Poe: Sa Vie et ses ouvrages.* Edited by W. T. Bandy. Toronto: University of Toronto Press, 1973.
———. *Les Fleurs du Mal.* Edited by Jacques Crépet and Georges Blin. Reedited by Georges Blin and Claude Pichois. Paris: José Corti, 1968.
———. *The Flowers of Evil.* Edited by Marthiel Mathews and Jackson Mathews. Rev. Ed., Norfolk, Conn.: New Directions, 1962.
———. *Oeuvres Complètes.* 2 vols. Edited by Claude Pichois. Paris: Bibliothèque de la Pléïade, 1975.
Beer, John. *Coleridge the Visionary.* London: Chatto and Windus, 1959.
———. *Coleridge's Poetic Intelligence.* London: Macmillan, 1977.
———. *Wordsworth and the Human Heart.* New York: Columbia University Press, 1978.
Beilharz, Richard. "*Fantaisie* et *Imagination* chez Baudelaire, Catherine Crowe et leurs prédécesseurs allemands." In *Baudelaire: Actes du Colloque de Nice*, pp. 30–40. Monaco: Minard, 1968.
Benedetto, L. F. "L'Architecture des 'Fleurs du Mal.'" *Zeitschrift für Französische Sprache und Literatur* 39 (1912): 18–70.
Benjamin, Walter. *A Lyric Poet in the Era of High Capitalism.* Translated by Harry Zohn. London: NBL, 1973.
Bernstein, Gene M. "Self-Creating Artifices: Coleridgean Imagination and Language." *Modern Philology* 76, no. 3 (1979): 240–58.
Bersani, Leo. *Baudelaire and Freud.* Berkeley and Los Angeles: University of California Press, 1977.
Bialostosky, Don H. "Coleridge's Interpretation of Wordsworth's Preface to *Lyrical Ballads.*" *PMLA* 93 (1978): 912–24.
Bloom, Harold. *The Anxiety of Influence: A Theory of Poetry.* New York: Oxford University Press, 1973.
———. "The Internalization of Quest Romance." *Yale Review* 58, no. 4 (Summer 1969): 526–36; rpt. in *Romanticism and Consciousness: Essays in Criticism*, edited by Harold Bloom, pp. 3–23. New York: W. W. Norton, 1970.
———. *Poetry and Repression: Revisionism from Blake to Stevens.* New Haven: Yale University Press, 1976.
———. *Shelley's Mythmaking.* New Haven: Yale University Press, 1959.
———. *The Visionary Company.* 2d ed. 1961; rpt. Ithaca, N.Y.: Cornell University Press, 1971.
———. *Yeats.* New York: Oxford University Press, 1970.
———. "Yeats and the Romantics." In *Modern Poetry: Essays in Criticism*, edited by John Hollander, pp. 501–2. New York: Oxford University Press, 1968.
Bonneville, Georges. *Les Fleurs du Mal: Analyse Critique.* Paris: Hatier, 1972.
Bopp, Léon. *Psychologie des Fleurs du Mal.* 4 vols. Geneva: Librairie Droz, 1964.
Borgal, Clément. *Baudelaire.* Paris: Editions Universitaires, 1961.

Bibliography

Bornstein, George. *Transformations of Romanticism in Yeats, Eliot, and Stevens.* Chicago: University of Chicago Press, 1976.
———. *Yeats and Shelley.* Chicago: University of Chicago Press, 1970.
Bostetter, Edward. "The Nightmare World of *The Ancient Mariner*." *Studies in Romanticism* 1 (1962): 241–54; rpt. in *Coleridge: A Collection of Critical Essays.* Edited by Kathleen Coburn, pp. 65–77. Englewood Cliffs, N.J.: Prentice-Hall, 1967.
Boulger, James D. "Christian Skepticism in *The Rime of the Ancient Mariner*." In *From Sensibility to Romanticism: Essays Presented to Frederick A. Pottle,* edited by Frederick W. Hilles and Harold Bloom, pp. 439–52. New York: Oxford University Press, 1965.
———. "Coleridge on Imagination Revisited." *Wordsworth Circle* 4 (1973): 13–24.
———. "Imagination and Speculation in Coleridge's Conversation Poems." *Journal of English and Germanic Philology* 64 (1965): 691–711.
Bradford, Curtis. *Yeats at Work.* Carbondale: Southern Illinois University Press, 1965.
———. "Yeats's Last Poems Again." In *The Dolmen Press Yeats Centenary Papers,* edited by Liam Miller, pp. 257–88. Dublin: Dolmen Press, 1966.
Brombert, Victor. "T. S. Eliot and the Heresy of Romanticism." *Yale French Studies* 13 (Spring-Summer 1954): 3–16.
Brooks, Cleanth. *Modern Poetry and the Tradition.* Chapel Hill: University of North Carolina Press, 1939.
———. *A Shaping Joy: Studies in the Writer's Craft.* London: Methuen, 1971.
———. "Yeats: The Poet as Myth-Maker." *Southern Review* 4 (Summer 1938): 116–42.
Broughton, Panthea Reid. "The Modifying Metaphor in 'Dejection: An Ode.' " *Wordsworth Circle* 4 (1973); 241–49.
Buchan, A. M. "The Sad Wisdom of the Mariner." *Studies in Philology* 61 (1964): 669–88.
Burns, Colin. " 'Architecture Secrète': Notes on the Second Edition of 'Les Fleurs du Mal.' " *Nottingham French Studies* 5 (October 1966): 67–69.

Cargo, Robert T. *Concordance to Baudelaire's Fleurs du Mal.* Chapel Hill: University of North Carolina Press, 1965.
Carter, A. E. "Baudelaire." *University of Toronto Quarterly* 29 (1959): 59–76.
Cheadle, B. D. "Yeats and Symbolism." *English Studies in Africa* 12 (September 1969): 132–50.
Clapton, G. T. "Baudelaire and Catherine Crowe." *Modern Language Review* 25 (1930): 286–305.
Cocking, J. M. "The Texture of Sensibility in 'Les Fleurs du Mal.' " *Essays in French Literature* 6 (November 1969): 18–35.
Coleridge, S. T. *Aids to Reflection.* Edited by H. N. Coleridge. Vol. 1, *The Complete Works of Samuel Taylor Coleridge.*
———. *Anima Poetae.* Edited by E. H. Coleridge. London: William Heinemann, 1895.
———. *Biographia Literaria.* Edited by H. N. Coleridge. Vol. 3, *The Complete Works of Samuel Taylor Coleridge.*
———. *Biographia Literaria and Aesthetical Essays.* Edited by J. Shawcross. 2 vols. Oxford: Oxford University Press, 1907; reprint ed., 1962.
———. *Coleridge on Logic and Learning, with Selections from the Unpublished Manuscripts.* Edited by Alice D. Snyder. London: Oxford University Press; New Haven: Yale University Press, 1929.
———. *Coleridge: Poetical Works.* Edited by E. H. Coleridge. New York: Oxford University Press, 1912; reprint ed., 1969.

Bibliography

———. *Coleridge's Miscellaneous Criticism.* Edited by Thomas Middleton Raysor. Cambridge, Mass.: Harvard University Press, 1936.
———. *Collected Letters of Samuel Taylor Coleridge.* Edited by E. L. Griggs. 6 vols. Oxford: Clarendon Press, 1956.
———. *The Collected Works of Samuel Taylor Coleridge.* Edited by Kathleen Coburn. London: Routledge and Kegan Paul; Princeton: Princeton University Press, 1969–.
———. *The Complete Works of Samuel Taylor Coleridge.* Edited by Shedd. 7 vols. New York: Harper and Brothers, 1853.
———. *Confessions of an Inquiring Spirit.* Edited by H. St. J. Hart, B. D. 3d ed. 1853; reprint ed., Stanford: Stanford University Press, 1957.
———. *The Friend.* Edited by Barbara E. Rooke. 2 vols. Vol. 4, *The Collected Works of Samuel Taylor Coleridge.*
———. *Lay Sermons.* Edited by R. J. White. Vol. 6, *The Collected Works of Samuel Taylor Coleridge.*
———. *Lectures, 1795: On Politics and Religion.* Edited by Lewis Patton and Peter Mann. Vol. 1, *The Collected Works of Samuel Taylor Coleridge.*
———. *Letters of Samuel Taylor Coleridge.* Edited by E. H. Coleridge. 2 vols. Boston, 1895.
———. *The Notebooks of Samuel Taylor Coleridge.* Edited by Kathleen Coburn. 3 vols. New York: Pantheon Books, 1957–62.
———. *The Philosophical Lectures of Samuel Taylor Coleridge.* Edited by Kathleen Coburn. New York: Philosophical Library, 1949.
———. *Shakespearean Criticism.* Edited by Thomas Middleton Raysor. 2 vols. London: Dent; New York: Dutton, 1960.
Cooke, Michael. "The Manipulation of Space in Coleridge's Poetry." In *New Perspectives of Coleridge and Wordsworth: Selected Papers from the English Institute,* edited by Geoffrey Hartman, pp. 165–94. New York: Columbia University Press, 1972.

Davie, Donald. "Yeats, Berkeley, and Romanticism." *Irish Writing* 31 (Summer 1955): 36–41.
Decaunes, Luc. "La Victoire esthétique de Baudelaire." *Cahiers du Sud,* no. 308 (1951), pp. 114–29.
Dekker, George. *Coleridge and the Literature of Sensibility.* London: Vision Press, 1978.
Dickstein, Morris. "Coleridge, Wordsworth, and the 'Conversation Poems.' " *Centennial Review* 16 (1972): 367–83.
Donoghue, Denis. *The Sovereign Ghost: Studies in Imagination.* Berkeley and Los Angeles: University of California Press, 1976.
———. "Tradition, Poetry, and W. B. Yeats." *Sewanee Review* 69 (1961): 476–84.
———. *William Butler Yeats.* New York: Viking Press, 1971.
———. "Yeats and Modern Poetry." In *The Integrity of Yeats,* edited by Denis Donoghue, pp. 9–20. Cork, Ireland: Mercier Press, 1964.

Eddins, Dwight. *Yeats: The Nineteenth-Century Matrix.* University: University of Alabama Press, 1971.
Edel, Leon. *The Modern Psychological Novel.* New York: Grosset and Dunlap, 1955; rev. ed., 1961.
Eliot, T. S. *For Lancelot Andrews: Essays on Style and Order.* London: Faber and Gwyer, 1928.
Ellmann, Richard. *The Identity of Yeats.* New York: Oxford University Press, 1954; reprint ed., 1975.
———. *Yeats: The Man and the Masks.* New York: Macmillan, 1948; reprint ed., New York: E. P. Dutton, n.d.

Bibliography

———. "Yeats without Analogue." *Kenyon Review* 26 (1964): 30-47; rpt. in *Modern Poetry: Essays in Criticism*, edited by John Hollander, pp. 395-410. New York: Oxford University Press, 1968.
Emmanuel, Pierre. *Baudelaire*. Bruges, Belgium: Editions Desclée de Brouwer, 1967.
Engelberg, Edward. *The Vast Design: Patterns in W. B. Yeats's Aesthetic*. Toronto: University of Toronto Press, 1964.
Engstrom, Alfred. "Baudelaire's Title for 'Les Fleurs du Mal.' " *Orbis Litterarum* 12, nos. 3-4 (1957): 193-202.

Feuillerat, Albert. "L'Architecture des 'Fleurs du Mal.' " In *Studies by the Members of the French Department of Yale University*, edited by Albert Feuillerat, pp. 221-330. New Haven: Yale University Press, 1941.
Fogle, R. H. "Coleridge's Conversation Poems." *Tulane Studies in English* 5 (1955): 103-10.
———. "Coleridge's Critical Principles." *Tulane Studies in English* 6 (1956): 57-69.
———. "The Genre of the Ancient Mariner." *Tulane Studies in English* 7 (1957): 111-24.
———. *The Idea of Coleridge's Criticism*. Berkeley and Los Angeles: University of California Press, 1962.
———. "Romantic Bards and Metaphysical Reviewers." *ELH* 12 (1945): 221-50.
Fondane, Benjamin, *Baudelaire et l'expérience du gouffre*. Paris: Editions Seghers, 1972.
Forstner, Lorne J. "Coleridge's 'The Ancient Mariner' and the Case for Justifiable 'Mythocide': An Argument on Psychological, Epistemological, and Formal Grounds." *Criticism* 18 (Summer 1976): 211-29.
Françon, Marcel. "L'Unité des *Fleurs du Mal*." *PMLA* 60 (1945): 1130-37.
Fruman, Norman. *Coleridge, the Damaged Archangel*. New York: George Braziller, 1971.
Frye, Northrop. *Anatomy of Criticism: Four Essays*. New York: Atheneum, 1967.
———. "The Drunken Boat: The Revolutionary Element in Romanticism." In *Romanticism Reconsidered: Selected Papers from the English Institute*, edited by Northrop Frye, pp. 1-25. New York: Columbia University Press, 1963.
———. *Fearful Symmetry: A Study of William Blake*. Princeton: Princeton University Press, 1947.
———. "Three Meanings of Symbolism." *Yale French Studies* 9 (1952): 11-19.
———. "Yeats and the Language of Symbolism." *University of Toronto Quarterly* 17 (October 1947): 1-17; rpt. in his *Fables of Identity: Studies in Poetic Mythology*. New York: Harcourt, Brace & World, 1963, pp. 218-37.

Galand, René. "Baudelaire, Formulary of the True Aesthetics." In *Baudelaire as a Love Poet and Other Essays*, edited by Lois Boe Hyslop, pp. 41-64. University Park: Pennsylvania State University Press, 1969.
———. *Baudelaire: Poétiques et Poésie*. Paris: Editions A. G. Nizet, 1969.
Gérard, Albert S. *English Romantic Poetry: Ethos, Structure, and Symbol in Coleridge, Wordsworth, Shelley, and Keats*. Berkeley and Los Angeles: University of California Press, 1968.
Grava, Arnolds. *L'Aspect métaphysique du mal dans l'oeuvre littéraire de Charles Baudelaire et d'Edgar Allan Poe*. Lincoln: University of Nebraska Press, 1956.
Grossman, Allen R. *Poetic Knowledge in the Early Yeats: A Study of The Wind among the Reeds*. Charlottesville: University Press of Virginia, 1969.

Bibliography

Grow, L. M. "*The Rime of the Ancient Mariner:* Multiple Veils of Illusion." *Notre Dame English Journal* 9 (Fall 1973): 23-29.

Hambly, Peter. "The Structure of *Les Fleurs du Mal:* Another Suggestion." *Australian Journal of French Studies* 8, no. 3 (1971): 269-96.

Harper, George McLean. "Coleridge's Conversation Poems." In *Spirit of Delight.* N.p.: Henry Holt, 1928; rpt. in *English Romantic Poets*, edited by M. H. Abrams, pp. 144-57. New York: Oxford University Press, 1960.

Harper, George Mills. "Yeats's Quest for Eden." In *The Dolmen Press Yeats Centenary Papers,* edited by Liam Miller, pp. 289-331. Dublin: Dolmen Press, 1966.

Hartman, Geoffrey. *Beyond Formalism: Literary Essays, 1958-1970.* New Haven: Yale University Press, 1970.

Haven, Richard. *Patterns of Consciousness: An Essay on Coleridge.* Amherst: University of Massachusetts Press, 1969.

Holstein, Michael E. "Poet into Priest: A Reading of Coleridge's 'Conversation Poems.' " *University of Toronto Quarterly* 48 (1979): 209-25.

Hough, Graham. *The Last Romantics.* London: Methuen; New York: Barnes and Noble, 1947; reprint ed., 1961.

House, Humphry. *Coleridge: The Clark Lectures, 1951-1952.* London: Rupert Hart-Davis, 1953.

Hughes, Randolph. "Une Etape de l'esthétique de Baudelaire: Catherine Crowe." *Revue de Littérature Comparée* 17 (1937): 680-99.

Jackson, J. R. de J. *Method and Imagination in Coleridge's Criticism.* Cambridge, Mass.: Harvard University Press, 1969.

Jakobson, Roman, and Claude Lévi-Strauss. " 'Les Chats' de Charles Baudelaire." *L'Homme*, no. 5 (January-April 1962), pp. 5-21.

James, D. G. *Skepticism and Poetry: An Essay on the Poetic Imagination.* London: George Allen and Unwin, 1937.

―――. "The Thought of Coleridge." In *The Major English Romantic Poets,* edited by Clarence D. Thorpe, Carlos Baker, and Bennett Weaver, pp. 100-112. Carbondale: Southern Illinois University Press, 1957.

Jones, A. R. "Coleridge and Poetry: II. The Conversational and Other Poems." In *Writers and Their Backgrounds: S. T. Coleridge,* edited by R. L. Brett, pp. 91-122. London: G. Bell & Sons, 1971.

Jones, P. Mansell. *The Background of Modern French Poetry: Essays and Interviews.* Cambridge: Cambridge University Press, 1951; reprint ed., 1968.

Katz, Marilyn. "Early Dissent between Wordsworth and Coleridge: Preface Deletion of October 1800." *Wordsworth Circle* 9 (1978): 50-56.

Kenner, Hugh. "The Sacred Book of the Arts." *Sewanee Review* 64 (1956): 574-90.

Kermode, Frank. *The Sense of an Ending: Studies in the Theory of Fiction.* New York: Oxford University Press, 1967.

―――. *Romantic Image.* London: Routledge and Kegan Paul, 1957; reprint ed., 1961.

Klimeck, Theodor. *Symbol und Wirklichkeit bei W. B. Yeats.* Bonn: H. Bouvier, 1967.

Langbaum, Robert. *The Mysteries of Identity: A Theme in Modern Literature.* New York: Oxford University Press, 1977.

―――. *The Poetry of Experience.* New York: Norton Library, 1957.

Leakey, F. W. *Baudelaire and Nature.* Manchester: Manchester University Press, 1969.

Bibliography

———. "Baudelaire: The Poet as Moralist." In *Studies in Modern French Literature Presented to P. Mansell Jones*, edited by Lloyd James Austin, Garnet Rees, and Eugène Vinaver, pp. 196–219. Manchester: Manchester University Press, 1961.
Leavis, F. R. *Revaluation*. London: Chatto and Windus, 1936.
Lentricchia, Frank. *The Gaiety of Language: An Essay on the Radical Poetics of W. B. Yeats and Wallace Stevens*. Berkeley and Los Angeles: University of California Press, 1968.
Levin, Harry. *The Gates of Horn: A Study of Five French Realists*. New York: Oxford University Press, 1963.
Levine, Bernard. *The Dissolving Image: The Spiritual-Esthetic Development of W. B. Yeats*. Detroit: Wayne State University Press, 1970.
Lipking, Lawrence. "The Marginal Gloss." *Critical Inquiry* 31 (1977): 609–55.
Littmann, Mark. "The Ancient Mariner and Initiation Rites." *Papers on Language and Literature* 4 (1968): 370–89.

Magaw, Malcolm. "Yeats and Keats: The Poetics of Romanticism." *Bucknell Review* 13, no. 3 (1965): 87–96.
Magnuson, Paul. *Coleridge's Nightmare Poetry*. Charlottesville: University Press of Virginia, 1974.
Marks, Emerson R. *Coleridge on the Language of Verse*. Princeton: Princeton University Press, 1981.
Matheny, Margaret Heinen. "Baudelaire's Knowledge of English Literature." *Revue de Littérature Comparée* 44 (1970): 98–117.
Mauron, Charles. *Le Dernier Baudelaire*. Paris: José Corti, 1966.
———. "La Personnalité affective de Baudelaire." *Orbis Litterarum* 12, nos. 3–4 (1957): 203–221.
———. "Premières Recherches sur la structure inconsciente des *Fleurs du Mal*." In *Baudelaire: Actes du Colloque de Nice*, pp. 131–37. Monaco: Minard, 1968.
McDonald, Daniel. "Too Much Reality: A Discussion of 'The Rime of the Ancient Mariner.' " *Studies in English Literature* 4 (1964): 543–54.
McFarland, Thomas. "The Origin and Significance of Coleridge's Theory of Secondary Imagination." In *New Perspectives of Coleridge and Wordsworth: Selected Papers from the English Institute*, edited by Geoffrey Hartman, pp. 195–246. New York: Columbia University Press, 1972.
———. *Romanticism and the Forms of Ruin: Wordsworth, Coleridge, and Modalities of Fragmentation*. Princeton: Princeton University Press, 1981.
Mellor, Anne K. "Coleridge's 'This Lime-Tree Bower My Prison' and the Categories of English Landscape." *Studies in Romanticism* 18 (1979): 253–70.
Mizener, Arthur. "The Romanticism of W. B. Yeats." *Southern Review* 7 (1941/42): 601–23.
Mossop, D. J. *Baudelaire's Tragic Hero: A Study of the Architecture of Les Fleurs du Mal*. London: Oxford University Press, 1961.

Oehler, Dolf. "Le Caractère double de l'héroïsme et du beau modernes." *Etudes Baudelairiennes* 8 (1977): 187–216.

Parker, Reeve. *Coleridge's Meditative Art*. Ithaca, N.Y.: Cornell University Press, 1975.
Parkinson, Thomas. "The Modernity of Yeats." *Southern Review* 6 (1969): 922–34.
———. *W. B. Yeats: The Later Poetry*. Berkeley and Los Angeles: University of California Press, 1971.
Parrish, Stephen Maxfield, ed., and James Allan Printer, programmer. *A Concor-*

Bibliography

dance to the Poems of W. B. Yeats. Ithaca, N.Y.: Cornell University Press, 1963.
Pearce, Donald. "Yeats and the Romantics." *Shenandoah* 8 (1957): 40–57.
Peyre, Henri. "Baudelaire as a Love Poet." In *Baudelaire as a Love Poet and Other Essays,* edited by Lois Boe Hyslop, pp. 3–39. University Park: Pennsylvania State University Press, 1969.
―――. *Qu'est-ce que le Romantisme?* Paris: Presses Universitaires de France, 1971.
Poulet, Georges. "Baudelaire, précurseur de la critique moderne." In *Journées Baudelaire: Actes du Colloque,* pp. 232–42. Brussels: Académie Royale de Langue et de Littérature Françaises, 1968.
Prickett, Stephen. *Coleridge and Wordsworth.* Cambridge: Cambridge University Press, 1970.

Rajan, Tilottama. *Dark Interpreter: The Discourse of Romanticism.* Ithaca, N.Y.: Cornell University Press, 1980.
Rees, Garnet. "Baudelaire and the Imagination." In *Modern Miscellany Presented to Eugène Vinaver,* edited by T. E. Lawrenson, F. E. Sutcliffe, and G. F. A. Gadoffre, pp. 203–15. Manchester: Manchester University Press; New York: Barnes and Noble, 1969.
Richards, I. A. *Coleridge on Imagination.* Bloomington, Indiana University Press, 1960.
Riffaterre, Michael. "Describing Poetic Structures: Two Approaches to Baudelaire's *Les Chats.*" In *Structuralism,* edited by Jacques Ehrmann, pp. 188–230. New York: Anchor Books, 1970.
Rogers, William Elford. "Yeats's 'Long-Legged Fly' and Coleridge's *Biographia Literaria.*" *Concerning Poetry* 8 (1975): 11–21.
Rudd, Margaret. *Divided Image: A Study of William Blake and W. B. Yeats.* London: Routledge and Kegan Paul, 1953.
Ruff, Marcel A. *Baudelaire.* Paris: Hatier, 1966.
―――. *L'Esprit du mal et l'esthétique baudelairienne.* Paris: Librairie Armand Colin, 1955.

Sabin, Margery. *English Romanticism and the French Tradition.* Cambridge, Mass.: Harvard University Press, 1976.
Saul, George Brandon. "In . . . Luminous Wind." In *The Dolmen Press Yeats Centenary Papers,* edited by Liam Miller, pp. 197–256. Dublin: Dolmen Press, 1966.
Savage, D. S. "The Aestheticism of W. B. Yeats." *Kenyon Review,* no. 7 (Winter 1945), pp. 118–34.
Scarfe, Francis. "Baudelaire angliciste?" *Etudes Anglaises* 21 (January-March 1968): 52–56.
Schulz, Max F. "Oneness and Multeity in Coleridge's Poems." *Tulane Studies in English* 9 (1959): 53–60.
Shaffer, Elinor S. *Kubla Khan and "The Fall of Jerusalem": The Mythological School in Biblical Criticism and Secular Literature, 1770–1800.* Cambridge: Cambridge University Press, 1975.
Shanks, Michael. "Coleridge et son influence sur la conception baudelairienne de l'imagination." In *L'Imagination créatrice: Actes mis en forme par Roselyne Chenu,* pp. 40–48. Neuchâtel, Switzerland: Editions de la Baconnière, 1971.
Spivak, Gayatri. "A Stylistic Contrast between Yeats and Mallarmé." *Language and Style* 5 (Spring 1972): 100–107.
Stauffer, Donald A. *The Golden Nightingale: Essays on Some Principles of Poetry in the Lyrics of William Butler Yeats.* New York: Macmillan, 1949.

Bibliography

Stevenson, W. H. "Yeats and Blake: The Use of Symbols." In *W. B. Yeats: Centenary Essays on the Art of W. B. Yeats*, edited by D.E.S. Maxwell and S. B. Bushrui, pp. 219–25. Ibadan, Nigeria: Ibadan University Press, 1965.
Stierle, Karlheinz. "Baudelaire and the Tradition of the *Tableau de Paris*." *New Literary History* 11 (1980): 345–61.
Stillinger, Jack. "The Order of Poems in Keats's First Volume." *Philological Quarterly* 48 (1969): 92–101.
Swiatecka, M. Jadwiga, O. P. *The Idea of the Symbol: Some Nineteenth-Century Comparisons with Coleridge*. Cambridge: Cambridge University Press, 1980.
Swinburne, Algernon Charles. *William Blake: A Critical Essay*. London: Chatto and Windus, 1906.
Symons, Arthur, trans. *Charles Baudelaire: Prose and Poetry*. New York: Albert and Charles Boni, 1926.
Symons, Arthur. *Figures of Several Centuries*. London: Constable, 1916.
———. *The Symbolist Movement in Literature*. Rev. and enlarged ed. New York: E. P. Dutton, 1919.

Tate, Allen. "Yeats's Romanticism: Notes and Suggestions." *Southern Review* 7 (1941–42): 591–600.
Teich, Nathaniel. "Coleridge's *Biographia* and the Contemporary Controversy about Style." *Wordsworth Circle* 3 (1972): 61–70.
Tindall, W. Y. "The Symbolism of W. B. Yeats." *Accent* 5 (Summer, 1945): 203–12; rpt. in *The Permanence of Yeats: Selected Criticism*, edited by James Hall and Martin Steinmann, pp. 264–77. New York: Macmillan, 1950.
Todorov, Tzvetan. *Théories du symbole*. Paris: Editions du Seuil, 1977.
Turnell, Martin. *Baudelaire: A Study of His Poetry*. New York: New Directions, 1953.

Unterecker, John. *A Reader's Guide to William Butler Yeats*. New York: H. Wolff, 1959; reprint ed., 1962.
Ure, Peter. *Towards a Mythology: Studies in the Poetry of W. B. Yeats*. Liverpool: University Press of Liverpool; London: Hodder and Stoughton, 1946.

Vendler, Helen Hennessy. *Yeats's Vision and the Later Plays*. Cambridge, Mass.: Harvard University Press, 1963.
Vigée, Claude. "La Conception de l'imagination chez Baudelaire." In *L'Imagination créatrice: Actes mis en forme par Roselyne Chenu*, pp. 15–39. Neuchâtel, Switzerland: Editions de la Baconnière, 1971.
Vivier, Robert. *L'Originalité de Baudelaire*. Brussels: Gembloux, J. Duculot, S.A., Imprimeur de l'Académie, 1952.
Vlasopolos, Anca. "*The Rime of the Ancient Mariner* as Romantic Quest." *Wordsworth Circle* 10 (Fall 1979): 365–69.

Ward, Patricia. "Coleridge's Critical Theory of the Symbol." *Texas Studies in Literature and Language* 8 (1966): 15–32.
Warren, Robert Penn. "A Poem of Pure Imagination." In *Selected Essays*, pp. 198–305. New York: Random House, 1941; reprint and rev. ed., 1951.
Wasserman, Earl R. "The English Romantics: The Grounds of Knowledge." *Studies in Romanticism* 3–4 (1964): 17–34.
Wellek, René. *A History of Modern Criticism: 1750–1950*. 4 vols. New Haven: Yale University Press, 1955–66.
Whalley, George. *Coleridge and Sara Hutchinson and the Asra Poems*. Toronto: University of Toronto Press, 1955.

Bibliography

Wheeler, Kathleen M. *The Creative Mind in Coleridge's Poetry*. Cambridge, Mass.: Harvard University Press, 1980.
Whitaker, Thomas R. *Swan and Shadow: Yeats's Dialogue with History*. Chapel Hill: University of North Carolina Press, 1964.
Wilson, Douglas Brownlow. "Two Modes of Apprehending Nature: A Gloss on the Coleridgean Symbol." *PMLA* 87 (1972): 42–52.
Wojcik, Manfred. "Coleridge: Symbolization, Expression, and Artistic Creativity." *Zeitschrift für Anglistik und Amerikanistik* (East Berlin) 19 (1971): 117–54.
Wordsworth, William. *The Prelude, Selected Poems and Sonnets*, edited by Carlos Baker. New York: Holt, Rinehart and Winston, 1954.

Yeats, William Butler. *The Autobiography of William Butler Yeats*. New York: Macmillan, 1969.
———. *Essays and Introductions*. New York: Macmillan, 1956.
———. *Explorations*. New York: Macmillan, 1962.
———. *The Letters of W. B. Yeats*. Edited by Allan Wade. London: Rupert Hart-Davis, 1954.
———. *Memoirs*. Edited by Denis Donoghue. New York: Macmillan, 1972.
———. *Mythologies*. London: Macmillan, 1959.
———. *Uncollected Prose by W. B. Yeats*. Edited by John P. Frayne and Colton Johnson. 2 vols. New York: Columbia University Press, 1970, 1976.
———. *The Variorum Edition of the Poems of W. B. Yeats*. Edited by Peter Allt and Russell K. Alspach. New York: Macmillan, 1971.
———. *A Vision*. New York: Macmillan, 1956.

Zwerdling, Alex. "W. B. Yeats: Variations on the Visionary Quest." *University of Toronto Quarterly* 30 (October 1960): 72–85; rpt. in *Yeats: A Collection of Critical Essays*, edited by John Unterecker, pp. 80–92. Englewood Cliffs, N.J.: Prentice-Hall, 1963.

INDEX

Abbey Theatre, 24, 153
Abrams, M. H., 35, 36, 60
Aesthetic movement, 14, 23, 28, 134, 139
Allegory, 13, 171, 172
Austin, L. J., 91
Axel (Villiers de l'Isle d'Adam), 147

Baker, James Volant, 34
Barth, J. Robert, 34
Baudelaire, Charles, 136, 139, 140, 141, 146, 152, 155, 156, 161, 167, 169, 170, 171, 188; beauty in, 87–88, 104, 191; and Coleridge, 19, 20, 21, 22, 28, 86, 87–88, 91, 94–95, 96, 98–99, 104, 134, 191; death in, 26, 134; fidelity to Romanticism, 88–89, 90, 91, 92; "forgetting" (*oubli*) in, 109, 116; "ideal beauty" in, 23, 104, 111, 133; "recollection" in, 21–22, 109, 116; subconscious in, 22, 134; and Yeats, 24, 137, 138, 140–47, 150–51, 162, 172–74, 175–76, 177, 188. See also Greater Romantic Lyric; Imagination; Nature; Romantic Quest; Symbol; Symbolization. Works: "Abel and Cain," 129; "All in One," 115; *Artificial Paradises*, 101, 125; "Balcony, The," 113; "Beacons," 110; "Beauty," 111; "Blessing, The," 107–9, 112, 115, 117, 118, 126, 180; "Blind, The," 122; "Carrion, A," 113–14; "Clock, The," 107, 109, 116–17, 118, 119, 122, 128; "Comes the Charming Evening," 122; "Confession," 115; "Conversation," 115; *Correspondance*, 90, 96, 99, 106, 119, 129; "Correspondances," 109–10, 112, 116; "Cracked Bell, The," 116; "Dance of Death, The," 96, 123; "Death of Lovers, The," 130; *De l'essence du rire*, 102; "Denial of Saint Peter, The," 129; "Destruction, La," 155; "Don Juan in Hell," 111; "Dream of a Curious Person," 131; "Ennemi, L' " ("The Ruined Garden"), 111; "Evening Harmony," 113–14; "Exotic Perfume," 112; *Exposition Universelle de 1855, L'*, 101; "Flask, The," 113–14; "Former Life, A," 111; "Fountain of Blood, The," 126; "Giantess," 111; "Good Sisters, The," 126; "Gypsies on the Road," 111; "Her Hair," 112–13; "Hymn to Beauty," 112, 113, 133; "Ideal, The," 111; *Intimate Journals*, 95; "Invitation to the Voyage," 130; "J'aime le souvenir" ("I love the thought"), 110; "Je te donne ces vers" ("If by some freak of fortune"), 113–14; "Landscape, A," 117–19, 120, 122, 123; "Litany to Satan," 129–30; "Love and the Skull," 105, 127–28, 129; "Lovers' Wine," 125, 126; "Man and the Sea," 116; "Martyr, The," 126; "Mask, The," 111; "Mists and Rains," 123; "Morning Twilight," 119, 124; "Murderer's Wine, The," 125, 131; "Music," 116; "My Beatrice," 126–27; *Nouvelles Fleurs du Mal*, 90; "Obsession," 116; *Oeuvres Complètes*, 88, 90, 91, 95, 96, 97, 98, 99, 100, 101, 102, 103, 104, 125, 128–29, 131; *Painter of Modern*

Index

Baudelaire, Charles (*cont.*)
  Life, The, 87, 99; "Parisian Dream," 122; "Phantom, A," 113-14; "Poem of Hashish, The," 131; "Punishment of Pride, The," 111; "Ragpickers' Wine, The," 124; "Red-Haired Beggar Girl, The," 120; *Rockets* (Fusées), 106; "Sadness of the Moon, The," 116; *Salon de 1859,* 91, 99, 114; *Salon de 1846,* 99, 100; "Sept Vieillards, Les," 122, 155; "Servant, The," 123; "Seven Old Men, The" (*see* "Sept Vieillards, Les"); "Skeletons Digging," 123; "Soul of Wine, The," 124-25; "Spiritual Dawn, The," 113-14; "Spleen," 116; *Spleen de Paris,* 89; "Sun, The," 120; "Swan, The," 120-21, 127, 132; *Théophile Gautier,* 95, 101; *Thoughts about Several of My Contemporaries,* 95, 103; "To a Madonna," 113, 115; "To the Reader," 105, 107-8, 128, 129, 131, 132; "Voyage, The," 22, 131-33, 148, 182, 188; "Voyage to Cythera, The," 127; "Wicked Monk, The," 111
—*Fleurs du Mal, Les,* 20, 22, 88, 91, 92, 99, 104-34, 138, 145, 148, 149, 162, 173, 174, 175, 176, 177, 188 (*see also* Greater Romantic Lyric; Romantic Quest; Symbolization); "Bile and the Ideal," 107, 108, 109, 110, 113, 116, 117, 118, 119, 120, 122, 132, 134; *Black Venus,* 112, 115; "Death," 22, 92, 107, 130-31, 133, 173; "Flowers of Evil," 22, 107, 124, 125-26, 127-28, 129; "Parisian Scenes," 21, 93, 107, 117, 118, 119, 122, 124, 125, 126, 132; "Revolt," 21, 107, 116, 124, 128-30, 173; *White Venus,* 115; "Wine," 107, 124, 125, 130
Beardsley, Aubrey, 136, 141, 143, 145
Beckett, Samuel, 191
Benjamin, Walter, 14-15, 94
Berkeley, George, 142, 166
Bersani, Leo, 94
Blake, William, 26, 27, 66, 89, 136, 138, 139, 140, 143
Bloom, Harold, 26, 138
Bowles, William Lisle, 30, 64
Byron, Lord George Gordon, 93

Coleridge, S. T., 89, 90, 110, 133, 136, 148, 151, 152, 156, 163, 170, 188, 189-90; and Baudelaire, 19-23, 28, 86, 87-88, 91, 94-95, 96, 98, 104, 134, 191; on fancy, 39-40, 43, 44, 74, 82; on *forma formata* and *informans,* 44; on *natura naturata* and *naturans,* 17, 18; Reason in, 17, 31, 41, 42, 43, 50, 52, 82; senses in, 17, 30, 32, 37, 40, 42, 43, 50, 53, 57, 59, 61, 65, 68, 74, 80, 82, 84, 85, 165; on Shakespeare, 166; swimming sensation in, 41, 42, 44; understanding in, 17, 31, 36, 42, 50, 82, 165; and Yeats, 24, 26, 28, 85, 86, 137-38, 139, 141-43, 150, 155, 162, 165-71, 175. *See also* Greater Romantic Lyric; Imagination; Nature; Romantic Quest; Symbol; Symbolization. Works: *Aids to Reflection,* 82-84, 85; "Dejection: An Ode," 19, 32, 33, 66, 70, 76-81, 155, 176; *Essays on Method,* 43, 166; "Fears in Solitude," 19, 32, 55, 59, 63-70, 77, 80; *Friend, The,* 43, 82, 166; "Frost at Midnight," 19, 32, 53-59, 62, 63, 66, 67, 69, 76, 80, 175; *Lay Sermons,* 18, 43, 86; *Lectures on Politics and Religion,* 82; *Letters,* 41, 46, 47, 52, 63, 169; "Letter to Asra," 80; *Logic,* 51; *Lyrical Ballads,* 48, 89, 93 (*see also* Wordsworth, William); *Miscellaneous Criticism,* 51; *Notebooks,* 29, 33, 34, 38-39, 42, 49, 50-51, 67-68; *On the Principles of Genial Criticism Concerning the Fine Arts,* 43-44, 51, 87; *Philosophical Lectures, The,* 45; "Reflections on Having Left a Place of Retirement," 19, 32, 33, 55, 59, 63-70, 77, 81; *Statesman's Manual, The,* 42, 43-44, 50, 83; "This Lime-Tree Bower My Prison," 19, 32, 53-59, 63, 66, 69, 76, 77, 78, 80; "What Is Life," 166
—*Biographia Literaria,* 46-50, 52-53, 176; imagination in, 37, 39, 48, 90; mind in, 37-38, 40, 81-82; symbol in, 13, 30, 44-45, 50
—"Eolian Harp, The," 34, 35, 63, 69-73, 74, 75, 76, 82, 94-95, 96; censored vision in, 19, 61
—*Rime of the Ancient Mariner, The,* 17, 32-33, 35, 36, 52, 53, 59, 70-76, 79, 93, 142, 190; circular structure in, 18, 32; imaginative failure in, 19, 32-33, 36, 73, 75-77; imaginative vision in, 18, 32, 74-75

214

Index

Conversation poems, 35, 53, 138. *See also* Greater Romantic Lyric
Crowe, Catherine, 20, 90–92

Delacroix, Eugène, 91, 101
Donoghue, Denis, 26, 138
Dowson, Ernest, 136, 140, 141, 143
Dream, 98; in Baudelaire, 99; in *Les Fleurs du Mal*, 22, 118–19, 122, 123, 125, 128; in Yeats, 142, 146, 149, 150, 151, 153, 154, 164, 174, 185

Eliot, T. S., 85, 86, 140
Experience, 15–16, 22, 56, 72–73, 93, 107–9, 117, 121–22, 126, 131–32, 163, 175, 180, 184
External nature, 14, 17, 21, 31, 77, 98, 119, 121, 122, 123, 165. *See also* Nature

Fancy, 17, 40, 43, 44, 74, 82, 90
Fondane, Benjamin, 93, 94
Frye, Northrop, 138

Gautier, Théophile, 95, 101
Gonne, Maud, 150, 153, 159, 179
Greater Romantic Lyric, 35–36, 74, 85, 137–38, 140; in Baudelaire, 14–15, 93, 120; circular structure of, 18, 32, 58, 169; in Coleridge, 15, 16–17, 28, 31, 35, 52, 53, 71, 190–91; *Collected Poems* as, 24, 169, 191; *Les Fleurs du Mal* as, 21, 24, 191; as genre, 14; imaginative vision in, 18, 32, 56–59, 77; movement of, 15, 66; symbol in, 18–19, 32; in Yeats, 15, 162, 169. *See also* Conversation poems
Guys, Constantin, 104

Hough, Graham, 139, 140
Hugo, Victor, 99, 104, 139

Imagination: god-like, 17, 37–38; primary, 17, 30, 34, 36, 37–38, 48, 90; secondary, 17, 34, 36, 37, 39, 41, 43, 44, 49, 51, 96, 165; symbolizing, 13–14, 15–16, 17, 115, 130, 177; triumph of, 16, 133. *See also* Symbol
—in Baudelaire, 20, 21, 90–92, 93, 96, 97, 98, 99, 102, 114, 117, 124, 126, 191; imaginative act, 21, 104, 134; lapses from, 16, 95; symbolizing, 13–14, 16, 132, 134
—in Coleridge, 36, 39–40, 48, 49, 56, 59, 68, 75, 76, 81, 86, 91; ambivalence about, 17, 31, 81–85; diminished importance of, 34–35, 45–46; theory of, 16–17, 28, 30, 31, 33, 34, 36, 41, 43, 48, 81–84, 98, 190
—in Yeats, 155, 172, 173, 183, 184, 185, 187; lapses from, 16, 135–36, 156–59; and passion, 150–52; as psychic reintegration, 135, 138
Ingres, Jean Auguste Dominique, 101
Innocence, 16, 73, 93, 100, 107, 116, 122, 130, 131–32, 180

Johnson, Lionel, 136, 140, 141
Joyce, James, 15, 189, 191

Keats, John: *Poems* (1817), 89
Kermode, Frank: "The Modern Apocalypse," 138, 139; *Romantic Image*, 140

L'Isle d'Adam, Villiers de, 137, 140, 143

Mallarmé, Stéphane, 27, 137, 140, 143, 166
Memory, 15, 17, 74, 88; in Baudelaire, 94, 98–99, 120, 121, 131, 132; in Yeats, 138, 162, 171. *See also* Baudelaire, "recollection" in
Modernism, 138, 139

Nature, 14, 88; in Baudelaire, 91, 98–104, 111–12, 115, 116, 123, 134; in Coleridge, 30, 31, 32, 33, 38, 40, 44, 48–49, 50, 76, 82–83, 84–85 (*see also* Coleridge, on *natura naturata* and *naturans*); in Greater Romantic Lyric, 15, 36, 54–70, 77–81; as *spectacle*, 94, 106–7, 120, 121, 134, 191; in Yeats, 136, 138, 139, 146–47, 168, 172, 188. *See also* External Nature
Nineties, 23, 136, 140, 146

Pagan School, The, 101, 111
Platonism, 42, 169, 170, 187
Poe, Edgar Allan, 20, 86, 90–91, 143
Proust, Marcel, 191

Recollection. *See* Baudelaire, "recollection" in
Reverie: in Baudelaire, 88, 94, 98, 99, 100, 120; in Yeats, 151, 174
Rhymers, 23, 136, 141, 152

Index

Richards, I. A., 34
Rimbaud, Arthur, 140, 146
Romanticism: Baudelairian, 16, 91–92, 129, 133–34; Coleridgean, 16, 26; English, 13, 20, 90, 138, 140, 142, 151, 153–54, 155, 172, 173–74, 188, 189–90; French, 20, 103, 189; and modern literature, 25, 26, 191; true inheritors of, 15, 135
Romantic Quest: in Baudelaire, 15, 16, 73; circular structure of, 57, 169; in Coleridge, 15, 16, 28, 31–32, 36, 190–91; *Collected Poems* as, 24, 146–47, 163, 164, 169, 173–74, 175, 176–77, 178–79, 180, 181, 182, 183, 187, 191; *Les Fleurs du Mal* as, 20–21, 22, 24, 26, 88–133, 173, 191; as genre, 14, 70–71, 140, 190–91; as psychic journey, 15, 85; two phases of, 16, 71; in Yeats, 15, 16, 24–25, 27, 73, 136, 153, 167, 169
Rossetti, Dante Gabriel, 136, 142

Shelley, Percy Bysshe, 25, 26, 27, 93, 138, 139, 142, 157, 158, 166, 172, 174, 175
Songs of Innocence and Experience (William Blake), 89
Stevens, Wallace, 85
Swinburne, Algernon, 143–44
Symbol, 19, 21; aesthetic of, 17, 33, 41, 81–85, 167, 189; circular, 18, 32, 42, 52, 58, 169–70; and creative process, 13, 86, 88, 138; diversity of meanings of, 13, 90, 140; as fusion of emotions and intellect, 18, 30, 40–41, 44, 49, 56–59, 78, 190; and imagination, 13, 16, 31, 34, 42–43, 44, 48; and imaginative vision, 17–18, 120; as unit of *oeuvre*, 14, 86
—in Baudelaire, 21, 91, 96, 101, 106, 116, 121, 124, 127, 134; as hunger and thirst, 21, 88; as system, 16, 19, 22, 95, 104–6, 191
—in Coleridge, 17, 21, 29–30, 39–46, 68, 87–88, 190; as symbolic method, 28, 30, 32, 191; as system, 16, 19, 71; as term, 13, 16, 17, 29–30, 31, 34, 36, 190
—in Yeats, 138, 140, 150, 151, 152, 153, 156, 162, 171–74; as system, 15, 16, 25, 86, 137, 137–38, 153, 171–72, 174–75, 180–83
Symbolist Movement, 13–14, 23, 28, 86, 109, 134, 140

Symbolization, 14, 28, 78, 82–83, 88, 191; in Baudelaire, 16, 22, 91–92, 95, 115, 127–33; Baudelaire's art criticism as, 22, 97–102, 191; in Coleridge, 18, 28, 30, 31–32, 36, 41, 46, 53, 54, 58–59, 74, 77, 79, 91, 168; Coleridge's theory of, 16, 19, 21, 50, 63, 71, 190; in *Collected Poems*, 24, 137–38, 169; in *Les Fleurs du Mal*, 21, 22, 24, 115, 116, 126–27; unachieved in Coleridge, 17, 19, 22, 33, 59, 60–63, 69–70, 76; in Yeats, 15, 24, 25, 167, 168, 169, 177, 191
Symons, Arthur, 136, 139–40, 143–45
Synge, John, 142

Tragic Generation, The, 140, 141, 142, 145, 151, 152, 188

Verlaine, Paul, 137, 140, 143, 182–83
Vigny, Alfred de, 106

Wilde, Oscar, 136
Wordsworth, William, 27, 30, 33, 46, 48–49, 85, 89, 90, 139, 142, 145, 156; cathedral as metaphor in, 16, 105, 106, 175; Coleridge's hopes for, 16, 47, 89, 171; *Preface to Lyrical Ballads*, 30, 46–47, 93; *Prelude, The*, 89; *Recluse, The*, 89.

Yeats, John Butler, 150
Yeats, W. B., 90, 93; and Baudelaire, 24, 137–38, 140–46, 150–51, 162, 172–76, 177, 188; birdsong in, 176, 177, 178, 179, 180–83, 191; and Coleridge, 24, 26, 28, 85, 86, 137–38, 141–43, 150, 155, 162, 165–72, 175; death in, 173, 189; departure from Romanticism in, 15, 137, 139, 145–46, 153–74, 166, 189; fidelity to Romanticism in, 15, 23, 25, 26, 92, 135, 138–40, 161, 167, 168, 187–88; heart in, 176, 177, 182, 183–87, 191; "ideal beauty" in, 141; and Nineties, 23, 136–37, 145; passion in, 22, 23, 137, 143, 145, 150–54, 157, 165, 179, 184, 185; "phantasmagoria" in, 171, 172–73; on Plotinus, 169; reverie in, 22, 138, 171; Rose as Image in, 23, 148; on Shakespeare, 166; Unity of Being in, 24, 25, 137, 143, 162, 164, 165–66, 170, 176, 181, 182, 187, 189; Unity of Culture in, 24, 137, 153,

Index

162, 170, 187. *See also* Greater Romantic Lyric; Imagination; Nature; Romantic Quest; Symbol; Symbolization. Works: "Adam's Curse," 179; "Adoration of the Magi, The," 148; "All Souls' Night," 181, 186–87; "Among School Children," 168, 169–70, 182, 186, 189; "Art and Ideas," 172, 173; *Autobiography*, 136–37, 142, 144, 145, 150, 174, 182; "Autumn of the Body, The," 146, 163; "Beggar to Beggar Cried," 178; "Broken Dreams," 185; "Byzantium," 181; "Cap and Bells, The," 149; "Celtic Twilight, The," 163; "Certain Noble Plays of Japan," 156; "Chosen," 170; "Circus Animals' Desertion, The," 169, 187; "Cold Heaven, The," 159, 167; "Colonus' Praise," 168; "Coming of Wisdom with Time, The," 154, 163; "Cuchulain Comforted," 178, 182; *Cutting of an Agate, The,* 183; "Dedication to a Book of Stories Selected from the Irish Novelists, The," 163, 164; "Demon and Beast," 167–68, 180; "Dialogue of Self and Soul, The," 187; "Discoveries," 153, 156; "Double Vision of Michael Robartes, The," 179, 185; "Easter, 1916," 179, 183; "Ego Dominus Tuus," 179, 185; "Ephemera," 147; *Essays and Introductions*, 142, 146, 152, 156, 157, 158, 166, 169, 171, 172, 174, 177, 183; *Explorations*, 161, 166, 170, 171; "Fascination of What's Difficult, The," 155, 168; "Folly of Being Comforted, The," 183; "Four Ages of Man, The," 176; "Friends," 167, 184; "Hero, the Girl, and the Fool, The," 164; "High Talk," 178, 187; "Holy Mountain, The," 166–67; "Hopes and Fears for Irish Literature," 151; "Image from Past Life, An," 179; "Indian to His Love, The," 164; "In Memory of Major Robert Gregory," 184; "Introduction to *The Resurrection*," 161; "Lamentation of the Old Pensioner, The," 163, 164; "Leda and the Swan," 160; *Letters*, 136, 143, 159, 175; "Living Beauty, The," 184; "Long-Legged Fly, The," 170–71; "Man Who Dreamed of Faeryland, The," 148; "Meditations in Time of Civil War," 182, 185–86, 187; *Memoirs*, 152, 156–57, 171, 182; "Memory for Youth, A," 179; "Men Improve with the Years," 184; "Miss Fiona Macleod as a Poet," 152; *Mythologies*, 146, 153; "Nationality and Literature," 151; "Nineteen Hundred and Nineteen," 181; "On a Picture of a Black Centaur," 164–65; "On a Political Prisoner," 179; *On the Boiler*, 189; "Paudeen," 178; "People, The," 184; *Per Amica Silentia Lunae*, 153; "Phases of the Moon, The," 141; "Philosophy of Shelley's Poetry, The," 172; "Poetry and Tradition," 153, 154; "Politics," 189; "Prayer for My Daughter, A," 180; "*Prometheus Unbound*," 158, 174; *Purgatory*, 189; "Reconciliation," 186; *Reveries over Childhood and Youth*, 150; "Ribh at the Tomb of Baile and Aillinn," 176; "Ribh in Ecstasy," 176; *Rosa Alchemica*, 146; "Sailing to Byzantium," 180–81, 185; "Second Coming, The," 156, 158–61; "September 1913," 178; "Solomon and the Witch," 179; "Song, A," 184; "Song of the Happy Shepherd, The," 183; "Sorrow of Love, The," 163; "Spur, The," 150; "Statues, The," 170; "Stolen Child, The," 147; "Stream and Sun at Glendalough," 159, 168, 187; "Symbolism of Poetry, The," 172; "There," 176; "Three Hermits, The," 178; "To a Friend Whose Work Has Come to Nothing," 178; "To a Wealthy Man," 178; "To a Young Girl," 184; "To Ireland in the Coming Times," 164, 183; "To the Rose upon the Rood of Time," 162; "Tower, The," 164, 181, 185; "Trembling of the Veil, The," 141, 143, 182; "Two Trees, The," 164; *Uncollected Prose*, 142, 147, 151, 152, 182; "Under Ben Bulben," 170; "Upon a Dying Lady," 185; "Vacillation," 168, 181, 187; *Variorum Edition of the Poems*, 148, 150, 159, 163, 172; *Vision, A*, 24, 135, 143, 144, 145, 157, 158, 159, 160, 165, 169, 173, 175, 176, 177, 181, 182; "What Then," 187; "Wild Swans, The," 185

Index

Yeats, W. B. (*cont.*)
—*Collected Poems*, 24, 89, 183 (*see also* Greater Romantic Lyric; Romantic Quest; Symbolization); *Crossways*, 147, 148; *From "A Full Moon in March,"* 187; *Last Poems*, 169, 176, 187; *Michael Robartes and the Dancer*, 159, 179; *New Poems*, 187; *Responsibilities*, 176, 178; *Rose, The*, 147, 148, 162; *Supernatural Songs*, 169, 176; *Tower, The*, 164, 175, 180, 182, 185, 187; *Wild Swans at Coole, The*, 179, 184, 185; *Wind among the Reeds, The*, 146, 147–50, 163; *Winding Stair and Other Poems, The*, 181, 185, 187; *Woman Young and Old, A*, 170

ANCA VLASOPOLOS IS ASSISTANT PROFESSOR OF ENGLISH
AT WAYNE STATE UNIVERSITY. SHE HOLDS THE PH.D. DEGREE IN
COMPARATIVE LITERATURE FROM THE UNIVERSITY OF MICHIGAN.

THE MANUSCRIPT WAS EDITED BY MIRIAM TILLMAN.

THE BOOK WAS DESIGNED BY SELMA TENENBAUM.

THE TYPEFACE FOR THE TEXT IS MERGENTHALER VIP TIMES ROMAN,
BASED ON A DESIGN BY STANLEY MORISON IN 1932.

THE DISPLAY FACE IS TIMES ROMAN.

THE TEXT IS PRINTED ON 60-LB. BOOKTEXT NATURAL TEXT PAPER.

THE BOOK IS BOUND IN HOLLISTON MILLS'
LINEN CLOTH OVER BINDER'S BOARDS.

MANUFACTURED IN THE UNITED STATES OF AMERICA.